LOS ANGELES

HALLI JASTARAN FAULKNER

CONTENTS

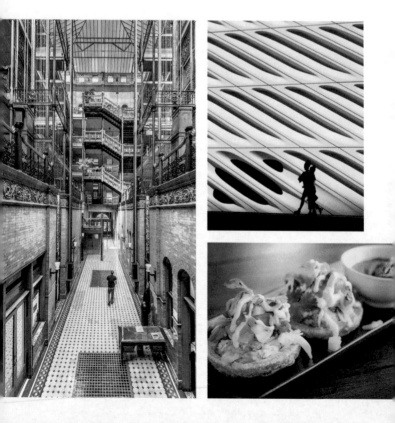

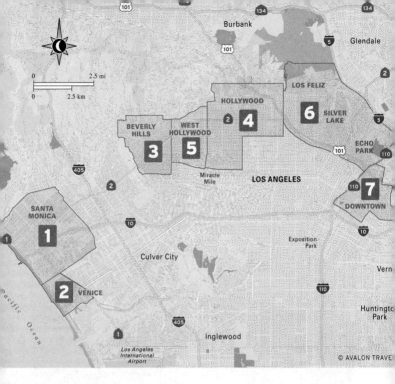

MAPS

1   Hollywood sign

2   surfboards for sale

3   Pacific Park in Santa Monica

4   Griffith Observatory

5   Rose Café in Venice

6   biking The Strand

DISCOVER
LOS ANGELES

Los Angeles has long been a beacon for dreamers. This is where countless individuals have come to escape, catch a big break or a sick swell, and reinvent themselves. Their stories have stoked the creative fuel that has made this city legendary to the world.

L.A. is often criticized for being too superficial—and it's true that the entertainment industry can be as brutal as the Cali sun. But this city revels in its cultural differences like no other American city. You'll find evidence of this in the art, entertainment, and food, which all celebrate innovative, creative, cultural fusion.

L.A. is also criticized for being too loud. Yes, there are honking cars, screaming producers, and vibrating nightclubs—but there's also the crackling of Guatemalan *papusas,* the gentle rustle of swaying palm trees, and the low buzz of a sidewalk café filled with focused writers.

It's the city's contradictions that make it such an exciting place to be. Even the landscape reflects this: highways sprawl into lush mountains and skyscrapers tower over the vast Pacific Ocean. Few major cities can compete with the recreational opportunities found here. Surf some of the best waves in Malibu, bike from Santa Monica to Venice, and hike to what feels like the top of the world in Runyon Canyon.

Don't be surprised if you find inspiration in L.A.'s many different energies. There's something special about the way this city reveres its softly lit silver-screen past while it charges head-first into the future. It's impossible to take it all in the first time—but don't let that stop you from trying, enjoying, and coming back for more.

11 TOP
EXPERIENCES

1 **Santa Monica Pier:** Bite into an ice cream cone, feel the salty ocean breeze, and gaze into the blue horizon from the iconic Ferris wheel (page 66).

2 **Hollywood Magic:** Find your fave celeb's star on the **Walk of Fame** (page 73), take a selfie with the **Hollywood Sign** (page 83), and go behind the scenes on a **movie studio tour** or **live TV recording** (page 76). Top it all off with a night clubbing on **Sunset Strip** (page 131).

3 **Venice Beach Boardwalk:** Walking, biking, or skating along this famous boardwalk—one of the coolest and edgiest L.A. scenes since the 1970s—is a quintessential California experience (page 68).

>>>

4 **Griffith Observatory:** Check out the space-related exhibits and state-of-the-art planetarium—or just admire the panoramic views of L.A. and the sky beyond, which are especially beautiful at twilight (page 82).

5 **Window-Shopping on Rodeo Drive:** Spend an afternoon window-shopping and people-watching in the playground of the rich and the famous (page 70).

>>>

6 **City of Art:** L.A. has a rich and eclectic art scene, from vibrant **street art** (page 156) to world-renowned **museums** (page 152).

>>>

7 **New Age L.A.:** Choose from the city's eclectic spiritual experiences, including oceanside yoga classes, reiki healing sessions, and wooded drum circles (page 166).

>>>

8 **Mexican Cuisine:** From $1.50 street tacos to decadent Oaxacan moles, the Mexican food in L.A. might be the best of any U.S. city (page 108).

<<<

9 **Beaches:** Bougie, funky, family-friendly...L.A. has just about every type of beach under the sun—and plenty of sun to be under (page 236).

>>>

10 Indie L.A.: Spend a day exploring one of L.A.'s funkier neighborhoods, like **Los Feliz** (page 54) or **Koreatown** (page 112).

11 Amusement Parks: Pal around with Mickey at **Disneyland** (page 224) or get your wizarding degree at **Universal Studios** (page 231).

<<<

EXPLORE
LOS ANGELES

THE BEST OF LOS ANGELES

This colorful three-day itinerary packs a lot into one trip, but it'll give you a well-rounded taste of what makes L.A. special, including movie-star glamour, up-and-coming artsy areas, and beach time. You'll need to rent a car or use a ride-hailing app to get from point to point in this itinerary.

▶DAY 1: BEVERLY HILLS AND HOLLYWOOD

Start your morning with a relaxing walk through **Beverly Gardens Park,** which will take you right to the beginning of **Rodeo Drive,** a high-end shopper's paradise. Stroll down Rodeo Drive, stopping in shops and drooling over dresses, leather bags, and suits. When you're ready for lunch, either head to **Spago** for high-end dining (reservation recommended) or to **Nate'n Al Delicatessen** for a casual home-style Jewish meal.

Once you've had your fill of Beverly Hills, drive northeast for about 25 minutes to **Hollywood,** checking into **The Hollywood Roosevelt Hotel** on Hollywood Boulevard, the perfect location from

Beverly Hills

BEST VIEWS

GRIFFITH OBSERVATORY
Come to the Griffith Observatory for the best views of the Hollywood sign and a panoramic picture of the San Gabriel Mountains, Downtown, and all of Hollywood (page 82).

THE GETTY CENTER
Perched at the top of the Santa Monica Mountains, this world-class art museum provides amazing, expansive views of L.A. and the Pacific Ocean. Plus there's a great lawn for picnics (page 84).

SANTA MONICA PIER
The Santa Monica Pier is *the* place to be at sunset—you'll get watercolor views of the Pacific Ocean and the entire South Bay (page 66).

OUE SKYSPACE
From the 78th floor of the Bank of America building, OUE gives visitors amazing views of all of Los Angeles—and even has a glass-bottomed slide for thrill seekers (page 81).

ROOFTOP AT THE STANDARD
The Rooftop at the Standard is the hippest place to sip a poolside cocktail among Downtown skyscrapers (page 135).

THE PENTHOUSE
This top-floor hotel restaurant in Santa Monica is where celebrities gather to clink fancy drinks and marvel at the 360-degree views (page 89).

Frank Grill. If you have the energy, continue the night in nearby West Hollywood with some dancing at **Avalon Hollywood** or laughs at **The Comedy Store.**

>DAY 2: SILVER LAKE AND DOWNTOWN

Who's in the mood for breakfast tacos? Start your day at **HomeState** in **Silver Lake,** about a 10-20-minute drive from Hollywood. Afterward, head across the street to check out **Soap Plant / Wacko,** a zany shop with a vibrant exterior.

From Silver Lake, drive another 20 minutes to **Downtown L.A.** to visit **The Broad** museum, which houses one of the world's greatest contemporary art collections. Afterward, you may want to take a walk around the **Walt Disney Concert Hall,** the iconic silvery structure across the street.

For lunch, check out the smorgasbord at nearby **Grand Central Market,** which has something for everyone. Take a quick walk through the **Bradbury Building**

which to explore the star-laden Walk of Fame.

Either hop on one of the many tour buses lining the **Walk of Fame** for a 1-2-hour tour of Hollywood and celebrity homes, or do a self-guided **tour** (see page 46). Keep your camera ready for shots of the famous white-lettered **Hollywood sign** up in the hills to the north.

End your day in Hollywood with old-school drinks at **Musso &**

Little Tokyo in Downtown L.A.

El Capitan Theatre

THE ENTERTAINMENT CAPITAL OF THE WORLD

MOVIES

- **ArcLight Cinema Hollywood** (page 145) has a state-of-the-art domed theater that makes every movie memorable.

- During warmer months, **Cinespia** (page 146) hosts weekly screenings of classic American films at the Hollywood Forever Cemetery—it's quite surreal to watch a movie surrounded by the ghosts of the big screen.

- **El Capitan Theatre** (page 146) is located right on Hollywood Boulevard and shows Disney's latest movies. There are also themed performances with live organ music.

MUSIC

- There's no better place in L.A. to catch a concert than the **Hollywood Bowl** (page 145), an outdoor amphitheater that attracts some of the world's biggest musical performers.

- Downtown's **Walt Disney Concert Hall** (page 157) is not only an iconic architectural landmark but also an inspiring place to hear the Los Angeles Philharmonic perform a wide range of classical tunes.

- Be a part of L.A.'s rich rock 'n' roll history at the famed **Troubadour** (page 150) club in West Hollywood.

COMEDY

- The three rooms at **The Comedy Store** (page 148) in West Hollywood are some of the greatest spots in the country to catch live comedy.

- **Upright Citizens Brigade** (page 144) in Hollywood is a small venue that packs a punch with its amazing improvisational talent.

- Come to **Groundlings Theatre** (page 144) in Hollywood for knee-slapping improv comedy with ample audience participation.

across the street—its unique 1930s design has been featured in a number of movies.

If you're looking for more art, spend the rest of the afternoon in the **Arts District.** For more shopping and snacking, check out **Little Tokyo.**

At night, check into the **Omni Los Angeles** for a traditional Downtown experience, or the **Ace Hotel** for a trendy stay. Have dinner at one of Downtown's decadent restaurants—**Bestia** for Italian cuisine or **Church & State** for French fare.

Venice Skate Park

>DAY 3: VENICE AND SANTA MONICA

Your last day is all about beach vibes. To get to **Venice** from Downtown, drive west for about 30-40 minutes (avoiding rush hour between 7:30am and 10:30am on weekdays).

Start your day on the bohemian Abbot Kinney Boulevard, grabbing some unique flavors at **Blue Star Donuts** before checking out the famous **Venice Beach Boardwalk.** Spend some time people-watching at the beach, viewing the public art walls, and checking out the skate park. Head over to **Jay's Rentals** and grab a bike or some roller skates to make your way down **The Strand,** a paved pedestrian path that will take you all the way to the **Santa Monica Pier.**

For lunch, take your pick of the cafés lining The Strand. Chill for the rest of the afternoon by spreading your towel on **Santa Monica State Beach** or practicing yoga at a nearby studio, such as **Bhakti Yoga Shala.**

When the sun starts going down, make your way to the **Ferris wheel** on the Santa Monica Pier to get one last good view of L.A. End your night casually with a juicy hot dog from a stand on the pier or go for an upscale seafood dinner at **The Lobster,** right near the entrance to the pier.

KIDS PLAY IN L.A.

Although L.A. sometimes feels like a playground for adults, there's plenty here for the little ones. Start at the Santa Monica Pier, spend some time at Griffith Park, then head south for a day at the ultimate kid destination—Disneyland.

>DAY 1: SANTA MONICA

Check into Santa Monica's **Casa del Mar** for a fun poolside scene that can keep the kids entertained. Once they get their swim in, walk to the **Santa Monica Aquarium** at the base of the Santa Monica Pier. Inside this small building, kids can touch sticky starfish and learn about the diverse marinelife living just yards away.

After the aquarium, walk down the pier to the amusements at **Pacific Park.** Kids can play arcade games, get painted in caricature, and ride a mini roller coaster.

If you still have some energy, you can walk down to the sands of **Santa Monica State Beach;** during

Pacific Park on the Santa Monica Pier

the summer there are lifeguards to keep kids safe while they play in the waves. You can also rent a bike from the stands lining the Santa Monica boardwalk (kids' bike seats are available) and cruise along **The Strand** bike path until you're all pooped.

Finish your beach day with a stroll down the **3rd Street Promenade,** just a few blocks from the beach. There are shops and restaurants for all tastes, and street performers on weekends.

>DAY 2: GRIFFITH PARK

Today will require a bit more driving, so start early. From Santa Monica, make your way northeast to Griffith Park, stopping in West Hollywood on the way for lunch at **Au Fudge.** (It will take about 30 minutes by car to get there, depending on traffic.) This kid-friendly restaurant opened by actress Jessica Biel has an adjoining child-care center so parents can enjoy a yummy (and quiet) California-inspired meal.

After lunch, drive for another 30-40 minutes until you reach **Griffith Park,** home to the **Los Angeles County Zoo** and the **Autry Museum of the American West.**

biking The Strand in Santa Monica

Each of these activities could take up a full afternoon, so pick whichever appeals more to your family. On your way out of the park, check out the Griffith Park Train Rides, which give short rides for only $2.25 per person.

Once you leave the park, I recommend heading to your **Anaheim hotel,** which will take about an hour by car. You'll avoid morning traffic and get a head start to your next day at Disneyland. Grab dinner at **Downtown Disney,** which doesn't require a ticket, and rest up at the hotel for the remainder of the evening.

> DAY 3: DISNEYLAND

The kids are you going to love you for this—it's time for **Disneyland!** To avoid crowds as much as possible, get an early start, and try to visit on a weekday. If you can spend two days exploring the park, that's even better.

If you want to pay upwards of $300 per night, the hotels on the Disney property—especially **Disney's Grand Californian Hotel & Spa**—are really fun and kid friendly. Otherwise, the **Hotel Indigo Anaheim** right outside the park is a bit cheaper and perfectly nice.

Purchase either a **one-day pass** for each family member, or, if you're spending two days here, upgrade to the Park Hopper pass, which gets you into both Disneyland and Disney California Adventure.

Finally, get to the **rides!** The Space Mountain roller coaster, Indiana Jones mine ride, and the Pirates of the Caribbean boat ride are sure to keep the kiddos (and adults!) entertained all day.

Disneyland fireworks

BEACH DAYS

Oh, the beaches you'll find! Southern California has some of the most beautiful and diverse beaches in the world. Follow the coastline from north to south, checking out three different beaches, each with its own unique charm.

Zuma Beach

>DAY 1: MALIBU

Start at the north end of Malibu at **Zuma Beach.** This is a spectacularly beautiful state beach that has plenty of solitude and room for beachgoers. Consider bringing a picnic lunch from **Malibu Farm** restaurant.

If you get restless, head to **Surfrider Beach,** about a 20-minute drive south along beautiful **Highway 1.** This popular beach has the best wave breaks in L.A. Watch the pro surfers from the shore and wait for the sun to go down before continuing on Highway 1 to get to your Santa Monica hotel. Prime beachside options include **Casa del Mar** and **Shutters on the Beach.**

>DAY 2: SANTA MONICA

Start your morning with a delicious, organic breakfast and cup

BEST PEOPLE-WATCHING

VENICE BEACH BOARDWALK
The Venice Beach Boardwalk is filled with colorful characters—some peddling handmade necklaces, others playing piano, still others doing impressive skateboard tricks (page 68).

GRAND CENTRAL MARKET
Come to Grand Central Market at lunchtime to get a feel for the diversity of our city—there will be *abuelos* selling *papusas,* businesswomen eating a quick meal, and baristas making latte art (page 114).

WALK OF FAME
On Hollywood Boulevard between Orange Avenue and Highland Boulevard, the Walk of Fame is filled with street performers, costumed superheroes, and your favorite movie star look-alikes (page 73).

RODEO DRIVE
Rodeo Drive is basically a runway for the world's most expensive cars and clothes; have lunch at one of its sidewalk cafes (either Nespresso or Blue Bottle) to truly enjoy the show of people passing by (page 70).

INTELLIGENTSIA
Intelligentsia in Silver Lake feels like the epicenter of L.A. hipster culture. Order a pour over coffee, sit at the counter, and pretend to read your tablet while watching the constant parade of fashionable twentysomethings (page 111).

of coffee at **Urth Caffé.** Follow up with a jog, power-walk, or bike ride through **Palisades Park,** which provides beautiful blufftop views of the ocean below.

Once the day starts to warm up around 10 or 11am, put on your bathing suit and head down to **Santa Monica State Beach.** My favorite part of the beach to lay a towel on is just south of the Santa Monica Pier, around Pico

Corona Del Mar State Beach

Boulevard in front of the Casa del Mar hotel; this area has full bay views and isn't as crowded as the beach space immediately surrounding the Santa Monica Pier.

If you're not content just lying on the beach, rent a boogie board, take a surf lesson, or roller skate around **The Strand.** There are multiple shops lining the Santa Monica boardwalk that rent these items and more.

Cap your day with a casual hot dog on the **Santa Monica Pier** or a fancy dinner at **The Lobster,** where reservations are recommended—ask for a table near the windows for ocean views. Spend another night in Santa Monica.

▶DAY 3: NEWPORT BEACH

Take your time waking up in Santa Monica—you'll want to leave after rush hour ends (around 10:30am). Drive south to **Newport Beach,** which will take about 60-90 minutes, depending on traffic.

Once you get to Newport, grab yummy banh mi sandwiches at the cheap **Saigon Beach Restaurant** and enjoy them on the beach. Either spend the day at Newport Beach and its family-friendly pier or continue driving for about 20 minutes to **Corona del Mar State Beach,** which is considered one of the most beautiful in Southern California. The sweeping cliffs and clear blue waters will make you feel like you're on the Mediterranean Sea. Whichever beach you choose, jump in—water here will be noticeably warmer than in either Malibu or Santa Monica.

Once the sun has done down, pack up your beach swag and head to **Mama D's Italian Kitchen** in Newport for delicious pizza and pasta.

ACTIVE IN L.A.

Hike up to the Griffith Observatory.

HIKING

- Hike up Hollywood's **Runyon Canyon** (page 168) to get a workout, take panoramic selfies, or spot a celebrity walking her adorable puppy.

- **Griffith Park** (page 174) is a spacious urban park that has dozens of hiking trails of varying difficulty—this is where you come to get some greenery and take a break from the bustling city.

- **Will Rogers Historical State Park** (page 175) is a west-side ranch with a moderate hike that leads to some of my favorite wide-lens ocean views.

BIKING, SKATING, AND SKATEBOARDING

- **The Strand** (page 162) is a paved bike path that runs from Malibu to Venice; most days, it's filled with bikers who have come for exercise, people-watching, and refreshing ocean breezes.

- **Venice Beach Boardwalk** (page 68) is my favorite place to roller skate. You can take in ocean views and also enjoy some of the most interesting people-watching in the city. There are a lots of bikers and skateboarders here, too.

- **Venice Skate Park** (page 165) is a fun place to either watch talented skaters attempt nail-biting tricks, or try out the concrete play area for yourself.

SURFING

- Malibu's famed **Surfrider Beach** (page 217) has both tame and fierce swells (depending on how far out you paddle)—and great people-watching to boot.

- **Zuma Beach** (page 217) on the northern end of Malibu is a pristine place to catch some beautiful, barreling waves.

- **Huntingon Beach** (page 234) in Orange County is called "Surf City U.S.A." for a reason.

PLANNING YOUR TRIP

WHEN TO GO

One of the best things about L.A. is the beautiful, balmy climate, which makes the city an appealing **year-round destination.**

Summer (June-August) is the **busiest time** of year for tourism. During this time, Santa Monica State Beach becomes packed with umbrellas, people flock to get into the pool deck at The Standard hotel, and hotel **prices peak.** You can expect to spend anywhere from $50 to $200 more per night than you would otherwise.

Busy holidays also bring crowds and inflated prices. If you can, avoid the week of spring break (late March/early April), Memorial Day weekend (last weekend of May), and Labor Day weekend (first weekend of September).

June is the grayest month in L.A. **"June gloom"** brings overcast skies but rarely brings rain, so it won't stop you from going to Disneyland, but it may ruin some of your "sunny California" pictures.

The **ideal time** to visit L.A. is **April-May** and **September-October.** The weather is usually in the 70s, skies are clear, and streets are not as crowded with tourists.

Winter (November-February) is still a nice time to visit, just a bit colder, cloudier, and rainier.

a lifeguard tower on Santa Monica State Beach

DAILY REMINDERS

For a list of **free-entry days** for museums, see page 140.

MONDAY

• The Getty Center and the Broad are closed.

TUESDAY

• The Museum of Contemporary Art (MOCA) Grand Avenue and the Getty Villa are closed.

WEDNESDAY

• The Los Angeles County Museum of Art (LACMA) is closed.

• The Santa Monica Farmers Market (the biggest in California) takes place 8:30am-1:30pm every Wednesday.

THURSDAY

• The Downtown Los Angeles Art Walk, which involves over 50 art galleries and a dozen food trucks, happens every 2nd Thursday of the month.

FRIDAY

• Jazz Fridays at LACMA happen 5pm-8pm every Friday April-November.

• First Fridays at the Natural History Museum of Los Angeles in Exposition Park happen year-round.

• L.A.'s heaviest traffic happens every Friday evening 4pm-7:30pm during the end-of-week rush hour.

SATURDAY

• Catch an outdoor flick on Saturday evenings May-June (seating is around 7pm; movie begins around 8:30pm) at the Hollywood Forever Cemetery.

SUNDAY

• Metered parking is free in some areas—but not all. Always check nearby parking signage.

ENTRY REQUIREMENTS

When visiting the United States from another country a **valid passport** is required. Depending upon your country of origin, a **visa** may also be required when visiting the United States. For a complete list of countries whose citizens are exempt from needing a visa, visit the State Department's website (http://travel.state.gov).

TRANSPORTATION

Most visitors will be flying into **Los Angeles International Airport** (LAX), the most trafficked airport in Southern California. Visitors also fly into **Hollywood Burbank Airport** (BUR) in Burbank or **John Wayne Airport** (SNA) in Orange County. Prices aren't as cheap at these airports, but Hollywood Burbank is more convenient to central L.A., and John Wayne is more convenient to Orange County (Disneyland and beaches).

Once you get to L.A., I highly recommend **renting a car** or hiring a **driving service.** Public transportation is slowly improving, but it's such an expansive city that there are many places that will take hours to get to by Metro or bus. The **traffic** here lives up to its infamous reputation. Try to avoid driving during **rush hour periods** (7am-10am and 3pm-7pm on weekdays) as much as possible. **Parking** can also be a struggle, but a little bit of planning can help save a lot of time and money. Scope out parking garages ahead of time and check venue websites for relevant parking prices and information.

That being said, if you're only staying in one neighborhood for a few days, you could definitely get away with just using taxis or rideshare apps, public transportation, or potentially walking.

For public transportation, the two main options are the **Metro rail** and the **Metro bus** systems. Both the rail and the buses have routes operating 24 hours a day. Find comprehensive route maps, timetables, and other resources online at www.metro.net. If you're going to use public transportation a lot during your trip, consider buying either a 7-day ($32) or 30-day ($121) unlimited Metro pass.

Despite the heavy traffic, L.A. is a somewhat **bikeable** city; there are bike racks on most buses, and bike-share operations in Downtown, Venice, and Santa Monica let you rent a bike for anywhere from 30 minutes to 30 days.

RESERVATIONS

The major thing you'll need to reserve in advance is your **accommodation**—hotels in L.A. tend to book up quickly, especially during summer.

Most mid-priced **restaurants** take same-week reservations, but a handful of upscale restaurants (like Spago in Beverly Hills) require reservations well in advance.

You can show up on the spot and get into almost all **museums** without reservations; the one exception is the Getty Villa, which has free admission but requires advance reservations. The Broad museum takes reservations but doesn't require them—your reserved ticket will simply let you skip the line.

If you're planning on rocking out at a **concert,** it helps to buy tickets in advance because popular artists usually sell out even large venues. Performances at the Hollywood Bowl, for example, almost always sell out in advance.

PASSES AND DISCOUNTS

There are two popular all-inclusive passes for the greater Los Angeles area. **GoCard Los Angeles** provides free entry to more than 30 entertainment venues for about $200; it's only worth buying if you'll go to three or more of the select attractions during your trip. **CityPass** includes entry to Disneyland, Disney California Adventure, SeaWorld San Diego, Legoland California, and the San Diego Zoo for about $300; it's only worth buying if you'll be spending four or more days at the aforementioned theme parks.

Los Angeles has a lot of great

museums, most of which either have free admission or select free-admission days. See page 140 for a comprehensive list of days.

the Chinese New Year Festival

GUIDED TOURS

There are plenty of tours all over Los Angeles that provide different glimpses of the city. **TMZ Tours** and **Legends of Hollywood** are both popular ways to see Beverly Hills and Hollywood—and perhaps peep a celebrity. **Starline Tours** runs tour buses with six routes that let you get on and off when you want, letting you explore the city at your own pace. For more information on these tours and more, see page 169.

CALENDAR OF EVENTS

JANUARY

On the first of each year, Pasadena hosts the annual **Rose Bowl Game** (www.tournamentofroses. com/rose-bowl) and the accompanying **Parade of Roses** (www. tournamentofroses.com/rose-parade). The football game is a rowdy event with partying sports fans from around the world. The Parade of Roses has beautiful floats

made of roses and other flowers. You'll need advance tickets for the Tournament of Roses; the Parade of Roses is free and open to all. Keep in mind that if January 1 falls on a Sunday, the game and parade happen on Monday, January 2.

FEBRUARY

Dragons galore! Every winter, the Chinatown area of Downtown L.A. hosts its **Chinese New Year Festival** (http://chinatownla.com/wp1/calendar), which has authentic Chinese food, music, martial arts demonstrations, and more. The highlight of the event is the Golden Dragon Parade, featuring some fierce fangs. Free admission.

To see movie stars in person, you can go to Hollywood's Dolby Theatre at dawn on the morning of the **Academy Awards** (http://www.oscars.org/oscars) and snag a bleacher seat. From there, you can watch hundreds of celebrities strut down the red carpet ushered by flashing lights. (FYI—famous people appear smaller in person!) The seats are free; it's first come, first served here on Hollywood Boulevard.

Parade of Roses

APRIL

Book lovers will adore the **L.A. Times Festival of Books** (http://events.latimes.com/festivalofbooks), which happens each year at the University of California, Los Angeles (UCLA) in Brentwood. Come learn about new literature, buy signed books, and attend panel discussions featuring your favorite writers. Free admission.

The world's largest Cinco de Mayo festival is called **Fiesta Broadway** (http://allaccess-la.com/fiesta-broadway) and it happens in Downtown L.A. each year. Brave crowds of more than 300,000 people to eat fantastic Mexican cuisine and dance to vibrant performances by well-known Latino artists. There are carnival-style rides and games for all ages. Free admission.

JUNE

L.A. Pride (https://www.lapride.org) is a weekend-long party. There are streamers and strobe lights and little rainbow-colored thongs celebrating all things LGBTQ. There's a Pride parade each year and festivities continue well into the night all along Santa Monica Boulevard in West Hollywood. The main strip is open for everyone to explore; some events, like concerts, require tickets.

JULY

Outfest (https://www.outfest.org) provides a cool opportunity to view LGBTQ films that may not receive the same spotlight as more mainstream movies. This weeklong festival takes place in multiple theaters throughout Hollywood and West Hollywood, and it's a

L.A. Pride

- **Downtown Los Angeles** is experiencing a revitalization that's bringing some fantastic shops, galleries, and restaurants to this once floundering neighborhood. The **Arts District** on the east side is particularly exciting—this is where you can check out street art from world-class artists, play Skee-Ball at local breweries, and buy $90 sweatpants at a pop-up boutique.

- In 2015, Los Angeles gained two professional football teams, the **L.A. Rams** and the **L.A. Chargers.** Angelenos are thrilled to have pro football teams back in our city, and the games for both these teams, particularly the Rams, are filled with energy. The Rams and Chargers will both start playing at the Los Angeles Stadium at Hollywood Park when it opens in 2020.

- In 2016, Los Angeles opened the **Expo Metro line,** which runs from Downtown to Santa Monica—a route that can take potential hours by car during rush hour. Since the line opened, tens of thousands of locals and visitors have used this glimmering new train to travel across the city in less than an hour.

good place to meet friendly and artsy Angelenos. Purchase tickets separately for each movie.

See some of the world's best surfers at the **Vans U.S. Open of Surfing** (http://www.vansusopenofsurfing.com) in Huntington Beach, a quaint surf town about 40 miles south of L.A. This area comes alive each summer for this surfing tournament, which also has pro and amateur skateboarding competitions. You can sit on either the sand or the beachside bleachers to watch the surfers and skaters compete.

AUGUST

Come to the **L.A. County Fair** (http://lacountyfair.com) for fried Oreos, Twinkies, and turkey legs. Oh, and other stuff, too—such as rides, lively musical performances, and a plethora of local livestock (who doesn't like petting a bunny?). The annual fair is a fun place to let loose and enjoy the less sophisticated side of Los Angeles. There's great people-watching from the top of the Ferris wheel. Tickets $8-14.

OCTOBER

Every year, West Hollywood hosts one of the country's largest Halloween bashes. The main attraction of this over-the-top **Halloween Carnival** (https://www.visitwesthollywood.com/halloween-carnaval) is the parade that runs down Santa Monica Boulevard from Doheny Drive to La Cienega Boulevard. Both paraders and revelers have elaborately fabulous costumes that look like they took months to prepare. The carnival is free and open to all.

Halloween Carnival

Dia de los Muertos at the Hollywood Forever Cemetery

NOVEMBER

Dia de los Muertos (http://www.ladayofthedead.com) is a special day for Mexicans to honor their dearly departed. Each year, the Hollywood Forever Cemetery hosts a huge weekend-long festival that is big and commercial, yet also authentically Mexican. Many attendees dress in gorgeous costumes of feathers and flowers, and each day is filled with Mexican music, food, and art. There's a craft area just for kids. Tickets $20.

The weeklong **AFI Los Angeles International Film Festival** (http://www.afi.com/afifest) shows new and classic films in some of L.A.'s favorite movie theaters. This is a great place to discover a buzz-worthy indie flick from Sweden, or rewatch *Casablanca* on the big screen. Some screenings require purchased tickets, but the majority are free and open to the public. Many screenings are followed by discussions with the film's directors and/or actors.

NEIGHBORHOODS

Santa Monica

Map 1

Santa Monica was born in the 1900s as a **seaside retreat,** and with its iconic **pier** and **Ferris wheel,** it still feels like L.A.'s playground.

Once home to silver-screen giants like Greta Garbo and Cary Grant, this beachy town is now an **eclectic mix** of hippie-surfers, business professionals, families, yogis, tech geeks, and celebs. It's no wonder this is one of the most popular places to live in L.A. County; Santa Monica embodies much of what people love about L.A., with its big **beaches,** great **shopping,** and delicious **dining.**

There's also California's biggest **farmers market,** inexpensive off-beach **motels,** a 22-mile **bike path,** and spectacular **sunsets** over the Pacific almost every night. What's not to love?

TOP SIGHTS
- Santa Monica Pier (page 66)

TOP NIGHTLIFE
- The Bungalow (page 122)

TOP SPORTS AND ACTIVITIES
- Learn to Surf L.A. (page 161)
- Palisades Park (page 161)
- The Strand (page 162)

TOP SHOPS
- McCabe's Guitar Shop (page 179)
- Mindfulnest (page 181)

TOP HOTELS
- Casa del Mar (page 204)

GETTING THERE AND AROUND
- Metro lines: Expo
- Metro stations: 26th Street/Bergamot, 17th Street/SMC, Downtown Santa Monica
- Major bus routes: 20, 33, 234, 720, 733, 734, 788, R3, R6, R7, C6, Big Blue Bus multiple routes

Venice

Map 2

Long known as the **funkiest** part of L.A., Venice comes to many visitor's minds when they think of the quintessential California experience. This is thanks in part to its **famous boardwalk,** which has provided the backdrop to an edgy, eclectic scene since the 1970s—both in films and reality.

Though the neighborhood has toned it down and become more **upscale** since then, it has managed to retain much of its colorful charm (and is still a magnet for L.A.'s quirkiest denizens—they just tend to be wealthier now). It's also a fantastic place for **walking, shopping, eating,** and **people-watching.**

Much of Venice was designed in the early 20th century by the famed Abbot Kinney, who wanted to bring the grandeur of Venice, Italy, to this then-small California town. You'll even find the Cali version of the Italian **canals** here.

TOP SIGHTS
- Venice Beach Boardwalk (page 68)

TOP RESTAURANTS
- Deus Ex Machina (page 94)
- Blue Star Donuts (page 95)

TOP ARTS AND CULTURE
- Venice Murals (page 141)

TOP SPORTS AND ACTIVITIES
- Venice Skate Park (page 165)

TOP SHOPS
- Mollusk Surf Shop (page 184)

TOP HOTELS
- The Rose Hotel (page 206)

GETTING THERE AND AROUND
- Metro lines: none (but you can take the Expo Line to Santa Monica and take a bus from there to Venice)
- Metro stations: none (but you can take the Expo Line to Santa Monica and take a bus from there to Venice)
- Major bus routes: 33, 733, R3, R7, BBB1, BBB3, BBB7, BBB8, BBB18

ABBOT KINNEY, VENICE BOARDWALK, AND THE CANALS WALK

TOTAL DISTANCE: 2 miles
WALKING TIME: 45 minutes

This is a perfect walk for lunchtime or late afternoon. Your walk starts on the famed **Abbot Kinney Boulevard** (a hipster shopper's dream), takes you along the iconic Venice Beach Boardwalk, and finishes up at the Venice Canals—a perfect place to be at sunset.

1 Start your journey at **Lemonade,** a delicious hangout for locals and visitors alike. If you're hungry, choose cafeteria-style from plenty of fresh sandwiches, salads, and hot entrees. Or, if you just need some fuel for the road, order Lemonade's namesake beverage to go; fun flavors include lavender, watermelon, and strawberry rhubarb.

2 Leave Lemonade and turn right to continue walking west along the north side of Abbot Kinney. At Palms Boulevard, cross to the south side of Abbot Kinney, turn left, and backtrack just a little to visit **Mystic**

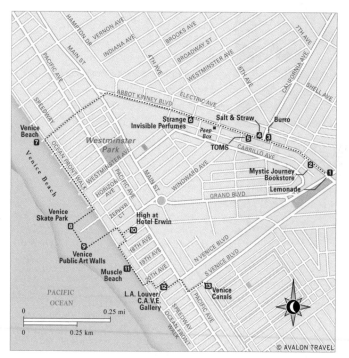

Venice Beach

Journey Bookstore. Here you can get in touch with your spiritual side via books, crystals, and sessions with in-house "intuitive readers."

3 Depart from your mystic journey, turn left, and keep walking west until you hit Millwood, then cross to the north side of Abbot Kinney. Keep walking to **Burro,** a gift buyer's paradise. You'll probably want to buy a bag or knapsack here just to hold all of your adorable purchases.

4 Once your bags are full, exit right, and you'll probably notice a line at **Salt & Straw** on the other side of California Avenue. If you're in the mood, go ahead grab a scoop of the sensational homemade ice cream.

Venice Canals

5 Cross the street at California Avenue to get to **TOMS,** a great place to sit, chill, and maybe buy some socially conscious shoes or sunglasses. When you leave TOMS, keep walking on the south side of Abbot Kinney; in roughly 150 feet, cross Andalusia Avenue. Once you cross, there will be a little **peep box** on your left—peer inside to get a glimpse of what Venice looked like circa 1910.

6 Keeping your eyes peeled for cool murals, walk past cute shops and boutiques to get to **Strange Invisible Perfumes.** Try out the unique scents in this Venice-only shop, and then keep walking west on Abbot Kinney to make your way to the beach!

7 Continue on Abbot Kinney for about a half mile, and you'll end up right in the heart of the **Venice Beach and Boardwalk.** This half mile isn't thrilling, but there are some cool houses to look at, and you can start to enjoy the fresh ocean breezes along the way. Once you make it to the boardwalk, take a moment to pause—gaze out at the horizon, breathe in the salt air, and marvel at the beautifully diverse throngs of people wandering (and biking and skating) by.

8 Turn left to walk south on the boardwalk. You'll pass all sorts of knickknack shops on your left and craft artists on your right. In 0.3 mile, you'll see the **Venice Skate Park** on your right (it looks like a huge concrete bowl). Walk over to check out the skaters, or rent a board and try out the park for yourself if you're so inclined.

9 Just beyond the skate park are the **Venice Public Art Walls,** which provide an excellent opportunity for a selfie.

10 Time to make your way back to the boardwalk. Note that if you turn down 17th Avenue at this point, you can walk a block and hit

Venice Public Art Walls

Venice Skate Park

High at Hotel Erwin, which has rooftop cocktails and some great views to end your walk with.

11 Keep walking south past people working out at **Muscle Beach.** This is a fun spot for a little people-watching.

12 Keeping walking south for about a quarter mile and then take a left on North Venice Boulevard. Just 1.5 blocks down on your left will be **L.A. Louver** and **C.A.V.E. Gallery,** two well-known and highly respected modern art galleries.

13 You can choose to end your walk here—and maybe getting a drink at Hotel Erwin—or continue onto the **Venice Canals.** To get to the canals, continue down North Venice Boulevard and cross Pacific Avenue. Make a right and walk for another two blocks before taking a left on South Venice Boulevard. Cross the street, continue for another two blocks, and you'll hit the Grand Canalway. The best way to enjoy the canals is to stroll them without a plan—have fun!

Beverly Hills

Map 3

Beverly Hills is unabashedly posh. Some of the entertainment industry's biggest stars and producers call this neighborhood home; as such, it's become synonymous with America's rich and famous. But we commoners are welcome here, too—which is a good thing, because there are **gorgeous homes** and **art galleries** to gawk at, **designer stores** to peruse, and **luxurious spas** and **restaurants** to splurge on.

Despite the many tourists, there are also a lot of people who *live* here—in the morning you'll find them in cafés sipping coffee, and in the afternoon on bistro patios, noshing on oversized Cobb salads. Like the shopping, the **people-watching** is endless (you may even catch a celeb behind an oversized pair of sunglasses).

TOP SIGHTS
- Rodeo Drive (page 70)

TOP RESTAURANTS
- Mastro's (page 97)

TOP ARTS AND CULTURE
- Galerie Michael (page 143)

TOP SPORTS AND ACTIVITIES
- Spa Montage (page 166)

TOP SHOPS
- Alo Yoga (page 185)
- What Goes Around Comes Around (page 185)

TOP HOTELS
- Hotel Bel-Air (page 213)

GETTING THERE AND AROUND
- Metro lines: None
- Metro stations: None
- Major bus routes: 4, 14, 16, 20, 17, 28, 316, 704, 720, 728, BBB5, CE534

BEVERLY HILLS

BEVERLY GARDENS PARK AND RODEO DRIVE WALK

TOTAL DISTANCE: 1 mile
WALKING TIME: 20 minutes

Beverly Hills's wide sidewalks make it not only a great place to people-watch, but also a great walking town. This walk starts at the beautiful Beverly Hills City Hall, strolls through Beverly Gardens Park, and then moseys down Rodeo Drive.

1 You'll start at **Beverly Hills City Hall** on the corner of Crescent Drive and North Santa Monica Boulevard. The building's eight-story, Spanish Renaissance-style tower makes it pretty hard to miss. Snap some pictures here and then wander through the perfectly manicured gardens, making sure to take a whiff of the rosemary bushes when they're in bloom.

2 Walk north on Crescent Drive toward the four-lane North Santa Monica Boulevard. Once you get to North Santa Monica, cross the street to **Beverly Gardens Park.** Once you're in the park, turn left (toward N. Canon Dr.) and take your time strolling down the park's soft

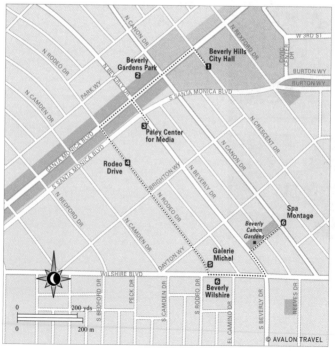

Beverly Hills City Hall

pathways. Enjoy the playful sculptures and big, leafy trees. After about a block you'll get to North Canon Drive; cross this street to continue in the park (use caution—it's a busy street). In the next block, don't miss getting a selfie with the Beverly Hills sign and lily pond, which is filled with tiny fish and bright purple, pink, and orange lotus flowers. A magical ficus tree also sits at the far end of the pond—marvel at the giant tree's gnarled roots and far-reaching branches before moving on. Cross Beverly Boulevard to explore one more sculpture-filled block of the park.

3 Had your fill of nature? Time to head to the **Paley Center for Media** for some cultural enrichment. Walk to the corner of Rodeo Drive and North Santa Monica Boulevard and cross back over North Santa Monica toward the town center. After you cross, walk one block to get to South Santa Monica Boulevard, where you'll turn left and walk 0.1 mile

Beverly Gardens Park

to get to North Beverly Drive. The Paley Center is a big, glassy building on the corner of North Beverly Boulevard and South Santa Monica Boulevard; turn right on Beverly Boulevard to get to its entrance. Once you're in the Paley Center, spend some time exploring the extensive collection of viewable TV shows and movies and three stories of exhibits, which feature costumes and props from popular productions.

4 Once you're done at the Paley Center, it's time to hit up *the* **Rodeo Drive.** Walk back to South Santa Monica Boulevard, turn right, and walk two blocks to Rodeo Drive. Turn left on Rodeo, and you'll be surrounded by huge flagship stores from the world's most famous high-end designers, including Ralph Lauren, Hermes, and Tory Burch. From Dior to Gucci, all the big-name brands are here, with big and beautifully de-

Rodeo Drive

signed stores to match. Even if you're not shopping, the stores themselves are so artful that they're fun to just ogle. To check out some smaller boutiques and lesser-known brands, wander down the side streets that extend in both directions off of Rodeo Drive.

5 After walking down Rodeo Drive for about 0.2 mile, you'll get to the intersection of Rodeo Drive and Dayton Way, where you'll see the impressive Louis Vuitton flagship store. Cross over Dayton Way to enter Two Rodeo Drive, a curving pedestrian walkway. Walk up this European-style street, passing Versace, Lanvin, and a Tiffany & Co. flagship, before reaching **Galerie Michael,** a must-see art gallery. You'll want to spend some time perusing the fine European art here, which ranges from the 17th century to present day and includes works from masters like Rembrandt and Matisse.

6 At the far end of Two Rodeo Drive is a sweeping marble staircase next to a multitiered marble foundation (another great picture spot). Walk down the staircase to the busy Wilshire Boulevard, right across the street from the **Beverly Wilshire,** built in 1928 when Beverly Hills was in its infancy. Cross over Wilshire Boulevard to enter the hotel. Once inside, snap a few pics in the lobby, made famous by the movie *Pretty Woman,* and check out its shops and restaurants.

7 End your walk with a late afternoon pampering at **Spa Montage,** considered by many to be the best spa in L.A. Continue east down Wilshire Boulevard past El Camino Drive and turn left onto the ride side of North Beverly Drive. Walk for a minute until you see **Beverly Cañon**

Beverly Wilshire

Gardens on your right—cut through this cute little park to reach North Canon Drive. Take a right on North Canon Drive and you'll be at the spa's entrance. You'll feel like a Beverly Hills socialite after splurging on a mani/pedi, facial, or massage at this tranquil oasis. Be sure to book a reservation in advance.

Hollywood

Map 4

Hollywood is where the **movie industry** was born, creating an image that would become synonymous with L.A. itself. All of the original studios except **Paramount** relocated in the 1970s, taking their wealth and creative energy with them. But in the past few decades, the **glitz and glam** that originally characterized the over-the-top town has returned, thanks to new businesses and investors. Today, celebrities attend **blockbuster premieres** at **historic movie theaters,** exclusive **restaurants** and **clubs** draw glamorous crowds after dark, and the huge, white-lettered **Hollywood Sign** is still the city's most iconic landmark. Yes, the touristy **Walk of Fame** can be rough around the edges, but it's all part of the over-the-top fun.

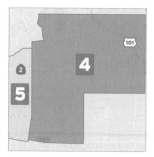

TOP SIGHTS
- Walk of Fame (page 73)

TOP NIGHTLIFE
- Musso & Frank Grill (page 128)
- La Descarga (page 129)

TOP ARTS AND CULTURE
- Groundlings Theatre (page 144)
- Hollywood Bowl (page 145)
- ArcLight Cinema Hollywood (page 145)
- Cinespia (page 146)

TOP SPORTS AND ACTIVITIES
- Runyon Canyon (page 168)
- Lucky Strike (page 169)

TOP SHOPS
- Melrose Trading Post (page 187)
- Supreme (page 187)
- House of Intuition (page 188)
- Nick Metropolis Collectible
  Furniture (page 189)

TOP HOTELS
- The Hollywood Roosevelt Hotel (page 208)

GETTING THERE AND AROUND
- Metro lines: Red
- Metro stations: Hollywood/Highland, Hollywood/Vine, Hollywood/Western
- Major bus routes: 2, 175, 180, 181, 204, 206, 207, 218, 210, 212, 217, 237, 302, 312, 656, 754, 757, 780, WH, LDHW

WALK OF FAME

TOTAL DISTANCE: 1.5 miles
WALKING TIME: 30 minutes

Once steeped in glitz and glamour, the Walk of Fame has been synonymous with Hollywood for decades. While a bit seedier (and
perhaps lowbrow) these days, it's nevertheless fun to spend a few
daytime hours checking out some of L.A.'s most famous sights
while spotting celebrity names cemented in sidewalk stars. I recommended walking in the morning or early afternoon, especially if you
have kids—crowds of tourists grow thick as the day wears on, and
evenings bring out more rowdy locals.

1 Start your tour just a bit off Hollywood Boulevard at the iconic **Capitol Records Building** on Vine Street. Tourists are not allowed inside
the building, but you can snap some pictures of the distinctive structure,
which is shaped like a tower of records. Scope out the beautiful *Hollywood Jazz* mural in the parking lot afterwards.

the Capitol Records Building and *Hollywood Jazz* mural

2 From Capitol Records, walk south on Vine (away from the hills) toward the busy intersection of Vine and Hollywood Boulevard. Go to the southwest corner of the intersection to fuel up at **The Pie Hole,** which has great coffee/tea drinks and—you guessed it—delicious sweet and savory pies.

3 Leave Pie Hole and continue walking west down the south side of Hollywood Boulevard. You'll pass by (or stop into) a bunch of stores that cater to a wide range of interests, including erotica, sneakers, souvenirs, and custom wigs. Terrazzo and brass stars, including those for Lucille Ball, Will Rogers, and Hank Williams, line the **Walk of Fame.** When you get to Wilcox Avenue, cross to the north side of Hollywood Boulevard and walk one block up on Hudson Street to check out the tribute mural to Mexican actress Delores del Rio.

4 Continue walking west on Hollywood Boulevard, past Duke Ellington's star, until you get to the **Museum of Broken Relationships** on the northwest corner of Hollywood Boulevard and McCadden Place. Stop in this bittersweet museum to peruse relics of relationships gone sour.

5 From the Museum of Broken Relationships, keep walking

Hollywood Boulevard

47

west on Hollywood Boulevard until you cross the always-busy intersection of Hollywood and Highland. Once you cross the street, the four-story **Hollywood & Highland** shopping complex will be on your right. Take the stairs or escalator into the complex to check out some of America's biggest chain stores, and then head up to the third- or fourth-level walkways for great views of the Hollywood sign.

6 When you leave Hollywood & Highland, keep walking west on Hollywood Boulevard—the **Dolby Theatre** will be immediately on your right. Enter through the grand marble walkway to see the world-famous theater that hosts the Academy Awards and other major entertainment events each year.

7 Continuing a few steps west on Hollywood Boulevard, you can't miss the **TCL Chinese Theatre** on your right. Here you can see the cemented palm prints of hundreds of stars, take a picture with people dressed up as your favorite movie characters (think *Star Wars, Pirates of the Caribbean*, etc.), and catch an IMAX film if your feet need a rest.

8 Leave the theater and continue west on Hollywood Boulevard for just a few paces until you get to Orange Street; use Orange to cross to the other side of Hollywood Boulevard to reach **The Hollywood Roosevelt Hotel.** If you're ready for a cocktail, the Roosevelt's classy bar

the Dolby Theatre

Four Ladies of Hollywood

is the place for it. If not, step inside anyway to take a look at this historic landmark.

9 Want more shopping, or just a refreshing break? Cross back over Hollywood Boulevard at Orange Street and continue a few hundred feet to the Hollywood Galaxy shopping center; tucked in the back of this mini-mall is **Muji Hollywood,** an impressive Japanese department store. Enjoy the lavender-scented mist blowing inside while you browse quality clothing, fun little gifts, and interesting home goods.

10 For your final stop, head to Hollywood Boulevard and Sycamore and cross to the south side of Hollywood Boulevard once more. Keep walking west (past Bob Marley's star) and in 450 feet arrive at the silver statute titled *Four Ladies of Hollywood,* a tribute to some original big-screen starlets.

West Hollywood Map 5

Affectionately known as WeHo, West Hollywood has all of the pizzazz of Hollywood proper, with more rock 'n' roll and more refinement. You'll find rock 'n' roll on the famous **Sunset Strip,** with its **legendary nightclubs** and **live music venues**, once home to mobsters, old-school Hollywood celebrities, and 1980s rock stars.

You'll find refinement in **upscale restaurants,** sophisticated **poolside lounges,** and **chic boutiques** in the Design District, home to **Melrose Avenue.**

WeHo is also home to a loud and proud **LGBTQ community.** There are also several ebullient bashes along Santa Monica Boulevard each year, including **Los Angeles Pride** in June and the **Halloween Carnival** in October.

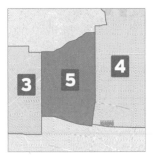

TOP SIGHTS
- Sunset Strip (page 78)

TOP RESTAURANTS
- The Little Door (page 104)
- Matsuhisa (page 104)

TOP NIGHTLIFE
- Pump (page 130)
- Skybar (page 130)
- The Abbey (page 131)

TOP ARTS AND CULTURE
- The Comedy Store (page 147)
- The Troubadour (page 150)

TOP SHOPS
- Fred Segal (page 191)
- Pacific Design Center (page 192)

TOP HOTELS
- Mondrian Los Angeles (page 210)

GETTING THERE AND AROUND
- Metro lines: No Metro line goes into West Hollywood, but WeHo's free CityLineX shuttle will take you from West Hollywood to the Hollywood/Highland Metro stop on the Red Line (http://www.weho.org/services/public-transportation-transit-options/cityline).
- Metro stations: none (see CityLineX above)
- Major bus routes: CityLine (WeHo's free mini bus), 2, 4, 10, 14, 16, 17, 30, 105, 217, 218, 302, 330, 316, 704, 705, 780
- WeHo Pickup: free weekend shuttle that runs along Santa Monica Boulevard between Robertson and La Brea Boulevards (www.wehopickup.com)

Echo Park, Los Feliz, and Silver Lake

Map 6

These once overlooked neighborhoods on the east side of Los Angeles are now destinations in their own right, filled with **hipster-chic boutiques, artsy coffeehouses,** and **fresh vegan and vegetarian restaurants.** If you want to pretend that you're a cool **local,** spend a day shopping, eating, and partying your way through the east side—you'll discover what's up-and-coming in Los Angeles.

Los Feliz sits at the bottom of one of L.A.'s best natural features—big, beautiful **Griffith Park,** home to the Griffith Observatory and

Greek Theatre. You'll find plenty of panoramic views and recreational opportunities in the park, including hiking, stargazing, and maybe even rocking out to an amazing concert.

TOP RESTAURANTS

- Guisado's (page 107)
- Jeni's Splendid Ice Creams (page 113)

TOP NIGHTLIFE

- Tiki-Ti (page 132)
- The Satellite (page 134)

TOP SPORTS AND ACTIVITIES

- Echo Park Lake & Boathouse (page 172)
- Los Angeles Dodgers (page 172)

TOP SHOPS

- Los Angeles County Store (page 194)

TOP HOTELS

- Hotel Covell (page 211)

GETTING THERE AND AROUND

- Metro lines: Red
- Metro stations: Vermont/Sunset, Vermont/Santa Monica
- Major bus routes: 2, 92, 96, 175, 180, 181, 201, 300, 302, 603, 704, 780

LOS FELIZ AND GRIFFITH PARK WALK

TOTAL DISTANCE: 1.5-4 miles
WALKING TIME: 30 minutes-2 hours

Choose a nice day for this walk and make sure you're in the neighborhood around 10:30am (prime brunch time). After an energizing meal, you can stick around Los Feliz and shop the day away, or, for the more intrepid, make a day of it by heading all the way to one of L.A.'s greenest places—Griffith Park.

1 Start your day with delicious breakfast tacos at **HomeState** on Hollywood Boulevard, which has indoor and sidewalk seating that's great for people-watching (but limited on weekends because this place is super popular). There's also great coffee and plenty of vegetarian taco options, too. Order at least three tacos—they're small and you'll need fuel for your walk!

2 Once you finish your delicious brunch, head next door and take a peek into **Bar Covell**, L.A.'s best wine bar. This is where you will

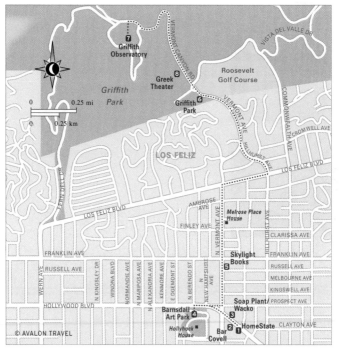

the Hollyhock House in Barnsdall Art Park

probably want to return *after* your walk for one of the best happy hours in the city.

3 Walk up to Vermont Avenue to the stoplight and cross Hollywood Boulevard to get to **Soap Plant / Wacko.** You can't really miss Soap Plant—its brick exterior is fully covered with flashy, technicolor murals. This is a one-of-a-kind knickknack shop/art gallery/bookstore that almost defies definition; it's funky and a bit gritty, and there's really nothing like it anywhere else in L.A.

4 After picking up a few gifts at Soap Plant, walk up Hollywood Boulevard (again toward Vermont Avenue) and cross back over Hollywood Boulevard at the light. Keep walking straight on Hollywood (it'll curve to your left) until you get to the entrance for **Barnsdall Art Park.** (The park is at the top of a hill, so from the bottom the entrance looks like just a parking lot.) Walk into the parking lot and up a winding road (or take the stairs) to get to this oasis of a park, which has amazing views of the Hollywood sign, Griffith Observatory, Downtown, Los Feliz, and Silver Lake. Walk around and check out the **Hollyhock House**, the majestic art deco mansion atop the hill. If you come during the right days/hours, you may be able to catch an art exhibit or even tour the Hollyhock House.

5 Leave Barnsdall Art Park the same way you came—down the hill and out onto Hollywood Boulevard. To get to some great shops on Vermont Avenue, head east on Hollywood Boulevard and cross over Hollywood Boulevard at Vermont Avenue, then keep walking north on

Vermont. Once you cross over Prospect Avenue, you'll get to a cute strip of shops, cafes, and bars. Take your time and peruse the scene. The one place you'll definitely want to check out while you're walking up Vermont is **Skylight Books,** a charming neighborhood book store with a live tree growing in the middle of the floor. This place has an outstanding selection of books that will make any reader feel at home.

Skylight Books

6 Vermont Avenue can be a great place to end your Los Feliz journey (perhaps with a beer at one of the neighborhood pubs?). But if you're in the mood for an adventure, keep going up Vermont (at a slight incline) to the shining emerald that is **Griffith Park.** To get to the park, you'll basically just keep walking up Vermont Avenue. (If you're a Melrose Place fan, swing a right on Greenwood Place while you're walking up Vermont—on the right you'll see the real **Melrose Place House.**) After about a half mile, you'll cross a major intersection at Los Feliz Boulevard, and then the neighborhood will become more residential. Continue walking up Vermont as it winds through this neighborhood (which

Griffith Park

Griffith Observatory

is landscaped quite beautifully), and in another half mile you'll get to the park entrance.

7 Once you're in Griffith Park, you can stroll around any number of its hundreds of pathways, which have different levels of incline. Find a nice lawn to lounge on, or, if you're still energized, veer to the left once you enter the park and hike all the way up to the gleaming **Griffith Observatory,** an incredible museum with an outdoor viewing deck that provides sweeping views of the city. (The hike up to the Observatory from the park entrance is another 1.5 miles with a 400-foot incline.)

8 Finally, if the timing is right, end your day with some live music at the **Greek Theatre,** an outdoor amphitheater nestled in Griffith Park. The Greek (as it's affectionately called) will be about 0.2 mile up the road on your left once you enter Griffith Park. Be sure to look at the venue's calendar and purchase tickets in advance.

Downtown Map 7

Downtown Los Angeles is experiencing a **rebirth.** Buildings that were thriving in the 1920s and shuttered in the 1990s are now bookshops, coffeehouses, restaurants, and pop-up shops selling locally made goods.

That being said, **DTLA** is still rough around the edges. The growing issue of homelessness is impossible to ignore here, and criminal activity is a bit higher than in other neighborhoods.

But that shouldn't stop you from exploring Downtown's **cool nightlife,** ever-growing **arts scene,** and **rich cultural history,** including fascinating ethnic neighborhoods such as **Chinatown, Little**

Tokyo, and **El Pueblo de Los Angeles,** a delicious slice of L.A.'s Mexican heritage.

TOP SIGHTS
- OUE Skyspace (page 81)

TOP RESTAURANTS
- Grand Central Market (page 114)
- Eggslut (page 115)
- Marugame Monzo (page 116)
- Bestia (page 117)

TOP NIGHTLIFE
- Upstairs Bar at the Ace Hotel (page 135)
- Rooftop at the Standard (page 135)

TOP ARTS AND CULTURE
- The Broad (page 154)
- Hauser & Wirth (page 155)
- The Container Yard (page 155)
- Walt Disney Concert Hall (page 157)

TOP SHOPS
- The Last Bookstore (page 200)

TOP HOTELS
- The Standard (page 212)
- Ace Hotel (page 212)
- Freehand Hotel (page 213)

GETTING THERE AND AROUND
- Metro lines: Blue, Purple, Red
- Metro stations: Little Tokyo/Arts District, Civic Center/Grand Park, Pershing Square
- Major bus routes: Downtown has the most bus coverage; go online (www.metro.net) to check for specific routes.

DOWNTOWN ARTS WALK

TOTAL DISTANCE: 2.5 miles
WALKING TIME: 1 hour

This walk will take you to a handful of L.A.'s best art museums and galleries. Along the way, you'll walk through three downtown neighborhoods: Bunker Hill, Little Tokyo, and the Arts District, where you'll see both highbrow modern art and spectacular alleyway designs. This is a good weekday walk, as some of the destinations are crowded on weekends. It's also a good idea to start in the morning and end before dark because it takes you past a few seedy corners.

1 Start your journey at the iconic **Walt Disney Concert Hall** at the corner of Grand Avenue and 2nd Street. The building is an architectural masterpiece; mosey around its perimeter and snap some photos in front of its looming, silvery arms. Tours are offered if you want to see the inside of the concert hall, but feel free to keep moving.

2 From the Disney Concert Hall, use the colorful crosswalk on 2nd Street to get to **The Broad,** another can't-miss structure. The Broad

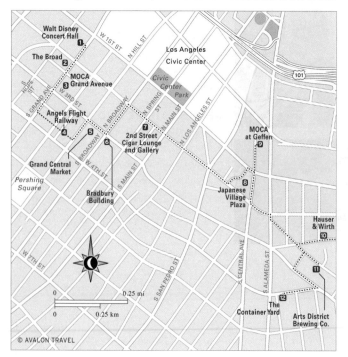

© AVALON TRAVEL

Walt Disney Concert Hall

is an enormous glass rectangle covered by a white concrete "veil." And while it's super-cool from the outside, you'll want to go inside and check out its incredible collection of contemporary art. You can reserve tickets in advance or show up unannounced and wait in line for entry—it's free to get in either way.

3 Once you leave The Broad, use the crosswalk to get to the other side of Grand Avenue. Turn right and walk just a few hundred feet to see more art at the **Museum of Contemporary Art (MOCA) Grand Avenue.** Buy your tickets to MOCA at its street-side box office and then spend some time wandering around its multiple galleries.

4 Once you're finished inside MOCA, continue to the **Angels Flight Railway.** To get to the railway, walk along MOCA's paved courtyard and past a few fountains—keep left and you'll get to an orange-red, old-timey ticket booth at the top of the railway. Buy a $1 ticket and ride the railway car to the bottom of Bunker Hill.

Angels Flight Railway

5 The Angels Flight Railway will let you off right at **Grand Central Market** just in time for lunch! Hopefully you brought your appetite, because Grand Central Market is *filled* with delicious treats from around the world—and great coffee, too. Fuel up and then exit onto Broadway (the opposite side of the market from which you entered).

6 Once you're on Broadway, you may want to step into the **Bradbury Building** right across the street to see its unique staircased architecture and wrought iron embellishments. The interior of this building is itself a work of art.

Grand Central Market

7 To get to your next destination in Little Tokyo, walk up Broadway and then turn right on 3rd Street. Take 3rd two blocks to Main Street (you might not want to do this portion after dark). Turn left on Main Street, walk up one block to 2nd Street, and turn right on 2nd. Keep walking southeast on 2nd Street; you'll pass the Los Angeles Police Department headquarters on your left, and the **2nd Street Cigar Lounge and Gallery** on your right. Pop in for a minute if you're tempted by the awning beckoning you to "Relax with Cigars & Art."

8 Keep walking down 2nd Street for about 0.3 mile, under a plethora of graceful trees providing some shade. As you cross Los Angeles Boulevard, you'll head into Little Tokyo, rapidly becoming a popular residential area. Continue on 2nd Street and cross the four-lane San Pedro Street to get to the **Japanese Village Plaza** on your left. Turn left to walk diagonally through the small plaza, which is filled with Japanese shops and cafés (*matcha*, anyone?).

Little Tokyo

9 After walking through the plaza for a few blocks, you'll come out onto 1st Street (maybe with a cute gift in hand). Cross 1st Street here to pass the Japanese Heritage Museum on your right and arrive at your next destination: **MOCA at Geffen,** a huge space that houses rotating contemporary art installations.

10 Once you leave MOCA at Geffen, you can start walking down Central Avenue. When you get to 2nd Street, turn left to head toward the Arts District. You'll pass a different plaza full of more Japanese shops. When you get to Alameda Street, keep walking in the same

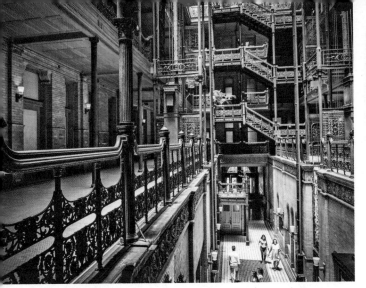

Bradbury Building

direction (southeast) onto Traction Avenue, a little diagonal street that will take you to 3rd Street. Enjoy the powerful street art and trendy pop-up shops lining Traction Avenue, and then turn left onto 3rd Street to get to **Hauser & Wirth,** one block down on your left. You'll enter Hauser & Wirth through big metal gates; take a quiet stroll around its three contemporary art galleries.

11 If all this art has worked up an appetite, end your walk with a well-deserved beer and a hot dog at one of the outdoor tables at **Arts District Brewing Co.** Just head back the way you came on 3rd Street and take a left to continue down Traction Avenue, and you'll see it on the right.

12 Either before or after your beer, get one last selfie in at **The Container Yard,** a former Japanese manufacturing company with brick walls that have been transformed by incredible street art. Just head back the way you came on Traction Avenue, make a left onto South Hewitt Street, then another left after one block onto East 4th Street. Continue briefly until you reach a funky intersection; make a slight right to continue down East 4th, passing Colyton Street. You'll see The Container Yard across the street (use the intersection a block further at South Alameda Street to cross). Be sure to check the venue's Facebook page ahead of time to see if there are any cool pop-up events happening during your visit.

SIGHTS

There are *lots* of photogenic spots here in Los Angeles.

On the west side, beaches offer up incredible vistas and sunsets. You can spend hours people-watching on the Venice Beach Boardwalk or strolling along the Venice canals. The Santa Monica Pier is one of L.A.'s most iconic landmarks, with its bright Ferris Wheel jutting above the Pacific.

Venice Beach Boardwalk

Beverly Hills is great for views of a different kind—like shop windows on Rodeo Drive. There are also gorgeous mansions to ogle, manicured parks to stroll, and Spanish-style architecture to photograph. Hollywood, on the other hand, is a bit grittier, but has the most popular sights in L.A. Its Walk of Fame is home to historic movie industry spots like the TCL Chinese Theater and Paramount Movie Studios.

Downtown L.A. is the city's most culturally diverse neighborhood. It also features the most diverse range of sights, from Olvera Street's Mexican marketplace to fascinating architectural marvels like the Bradbury Building.

For some of L.A.'s best sights, head to the hills—the Getty Center is tucked into the Santa Monica Mountains and Griffith Park, perched above Los Feliz, is home to the Griffith Observatory and the Hollywood Sign.

Make sure to bring your camera!

HIGHLIGHTS

✪ **BEST PLACE TO WATCH THE SUNSET:** Take a ride on the **Santa Monica Pier** to watch an amazing Pacific Ocean sunset (page 66).

✪ **BEST PEOPLE WATCHING:** The **Venice Beach Boardwalk** is a lot of things, but shy is not one of them. Let your freak flag fly and meet some of L.A.'s most eccentric residents (page 68).

✪ **BEST WINDOW-SHOPPING:** Even if you're just window-shopping or people-watching, **Rodeo Drive** will give you a taste of what it's like to be rich and famous (page 70).

✪ **BEST TOURISTY CHARM:** You can't leave L.A. without visiting the **Walk of Fame**—join in the touristy fun by taking a pic with your fave celeb's star (page 73).

✪ **BEST SLICE OF ROCK 'N' ROLL HISTORY:** The infamous **Sunset Strip** is lined with neon billboards, historic music venues, and at night, drunk tourists (page 78).

✪ **BEST PLACE TO RIDE A SLIDE:** At the **OUE Skyspace** observation deck, you can see all of L.A.—and ride a glass slide above it (page 81).

✪ **BEST STARGAZING: Griffith Observatory** offers free panoramic views of L.A. and the night sky from one of the biggest telescopes in the country (page 82).

✪ **BEST PICTURE TO BRING HOME:** Perhaps the most iconic landmark in L.A., the **Hollywood Sign** deserves at least one selfie (page 83).

✪ **BEST ART COLLECTION WITH A VIEW:** Art-lover or not, a trip to the **Getty Center** is worth it for its amazing views and beautiful architecture (page 84).

Griffith Observatory

✪ Santa Monica Pier

With its iconic Ferris wheel and lively beach scene, the Santa Monica Pier is a quintessential L.A. experience. Yes, it can get crowded with tourists (especially during summer), and yes, you will pay $12 for a cheesy pretzel, but the pier is just too darn fun to miss. This 100-plus-year-old wooden pier houses six restaurants, a mini aquarium, and even a small amusement park. This is also a great spot for people-watching—plop down on a bench and watch caricature artists, anglers, and tourists from all over the world.

Kids especially love the pier. Take them to pet starfish in the local aquarium (1600 Ocean Front Walk, 310/393-6149, https://healthebay.org/aquarium), take a spin on the carousel, cool off with some hand-dipped ice cream, and then try your luck at the pier arcade. At the end of the pier is the grand finale: Pacific Park (380 Santa Monica Pier, 310/260-8744, www.pacpark.com), a small amusement park featuring a Ferris wheel, a miniature roller coaster, kiddie rides, and midway games.

For adults, the views are the biggest reward. The best time to visit is right around sunset, when the ocean cool starts to set in. Ride the Ferris wheel then for unbeatable Pacific views.

During the summer, there's a free twilight concert at the pier every Thursday night.

MAP 1: Ocean Ave. and Colorado Ave., 310/458-8901, http://santamonicapier.org; daily 24 hours; free

NEARBY:

- Shop or dine at the popular 3rd Street Promenade (page 66).
- Get a different perspective on Santa Monica at Camera Obscura (page 67).
- Rent a bike or roller blades at Santa Monica Beach Bicycle Rentals and cruise The Strand (page 162).
- Make reservations for a luxe dinner at The Lobster (page 90).
- Grab a cocktail with a view at Onyx Rooftop Bar (page 122).

Santa Monica Pier

3rd Street Promenade

In a city that gets almost 300 sunny days annually, outdoor malls make a lot of sense, and the 3rd Street Promenade is one of the best. In 1989, the city of Santa Monica closed four blocks of 3rd Street to all motorized vehicles and turned it into a palm tree-lined pedestrian thoroughfare. You'll mostly find big chain stores here (Nike, Rip Curl, Banana Republic, and so forth), but there's also a handful of local retailers selling books, jewelry, and other wares. There's also quite a few restaurants, many of which have big patios that enable full-force people-watching. On weekends, talented street performers sing and dance throughout the fountain-filled promenade.

MAP 1: 3rd Street between Broadway and Wilshire Blvd.

3rd Street Promenade

Camera Obscura

The phrase *camera obscura* (Latin for "dark room") refers to the optical phenomenon that happens when an image is projected through a small hole and appears backwards and upside down on an opposite wall. At Santa Monica's Camera Obscura, located in a small building in Palisades Park, you can experience this phenomenon up close. You'll walk up a flight of stairs to a small, dark room that houses the optical device and its projected image. You can navigate the outside lens yourself to see different views of your surroundings, like a unique angle of the ocean or a palm tree-lined street. There are also regular arts and crafts classes and programs offered for all ages.

MAP 1: 1450 Ocean Ave., 310/458-2239; Mon.-Fri. 9am-3pm, Sat. 11am-4pm; free

Gehry House

Gehry House is the home of world-renowned architect Frank Gehry, who designed the Walt Disney Concert Hall and other landmark buildings. In the late 1970s, Gehry bought this pink Colonial-style home in one of Santa Monica's residential neighborhoods. A few years later, he began building a modern gray structure around the original home, using unconventional materials like corrugated steel, plywood, and chain-link fencing (much to the chagrin of his neighbors). Today, this one-of-a-kind house is a popular Santa Monica destination. You can take pictures from the road, but don't step on the property—the Gehrys still live here.

MAP 1: 1002 22nd St.

Venice

Map 2

TOP EXPERIENCE

✪ Venice Beach Boardwalk

A people-watching paradise, the Venice Beach Boardwalk is full of life, welcoming artists, bohemians, and weirdos alike. This sandy strip stretches about two miles, from the Venice Pier in the south to Santa Monica in the north. According to Los Angeles Parks and Recreation, Venice Beach, the heart of which is its boardwalk, is the second-most visited tourist destination in Southern California. And it's easy to see why—the boardwalk is like an adult amusement park, with something to offer everyone.

Into fitness? Check out the beach's skate park, lively basketball courts, or Muscle Beach. Want to shop? Peruse the numerous stores lining the boardwalk or the artist stalls set up all summer and on weekends. Feeling rhythmic? Look for the huge drum circle that happens most Saturdays and Sundays from noon to sundown. If you're looking for a subdued afternoon, this is definitely not the place. But if you're thirsty for some spontaneous, California-style fun, look here first. You never quite know what you'll find.

For decades, the Venice Beach Boardwalk was a place for creative spirits to convene. This is still true, although there are some changes happening because wealthy tech companies have been buying up properties all around Venice, especially along its beloved boardwalk. The Venice Beach

Venice Beach Boardwalk

Freakshow, a boardwalk icon for over a decade, was forced to shut down in 2017 when its building was bought by new owners who declined to renew its lease (much to the chagrin of many Angelenos).

MAP 2: 1800 Ocean Front Walk, 301/396-6764

NEARBY:

- Pump iron (or pretend to) at **Muscle Beach** (page 69).
- Watch graffiti artists work their magic at the **Venice Public Art Walls** (page 141).
- Sip on cocktails and watch the sunset at **High at Hotel Erwin** (page 124).
- Admire the contemporary art at **C.A.V.E. Gallery** and **L.A. Louver** (page 142).
- Rent a bike or roller blades at **Jay's Rentals** (page 165).

Muscle Beach

In its heyday, Muscle Beach was frequented by many tanned men and women in small bathing suits, including movie star and former California governor Arnold Schwarzenegger. Today, the scene is a bit more subdued, but you will still find some super-strong and athletic people working out here, both in the weightlifting

section and in the gymnastics training area on the beach (where you may see some really cool moves). You can even work out here yourself for a small fee.

MAP 2: 1800 Ocean Front Walk, 301/399-2775, www.musclebeach.net; Mon.-Sat. 8am-7pm; $10 per day for use

Venice Canals

Inspired by the canals of Venice, Italy, the canals of Venice, California, are not nearly as grand, but do offer a beautiful place for a peaceful stroll. In 1905, Abbot Kinney designed these 12 acres of canalways as part of his plan to bring Italy to America. They are lined with lovely homes and white pedestrian bridges. The early mornings are a particularly good time to take a stroll, and evenings are nice, too. In December, there is an annual Holiday Boat Parade, and the canals' Christmas lights are pretty when reflected on the water.

MAP 2: 200 Linnie Canal; daily 24 hours

Abbot Kinney Boulevard

Once named the "coolest block in America" by *GQ*, Abbot Kinney

Abbot Kinney Boulevard

Boulevard is a hipster's paradise. While some lament the commercialization that has taken place since, others rejoice in the growth of new restaurants, boutiques, organic apothecaries, and so much more. The main strip of Abbot Kinney is only about a mile long, so prepare for a leisurely walk and come hungry—delicious eats abound for all budgets. Your best bet is to get a coffee and sit outside, as this strip offers some of the best people-watching in all of L.A.

MAP 2: Abbot Kinney Blvd., www. abbotkinneyblvd.com

Rose Avenue

If Abbot Kinney Boulevard had a subdued younger sister, it would be Rose Avenue. The one mile of Rose Avenue from Lincoln Boulevard to the beach is filled with delightful shops and restaurants, capturing much of the understated elegance that certain parts of Venice are known for. Take a stroll here to buy some unique threads or grab a sidewalk table at one of a number of cafes to enjoy a sunny afternoon, filled with flowers and top-notch people-watching.

MAP 2: Rose Ave. between 7th Ave. and Pacific Ave.

Beverly Hills   Map 3

TOP EXPERIENCE

✪ Rodeo Drive

First glamorized in the 1970s, Rodeo Drive was once the place to be rich and famous. Today, it's the central channel that runs down Beverly Hills's commercial center, and even though L.A.'s uber-rich have dispersed across the city, Rodeo Drive and its surrounding streets still have a loyal following of people who like to drink coffee, eat salad, and sip rosé in style.

Rodeo Drive has become particularly popular with international visitors who are looking to do some serious shopping. This is where you'll find huge designer stores, many of them flagships, and all of them works of art unto themselves. Whether you're browsing or buying, Rodeo is definitely an entertaining place to spend an afternoon.

While you're here, make sure to check out **Two Rodeo Drive,** a charming pedestrian walkway that branches off Rodeo Drive's main drag. It includes galleries, antique stores, and more designer shops.

MAP 3: http://rodeodrive-bh.com; 24 hours daily

NEARBY:

- Stroll through lush **Beverly Gardens Park** (page 71).
- Grab a huge lox-and-bagel sandwich

at Nate'n Al Delicatessen (page 95).

- Drink martinis with the cool kids at The Honor Bar (page 96).
- Escape with an espresso at Nespresso Boutique & Cafe (page 97).
- View pieces from 17th century masters at Galerie Michael (page 143).
- Step off Rodeo for vintage goods at What Goes Around Comes Around (page 185).

Beverly Gardens Park

Beverly Gardens Park is a thoughtful, pedestrian-minded park with meandering walkways that pass modern statutes, a rose garden, and a lotus-filled fountain perfect for snapping selfies. About two miles long, it runs alongside North Santa Monica Boulevard, right in the heart of Beverly Hills. It's a good place to get some exercise in the morning, or take a break from shopping on Rodeo Drive. Beverly Gardens Park is also the location for the Beverly Hills Art Show, an outdoor fair that happens in May and October.

MAP 3: Santa Monica Blvd. between Wilshire Blvd. and Doheny Drive, www.beverlyhills.org/exploring/cityparks/beverlygardenspark; 24 hours daily

Greystone Mansion & Park

Greystone is a mansion-turned-park that has been featured in dozens of films, including *Spiderman, The Social Network,* and *Ghostbusters.* Built in 1928 by the oil-rich Wilkins family, this palatial estate sits on 18 acres of prime Beverly Hills real estate. The city of Beverly Hills bought the mansion and its surrounding property in 1965, and made it into a public park in 1971. Since then, Greystone's grounds have been open to the public for strolling, picnicking, weddings, and more.

Rodeo Drive

CELEBRITY HOMES

There is something oddly enticing about seeing celebrity homes. Yes, celebrities are normal people just like the rest of us, but it can be *fun* to see where they live—just imagine all the glamour inside those homes! Celebrity home tours are not for everyone, but if you're even remotely interested in celebrity culture, Beverly Hills and Hollywood are the epicenter.

There are two options for touring celebrity homes—do a self-guided driving tour, or hop on a bus for a narrated tour. I recommend the bus tours because they're entertaining. But, if you'd rather guide yourself, you can look online for a map of celebrity homes or buy one from people selling them alongside the Walk of Fame in Hollywood. Once you have your map, drive around and view the homes at your own speed.

If you decide to do a guided tour, there are plenty to choose from. You can find many of them on the Walk of Fame—they drive the same routes and take walk-ups. If you want to book ahead of time, go online and check out **Access Hollywood Tours** (www.ac-cesshollywoodtours.com) or **A-List Hollywood Tours** (www.alisthollywoodtours.com), which have popular celebrity home tours.

The interior of the mansion is only open for ticketed events—check the online calendar for details.
MAP 3: 905 Loma Vista Dr., 310/286-0119, www.greystonemansion.org; grounds open daily 10am-6pm; event ticket prices vary

Beverly Hills Library

Beverly Hills Library is clean and beautiful, with vaulted ceilings, real wooden reading desks, and ample natural lighting. There's a café inside and a handful of story-time activities for kids each week.
MAP 3: 444 N. Rexford Dr., 310/288-2222, www.beverlyhills.org; Mon.-Thurs. 9:30am-9:30pm, Fri.-Sat. 10am-6pm, Sun. noon-6pm

Beverly Hills City Hall

Right next to library is the tall tower of Beverly Hills City Hall, a 1930s Spanish Revival building with an eight-story tower topped with an intricately designed blue-and-green-tiled cupola. This local landmark and its palm-shaded front lawn are popular places for wedding photos.
MAP 3: 455 N. Rexford Dr., 310/285-1000, www.beverlyhills.org; Mon.-Thurs. 7:30am-5:30pm, Fri. 8am-5pm

Beverly Hills City Hall

TOP EXPERIENCE

⊙ Walk of Fame

Walk of Fame

Every Hollywood visitor should probably plan to spend about one to three hours exploring the Walk of Fame. Yes, it can be crowded with tourists, but there is something undeniably fun about seeing its more than 2,000 paved stars for yourself. The Walk of Fame starts at the intersection of Hollywood Boulevard and La Brea Avenue and ends at Hollywood Boulevard and Gower Street, a total of 1.3 miles (there's also a small stretch that runs 0.4 mile down Vine Street). If there's a specific celebrity star you want to see, look up their star location online ahead of time to save yourself the hassle of searching (http://projects.latimes.com/hollywood/star-walk/list). Check out the Walk of Fame website to see the schedule of public star dedication ceremonies, which happen about twice per month.

Along the Walk of Fame, you'll find plentiful entertainment options like the TCL Chinese Theatre, *Jimmy Kimmel Live!,* and Lucky Strike bowling. You'll also encounter lots of local performers in full costume—we're talking Darth Vader, Marilyn Monroe, and Willy Wonka. Give them a few bucks to take your picture with them. There are a lot of restaurants along the Walk of Fame, but most are mediocre and overpriced, so head *off* of the strip to eat once you're done exploring.

MAP 4: Hollywood Blvd. between La Brea Ave. and Gower St., www.walkoffame.com

NEARBY:

- Snap a selfie in front of the red-carpet worthy **TCL Chinese Theatre** (page 74).
- Take the kids to see a Disney film at the fun **El Capitan Theatre** (page 146).
- Drink to old Hollywood glamour at **Musso & Frank Grill** (page 128).
- Enjoy fine-dining in style at **Gwen** (page 99).
- Bowl, drink, and listen to live music at **Lucky Strike** (page 169).
- Peruse minimalist home goods at **Muji Hollywood** (page 190).

TCL Chinese Theatre

Formerly Grauman's Chinese Theatre, this iconic movie palace has been a Hollywood landmark since 1927. This is where some of the most prominent red-carpet movie premieres take place. Wander around the theater's forecourt to see the handprints/footprints/other parts of over 200 celebs, including George Clooney, Judy Garland, John Wayne, and Will Smith. Afterward, see a movie in one of the numerous IMAX theaters, one of which seats more than 900 people. If you don't want to see a movie but want to see the inside, pop into the gift shop to take a 30-minute tour.

MAP 4: 6925 Hollywood Blvd., 323/461-3331, www.tclchinesetheatres.com; free to walk around, movie tickets $14-$16; validated parking in adjacent Hollywood & Highland garage

Museum of Broken Relationships

Dedicated to love and loss, this newer museum is filled with donated objects that tell the story of, yes, broken relationships. Although it may sound depressing, the exhibits are actually quite poignant, and speak to one of the most shared human experiences—heartbreak. The museum is pretty small and located right in the center of the Walk of Fame, so you can make it part of your jaunt down Hollywood Boulevard.

MAP 4: 6751 Hollywood Blvd., 323/892-1200, https://brokenships.com; Mon.-Wed. 11am-6pm, Thurs. 11am-7pm, Fri.-Sat. noon-8pm, Sun. 11am-7pm; admission $15-18

The Four Ladies of Hollywood

This stainless steel public art installation depicts four important "ladies of Hollywood"—Judy Garland, Delores del Rio, Dorothy Dandridge, and

Paramount Pictures Studios

Anna May Wong—some of America's first movie stars. Created in 1994, this piece of art, which is also known as the "Hollywood Gateway," is on the same street corner as two of the most popular sidewalk stars—those of Elvis and the Beatles. It's a straightforward sculpture that's not worth its own trip (unless you happen to be a huge fan of one of those women), but it can be a fitting place to start or end your walk down Hollywood Boulevard and the Walk of Fame.

MAP 4: Corner of Hollywood Blvd. and La Brea Ave.

Paramount Pictures Studios

Visitors can explore one of Hollywood's oldest movie production studios on guided tours of this 65-acre lot. Tours allow access to some of Hollywood's most iconic movie and television filming locations, as well as the prop warehouse, home to thousands of props like old-school telephones, leather chaps, and enormous bearskin rugs. Choose either the Studio Tour ($55pp, every 30 minutes 9:30am-3pm Mon.-Fri., 2 hours), the VIP Studio Tour ($178pp, 9:30am or 1pm Mon.-Fri., 4.5 hours, gourmet lunch included), or the After Dark Studio Tour ($78pp, 8pm Fri.-Sat., 2.5 hours, champagne included). The Studio Tour and VIP Studio Tour take visitors around by cart, but the After Dark Studio Tour is a walking tour. Advance reservations are required for the VIP Studio Tour. Parking is complimentary for the VIP and After Dark tours.

MAP 4: 5515 Melrose Ave., 323/956-1777, www.paramountstudiotour.com; tour times vary; tickets $55-178, parking $12

Madame Tussauds Hollywood

When in Hollywood, you may as well go full tourist and pop by Madame Tussauds for some gratuitous pics with your favorite (wax) celebrities. This branch of Madame Tussauds, which was born in London in 1843 and now has dozens of international locations, is located right on the Walk of Fame, and includes replicas of Marilyn Monroe, Michael Jackson, Tom Hanks, and Taylor Swift. Look for people passing out vouchers in front of the museum—they can make your admission as cheap as $10.

MAP 4: 6933 Hollywood Blvd., 323/798-1670, www.madametussauds. com/hollywood; Mon.-Thurs. 10am-7pm, Fri.-Sat. 10am-5pm, Sun. 10am-10pm; admission $15-31

Dolby Theatre

Home to the Academy Awards since 2002, the Dolby Theatre is a grand homage to American cinema and one of the world's premier entertainment venues. Enter through its towering marble portal and wander down the limestone "Awards Walk" that movie stars use for their red-carpet entrance each year. To get into the theater itself, you'll need to either take a guided tour ($18-23, every 30 minutes 10:30am-4pm, 30 minutes long) or attend one of its many live performances (see the theater's website for tickets).

MAP 4: Hollywood & Highland, 6801 Hollywood Blvd., 323/308-6300, http://dolbytheatre.com; tours daily 10:30am-4pm; $18-$23

Hollywood Forever Cemetery

This picturesque cemetery was founded in 1899, and its 62 acres include a wide variety of old-fashioned standing headstones, monuments, mausoleums, and statues. Most

MOVIE AND TELEVISION STUDIOS

Hollywood produces more movies, music, and TV shows than any other town on the planet. The initial seeds for this creative explosion were sown in the 1920s, when movie studios first settled in the then-spacious Hollywood Hills. In 1929, the first Academy Awards ceremony was held in The Hollywood Roosevelt Hotel on Hollywood Boulevard. Subsequently, as recording technology improved, Hollywood films only grew—in terms of budget, visual sophistication, and global reach.

Hollywood entered its first Golden Age in the 1930s and 1940s, and continued its stride through the 1960s. Alongside the growth of the movie industry came increased TV show production, as well as the creation of big-name, L.A.-based music labels like Capitol Records and Tower Records. There are still some movie, television, and recording studios in Hollywood, but they have also expanded across L.A. and into areas like Studio City and Century City.

Today, Hollywood manages to be glamourous, seedy, and everything in between. It's a place where dreamers flock, hoping to rub elbows with just the right executive to land them a leading role in a hot indie film. Experience Hollywood for yourself by touring a movie studio or sitting in the audience of a live television recording. These are experiences that Los Angeles offers like no other place in the world.

MOVIE STUDIO TOURS

For all tours, look online for tour times, and try to purchase tickets in advance, especially during the summer and holidays.

- In Hollywood proper, **Paramount Pictures Studios** (5515 Melrose Ave., 323/956-1777, www.paramountstudiotour.com; tour times vary; tickets $55-178, parking $12) has a great tour (with a VIP option). This is where critically-acclaimed movies such as *True Grit* and *The Fighter* were filmed.

- In Burbank, **Warner Bros. Studios** (3400 W. Riverside Dr., 818/977-8687, www.wbstudiotour.com; 8am-4:30pm daily, extended summer hours; tours range $55-295) in North

people visit Hollywood Forever to see the grave sites of famous people, including rockers Johnny and Dee Dee Ramone, director Cecil DeMille, and actress Jayne Mansfield. The cemetery's large foundation and trees also make Hollywood Forever a nice place to take a leisurely stroll. In spring and summer check out the outdoor films hosted by Cinespia here; in the fall, join the cemetery's Dia de Los Muertos (Day of the Dead) celebration for great Mexican food, costumes, and musical performances. Guided walking tours are available ($15 pp); check online at www.cemeterytour.com.

MAP 4: 6000 Santa Monica Blvd., 323/469-1181, www.hollywoodforever.com; daily 8:30am-5pm; free

Capitol Records Building

Built in 1956, this round, 13-story building (which looks like a stack of records) will put a smile on your face. There's something undeniably charming about this office space where some of the biggest musical artists in history have come to do business. Tourists aren't allowed in the building itself,

Hollywood Forever Cemetery

Hollywood offers a fun and colorful tour, including a gigantic prop room where you can view props and costumes from memorable movies and TV shows; shows filmed here include *Friends, Gilmore Girls,* and *Big Bang Theory.*

- If you want to see Dorothy's yellow-brick road, head to **Sony Studios** (10202 W. Washington Blvd., Culver City, 310/244-8687, www.sonypicturesstudiostours.com; 9:30am, 10:30am, 1:30pm, and 2:30pm Mon.-Fri.; $50pp; ages 12 and up only). Reservations are required.

- To see the Bates Motel from *Psycho* and the shark from *Jaws,* visit **Universal Studios Hollywood** (100 Universal City Plaza, Universal City, 800/864-8377, www.universalstudioshollywood.com; $109-119) and take the studio tour, which is included in the entrance fee to the theme park. Discounts are available for kids ages 3-9, CA residents, and on less busy dates.

LIVE TELEVISION RECORDINGS

Have you ever wanted to be in the audience for *The Ellen DeGeneres Show, Jimmy Kimmel Live!, The Price is Right, Dancing with the Stars, Conan* or *The Voice?* Well, you're in luck—these shows (and many, many more) are recorded right here in L.A. To get a spot, you won't need to pay anything, but you will need to plan in advance.

The trick to getting these coveted tickets is to go on each show's website well in advance of your trip and reserve tickets for the dates of your visit. Most shows are recorded at either CBS Television City or one of the major studios mentioned above, but some have their own filming locations; check each show's website for location details. You can also go to one of these general ticket sites and browse tickets for dozens of shows: www.on-camera-audiences.com, www.tvtickets.com, www.1iota.com.

If you're traveling with kids or young adults, be aware that shows have different age minimums ranging from 10 to 21 years old. Some shows film year-round, while others take breaks during certain times of the year, especially summer.

but you're welcome to come by and take pictures. Check out the restored *Hollywood Jazz* mural in the parking lot, and if you're here in December, don't miss the Christmas tree on top of the building.

MAP 4: 1750 Vine St.

CBS Television City

If you're dying to see a live taping of a hugely popular television show, this is the place to visit. You can reserve free tickets online to be part of a live talk show audience, such as for *The Late Late Show with James Corden.* If you want to be in the audience for *The Price is Right* game show, however, you'll need to stand in line, potentially for a few hours. Go to the studio's website to find out what shows

are currently filming and when. No tours are available.

MAP 4: 7800 Beverly Blvd., 323/575-2345, www.cbstelevisioncity.com

High Voltage Tattoo

Founded by famed tattoo artist Kat Von D and formerly known as L.A. Ink, High Voltage Tattoo turns out some of the best-looking tattoos in town (all of which is reflected in the rates). The shop even used to have its own reality TV show. If you're in the neighborhood, it's worth stopping by to check out the fun, colorful vibe. And if you want to go home with an awesome tattoo, be sure to make an appointment well in advance, as the best artists book up quickly. (FYI—none of the original artists from the television show are still there.)

MAP 4: 1259 N. La Brea Ave., 323/969-9820, www.highvoltagetattoo.com; Mon.-Fri. noon-10pm, Sun. 1pm-5pm

Egyptian Theatre

Opened in 1922, the Egyptian Theatre is a great place to experience Old Hollywood glamour. Located right on the Walk of Fame, it shows one or two movies per night, both classic and current. Built in Egyptian Revival style, the theater has become just a bit worn over the years, but still retains much of its kitschy, hieroglyphic splendor.

Check the website to find out about special events and current film series with focuses like legendary directors, film noir, and modern European cinema. Tours happen infrequently—call or check the website to find out when the next one is happening.

MAP 4: 6712 Hollywood Blvd., 323/461-2020, www.americancinemathequecalendar.com/egyptian_theatre_events; evening screenings 2-4 nights per week; movies $12, tours $9

West Hollywood Map 5

✪ Sunset Strip

Sunset Boulevard is one of the longest and most famed streets in L.A. There are many worthwhile stretches of this popular street, one of which lies right in the heart of West Hollywood—the Sunset Strip. Made famous in the late 1970s by hard-partying rockers, the Sunset Strip has one foot in its notorious past and another in the high-rises of the future.

The Sunset Strip's 1.5 miles run from Crescent Heights Boulevard in the east to Sierra Drive (and the edge of Beverly Hills) in the west. You'll know you've reached the Sunset Strip when you start seeing huge and vivid billboards in every direction. Along this jaunt, you'll find iconic clubs including the Whisky a Go Go, the Roxy Theatre, and the Viper Room. All of these clubs are still hot today, regularly hosting sold-out live shows. You'll also find world-famous comedy clubs the Laugh Factory and The Comedy Store, as well as newer, trendier spots like Skybar at the Mondrian Los Angeles.

For potential celebrity sightings, head to the famous Chateau Marmont hotel. Throughout the Sunset Strip there are some delicious restaurants, fun bars, and cute shops, making it a great place to spend an afternoon.

If you want to explore the Sunset Strip's famous nightlife for yourself, check out an itinerary on page 131.

Sunset Strip

MAP 5: Sunset Blvd. between Crescent Heights Blvd. and Sierra Drive, www.thesunsetstrip.com

UNION STATION/ CHINATOWN

El Pueblo de Los Angeles

El Pueblo, which means "the town," is L.A.'s preserved town center from the 1780s. Some of L.A.'s oldest buildings are here, and there's also a beautiful square with magnolias and statues of historical figures. The plaza is often hosting some sort of festivity, especially on holidays like Cinco de Mayo or Dia de los Muertos.

Notable attractions in this small district include the **Museum of Social Justice** (115 Paseo de la Plaza, www. museumofsocialjustice.org, 213/613-1096; 10am-3pm Thurs.-Sun), where you'll learn about some of L.A.'s early social justice pioneers and see murals depicting the struggles along the U.S.-Mexico border; the **Plaza de Cultura y Artes** (501 N. Main Street, 888/488-8083, www.lapca.org; Mon., Wed. and Thurs. noon-5pm, Fri.-Sun. noon-6pm), which has beautiful exhibits highlighting the Mexican American experience in Southern California; and **Olvera Street** (125 Paseo de la Plaza, 213/485-6855, www.calleolvera. com; daily 10am-7pm), a marketplace where you can buy some authentic Mexican souvenirs.

MAP 7: 125 Paseo De La Plaza, 213/628-1274, http://elpueblo.lacity.org; free

Union Station

Union Station

Union Station is a beautiful 1930s structure with access to Metro, Amtrak, and MARC trains. When it opened in 1939, Union Station was the largest rail terminal in the western United States—and it still is today! Perhaps its most remarkable space is the grand waiting room, which has towering 40-foot windows, art deco chandeliers, inlaid marble floors, and hand-painted tiles. Visitors can take guided tours of Union Station to learn about its history and architecture on the second Sunday of each month; see the website for details.

MAP 7: 800 N. Alameda St., www. unionstationla.com; daily 4am-1am

Chinatown

While not as extravagant as San Francisco's Chinatown, L.A.'s version has its own special charm. The best time to visit Chinatown is during

Olvera Street

the annual Chinese New Year celebration, which has happened here for over a century. Sometime in the winter (see online calendar for details), you can come to this celebration to experience a dragon parade, nosh on tasty eats, and hear performances from traditional Chinese musicians. Outside of this celebration, you can walk around Chinatown by day for some good, greasy food and discount shopping on uniquely Chinese items.

MAP 7: 727 N. Broadway, http://chinatownla.com/wp1

CIVIC CENTER
Los Angeles City Hall

City Hall is a downtown landmark and a good place to visit if you're interested in history and architecture. This three-story tower, built in 1928, houses the mayor's offices and the L.A. City Council. The building, which used to be the tallest in L.A., has a 360-degree observation deck on the 27th floor that's free and open to visitors. The corridors of the building are less impressive but also open to the public. It's closed on weekends.

MAP 7: 200 N. Spring St., 213/473-3231, www.lacity.org; Mon.-Fri. 8am-5pm

Cathedral of Our Lady of the Angels

If you're looking for a calming space to spend an hour downtown, come to the Cathedral of Our Lady of the Angels. This 65,000-square-foot postmodern cathedral was designed by Pritzker Prize-winning architect Rafael Moneo. It includes a mausoleum, gift shop, cafeteria, conference center, and clergy residences. The church itself is strikingly modern, and the peaceful grounds a perfect place for a meditative stroll. Worshipers can

See a 2,000-pound cast-bronze chandelier (Lee Lawrie) and mosaic decorations (Julian E. Garnsey) at the Los Angeles Central Library.

take part in the daily morning mass at 7am Monday-Saturday, or the multiple Sunday masses, including one in Spanish.

MAP 7: 555 W. Temple St., 213/680-5200, www.olacathedral.org; Mon.-Fri. 6:30am-6pm, Sat. 9am-6pm, Sun. 7am-6pm

BUNKER HILL
Bradbury Building

If you love creepy-cool architecture, check out the Bradbury Building. From the outside, you wouldn't know it's anything special; once you step in, you'll see sunlight streaming through a full glass roof, open-cage elevators, and geometrically patterned iron staircases circling marble floors. Featured in the 1982 movie *Blade Runner*, the Bradbury Building has something special (and perhaps haunted) about it. There's not much to do here besides walk in and marvel, so it'll be a short stop on your Downtown journey.

MAP 7: 304 S. Broadway, 213/626-1893; daily 9am-5pm; free

Los Angeles Central Library

If you love libraries, this is one for the books (so to speak). L.A.'s Central Library has several entrances, all of which will eventually take you to its grand atrium—eight stories high and filled with over six million titles. I love the classic fiction and travel writing sections, but I'm sure this place has tomes for just about anyone. There's also a dynamic children's literature section, and lots of quiet nooks that provide a peaceful place for reading or laptop time.

MAP 7: 630 W. 5th St., 213/228-7000, www.lapl.org/branches/central-library; Mon.-Thurs. 10am-8pm, Fri.-Sat. 9:30am-5:30pm, Sun. 1pm-5pm; free

✪ OUE Skyspace

OUE is the place to get full 360-degree views of our beautiful city. Ride multiple elevators up to the 70th floor of the U.S. Bank Tower, almost 1,000 feet above the city streets, and take in the vistas from the floor-to-ceiling windows. OUE's multiple outdoor patios offer some of the best sunset views in the city—you'll see the Santa Ana Mountains, the rolling hills of Hollywood, and the tops of Downtown's skyscrapers. The glass-bottomed slide will bring out the kid in you; it costs $10 extra, and it's worth every penny.

MAP 7: 633 W. 5th St., 213/894-9000, https://oue-skyspace.com; daily 10am-9pm; $19-22

LITTLE TOKYO
Japanese Village Plaza

Japanese Village Plaza is a sweet, if manufactured, homage to the significant influence that Japanese food and culture has had on Southern California. This small plaza in Little Tokyo is just a few blocks long and completely closed to cars; you can wander around, shop for some moisture-rich Japanese skin-care products, indulge in a green tea doughnut, and slurp some thick udon noodles, all under dangling paper lanterns.

MAP 7: 335 E. 2nd St., 213/617-1900, http://japanesevillageplaza.net; Sat.-Wed. 7am-7pm, Thurs.-Fri. 7:15am-7:45pm

James Irvine Japanese Garden

Need a break from Downtown's hustle and bustle? James Irvine Japanese Garden has just what you need to recharge. A part of L.A.'s Japanese American Cultural & Community Center, this compact garden is filled with a variety of plants, flowers, and stone lanterns, all arranged in

BUDDHIST TEMPLES IN LITTLE TOKYO

Los Angeles is home to the second largest number of Japanese Americans in an American city (after Honolulu). You'll see this cultural heritage manifested in some beautiful Buddhist temples scattered throughout the city; there's a particularly dense concentration in Downtown's Little Tokyo.

- Start by visiting the **Koyasan Buddhist Temple** (342 E. 1st St., 213/624-1267, www.koyasanbetsuin.org), where you can take a meditation class, buy sacred trinkets, and chat with monks.

- Down the street from Koyasan are two **Buddhist Missions:** the **Jodoshu North American Buddhist Mission** (442 E. 3rd St., 213/346-9666, www.jodo.org/js) and the **Zenshuji Soto Mission** (123 S. Hewitt St., 213/624-8658, www.zenshuji.org), where you can meditate and attend beautiful services and ceremonies throughout the year.

- On the outskirts of Little Tokyo is the **Nishi Hompa Honwanji Temple** (815 E. 1st St., 213/680-9130, www.nishihongwanji-la.org), a gorgeous, tranquil space that's welcoming to visitors.

traditional Zen style. Enter through the basement of the community center, and walk into the garden to dip your fingers in the handwashing fountain, take a leisurely stroll, and meditate on the sound of a cascading stream.

MAP 7: 244 S. San Pedro St., 213/ 628-2725, www.jaccc.org/jamesirvinejapanesegarden; Tues.-Fri. 10am-5pm, Sat.-Sun. 10am-4pm; free

SOUTH PARK
L.A. Live

L.A. Live is a dynamic outdoor entertainment complex. Here you can find the Grammy Museum, the Staples Center (home to four pro sports teams), multiple concert venues, a bowling alley, movie theater, and more than 15 bars, clubs, and restaurants. L.A. Live premiered in 2007, its centerpiece a 40,000-square-foot open-air space featuring six 75-foot LED towers. Whether you're cheering on the Lakers or salsa dancing at Club Conga, L.A. Live is a fun place for a night out.

MAP 7: 800 W. Olympic Blvd., 866/548-3452; hours vary for each venue; free

Greater Los Angeles   Map 8

TOP EXPERIENCE

✪ Griffith Observatory

Since 1934, visitors have come to the Griffith Observatory day and night for sweeping views of both Los Angeles below and the cosmos above. Perched atop Griffith Park, this iconic L.A. landmark has provided the background in so many Hollywood films, including the acclaimed 2016 film *La La Land*.

The observatory offers a handful of space-related exhibits, a state-of-the-art planetarium (the third opened in the country), and stargazing via multiple heavy-duty telescopes. Its Zeiss telescope, which takes up a whole room, provides particularly awesome views of the moon, stars, and more. On

Griffith Observatory

and climb around the animal-themed playground. To be clear, this is no San Diego Zoo (which is one of the world's greatest zoos), but it's a nice place to spend a family afternoon. Once you're there, check out the zoo's many daily demonstrations, including elephant training and hippo encounters. The L.A. Zoo is tucked into Griffith Park, so you can pack a picnic and hang out in the park after your animal adventure.

MAP 8: 333 Zoo Dr., 323/644-4200, www. lazoo.org; daily 10am-5pm; adults $20, children $15, under two years old free

one Saturday each month, the Griffith Observatory hosts a "Star Party" in which the whole family can try out different telescopes, view celestial objects, and chat with astronomers (see website for dates). This is one of the best places in the city to get relatively close views of the Hollywood sign—bring your camera!

Admission to the observatory building, grounds, and telescopes is free, but you must purchase a ticket to see one of the shows in the planetarium ($7 adults, $5 students and seniors, $3 ages 5-12). The shows Children under 5 years old are only admitted to the first show of the day and must sit on an adult's lap.

MAP 8: 4730 Crystal Springs Dr., 323/913-4688, www.laparks.org/ griffithpark; noon-10pm Tues.-Fri., 10am-10pm Sat.-Sun.

Los Angeles Zoo and Botanical Gardens

The L.A. Zoo is home to more than 250 different animal species, 29 of which are endangered. It's a great place to bring children—they can feed and pet some animals, take a carousel ride,

✪ Hollywood Sign

In 1923, the iconic white-lettered "Hollywoodland" sign was erected atop Mount Lee. Twenty-six years later, "land" was removed, and the 50-foot-tall letters that remained became a permanent feature of the Los Angeles landscape. In 2010, the original wooden letters were auctioned off and replaced with new 45-foot-tall letters made of sheet metal.

There are a few options for getting up close to the iconic white-lettered Hollywood Sign. You can hike up near the sign via Griffith Park; get a good view of the sign from the Griffith Observatory or the visitors center at Hollywood & Highland; or take a van tour, which will provide a few nice lookout points (but won't take you next to the sign—it's closed to vehicles). For a different perspective altogether, book a helicopter tour for a bird's eye view of the L.A. landmark. If you're visiting on foot, don't even think about climbing the fence around it—the area is covered in motion detectors, security cameras, and barbed wire.

the Hollywood Sign

MAP 8: https://hollywoodsign.org; hiking trails open daily sunrise to sunset

☻ The Getty Center

The Getty Center sits high in the Santa Monica mountains, overlooking Los Angeles and the Pacific Ocean. The expansive art museum houses the eclectic art collection of billionaire J. Paul Getty; you'll find a different theme in each of the five modern white buildings that make up the compound, from Renaissance-era paintings to pop art. Getty is also responsible for the The Getty Villa in Malibu, which was his estate in the 1950s.

In addition to the permanent collection, which includes sculptures, drawings, and paintings from artists including Degas and Rembrandt, there are always new rotating exhibitions. After you've gotten your fill of art, be sure to enjoy the beautiful outdoor terraces and gardens as well. Pack a picnic or grab some fare at the onsite cafeteria and restaurant.

To get to The Getty, you'll have to drive or take Metro bus 761 to the museum's parking lot, where you'll catch a private tram to the hilltop compound. If you drive, you'll have to pay $15 to park. If you don't want to take the tram, you can walk a 0.75-mile pedestrian path from the parking structure to the compound; it's uphill and takes about 20 minutes.

MAP 8: 1200 Getty Center Dr., 310/440-7300, www.getty.edu/visit/center; Tues.-Fri. 10am-5pm, Sat. 10am-9pm, Sun. 10:30am-5pm; free admission, $5 audio tour, $15 parking

The Getty Center

Sony Studios

Sony Studios is one of the major film studios, with a long, star-studded history dating back to the Golden Age of Hollywood. If you're interested in this history, make the trek to Culver City to take Sony's tour, where you can visit soundstages once home to iconic films like *The Wizard of Oz* and *Men in Black*. Advance reservations are required.

MAP 8: 10202 W. Washington Blvd., Culver City, 310/244-8687, www.sonypicturesstudiostours.com; 9:30am, 10:30am, 1:30pm, and 2:30pm Mon.-Fri.; $50pp; ages 12 and up only

Exposition Park

Whether you want to explore dinosaur fossils, learn about African American history, or stop and smell the roses, Exposition Park has you covered. This 160-acre space south of downtown is home to a few notable museums; a seven-acre sunken Rose Garden, which is a nice place to enjoy an afternoon picnic; and the Los Angeles Coliseum, which hosts football games and other large events.

The Natural History Musuem of Los Angeles County (213/763-3466, www.nhm.org; daily 9:30pm-5pm; adults $15, seniors/students $12, children ages 3-12 $7) features millions of years of the earth's history, including one of the best dinosaur exhibits in the country. Special exhibits have included the history of tattooing and a butterfly pavilion. The museum also hosts the cool First Fridays for adults. There are behind-the-scene tours, themed discussions, two bars, live music, DJs, and food trucks. This event can be pretty popular, so buy tickets in advance.

Founded in 1977, the California African American Museum (600 State Dr., 213/744-7432, www.caamuseum.org; Tues.-Sat. 10am-5pm, Sun. 11am-5pm; free) was the first African American museum fully supported by a state. The museum researches, collects, and displays African American history, art, and culture, with an emphasis on the American West. Exhibits have examined such topics as the history of hip hop photography and the role of African American women in silent films.

The California Science Center (700 Exposition Park Dr, 323/724-3623, www.californiasciencecenter.org; daily 10am-5pm; free) has fun, interactive exhibits on everything from the human body to how we interact with modern technology. Kids will especially enjoy this museum.

MAP 8: 700 Exposition Park Dr., 213/744-7458, http://expositionpark.ca.gov; park open 6am-10pm, see venues for specific hours

RESTAURANTS

Chefs from around the world call Los Angeles home, which is good news for you. As an international melting pot, especially for Mexican, South American, and Asian cultures, Los Angeles has some of America's most delicious and inventive cuisine. Some restaurants here pride themselves on authenticity ("tacos like my *abuela* made in Mexico"), while others infuse elements of multiple cultures to create fresh new dishes like Korean BBQ short rib tacos.

The Little Door

There's an incredible variety of international cuisines in L.A., but if you could only try one, it should be Mexican. From steaming $1.50 street tacos to delicately prepared mole-filled dishes, the Mexican cuisine here spans a diverse range of prices, specialties, and venues, but is almost always creative, authentic, and delicious. We Angelinos are lucky to be able to enjoy so many rich tastes from our neighbors to the south.

Which is not to say that L.A. doesn't also excel in its homestate fare—there's a big focus on uniquely California cuisine, which means fresh, local produce that's often organic; meats from nearby farms; and fresh-caught seafood from the Pacific Ocean. Many of these Cali-centric restaurants are run by celebrity chefs (and are great places for celebrity sightings).

The best part about eating in L.A. is how affordable many of these delicious options are. Whether you want to spend just a few bucks on tasty tacos or splurge on a decadent tasting menu, Los Angeles will satisfy your craving.

HIGHLIGHTS

✪ **BEST SURF, BIKE, *AND* COFFEE SHOP:** Head to **Deus Ex Machina** for the Venice essentials...iced lattes, surfboards, and motorcycles (page 94).

✪ **BEST FOR THE SWEET-TOOTHED:** Opt for unique flavors and high quality ingredients at **Blue Star Donuts** or **Jeni's Splendid Ice Creams** (pages 95 and 113).

✪ **BEST RITZY STEAKHOUSE:** Buttery mashed potatoes and perfectly prepared steaks are served to the rich and famous at **Mastro's** in Beverly Hills (page 97).

✪ **BEST FOR ROMANCE:** You'll find a candle-lit garden and lovely French-Moroccan cuisine inside **The Little Door,** West Hollywood's favorite spot for a cozy date night (page 104).

✪ **BEST SUSHI EXPERIENCE:** Splurge on *omasake* at **Matsuhisa,** the birthplace of the Nobu sushi experience (page 104).

✪ **BEST TACOS:** There's stiff competition amongst taco purveyors in L.A. But **Guisado's** stands out as one of the best (page 107).

✪ **BEST TRADITIONAL KOREAN BBQ:** Order the *bulgogi* at **Gwang Yang BBQ** and you'll be in beef heaven (page 112).

✪ **BEST LOCAL SMORGASBORD:** Come hungry to **Grand Central Market,** a buzzy warehouse packed with some of the city's best food stalls (page 114).

✪ **BEST BREAKFAST SANDWICH:** **Eggslut**'s cheesy, yolky, perfectly grilled breakfast sandwiches are a great way to start the day (page 115).

✪ **BEST FRESHLY PULLED NOODLES:** **Marugame Monzo** in Little Tokyo has some of the freshest and most affordable noodles in town, and probably in the state (page 116).

✪ **BEST ITALIAN: Bestia** serves superb, seasonal pasta in a modern, industrial space (page 117).

PRICE KEY

$	Entrées less than $15
$ $	Entrées $15-25
$ $ $	Entrées $25-40
$ $ $ $	Entrées more than $40

Santa Monica

Map 1

CALIFORNIA CUISINE

Rustic Canyon $$$

Rustic Canyon Wine Bar & Seasonal Kitchen grew from dinners hosted by founder Josh Loeb at his family home. This small and classy restaurant maintains that homey feel, serving fine food and wine in a cozy, kitchen-like setting. Rustic Canyon's menu changes regularly and features ingredients that come from local farmers, ranchers, and fishermen who practice sustainable agriculture. The food is made with sharing in mind, so order for the table and taste different dishes. There are also regularly rotating cocktails and rich wines by the glass.

MAP 1: 1119 Wilshire Blvd., 310/393-7050, http://rusticcanyonwinebar.com; Sun.-Thurs. 5:30pm-10:30pm, Fri.-Sat. 5:30pm-11pm

Fig $$$

Fig, the Fairmont Miramar Hotel's crown jewel, feels like a Middle East-meets-Paris oasis. Renovated in 2016, Fig is now fresh and airy, with an open wall during warmer months, potted succulents hanging from the ceiling, and prime tables overlooking the Fairmont's playful pool deck. Fig's food is Mediterranean-inspired and everything on the menu is good (especially the cheese selections from the in-house fromagier), but Fig's hot-from-the-oven bread balloons take the cake (so to speak). Order a balloon for the table with all of the sides—eggplant salad, charred green onions, hummus, *labneh*, and warm curried lentils.

MAP 1: 101 Wilshire Blvd., 310/319-3111, www.figsantamonica.com; Mon.-Fri.

7am-2pm and 5pm-10pm, Sat.-Sun. 7am-2:30pm and 5pm-10pm

Urth Caffé Santa Monica $

Urth is a Los Angeles institution, and this location in Santa Monica has a big outdoor patio where you can sit and luxuriate over pastries, salads, and L.A.'s most exquisitely roasted organic coffee. Urth does every meal well, so there will almost always be a line out the door at this counter-service restaurant. For breakfast, try the salmon scramble made with organic eggs, Roma tomatoes, chives, and naturally smoked salmon. For lunch or dinner, order any of Urth's pizzas, entrée salads, or grilled panini. And you simply can't leave without dessert—Urth makes all of its cakes daily using only organic ingredients.

MAP 1: 2327 Main St., 310/314-7040, https://urthcaffe.com/caffe/locations/urth-santa-monica; Sun.-Thurs. 6am-11pm, Fri.-Sat. 6am-midnight

M Street Kitchen $$

The food at M Street Kitchen is just what California cuisine should be: fresh, creative, delectable, digestible, and downright delicious. I like to think of it as fancy-healthy. Hearty sandwiches, full salads, and yummy lunch bowls (especially the one with grilled organic salmon) make M Street Kitchen a great place to stop for lunch while you're cruising Main Street. Locals love to brunch here. The dining room is filled with big wooden tables and there's a generous patio space for outdoor dining (and people-watching).

MAP 1: 2000 Main St., 310/396-9145, http://mstreetkitchen.com; Sun.-Thurs. 8am-10pm, Fri.-Sat. 8am-11pm

The Penthouse $$$

Dine at the Penthouse at the Huntley Hotel and you might be seated next to a Real Housewife of Beverly Hills. To be fair, the food at the Penthouse can be topped, but it's not the food you're paying for—it's the thick cocktails, the snazzy ambience, and the panoramic Santa Monica views. Because those views are the main attraction, you'll want to dine here during the daytime to take in the full 360 degrees. For a special occasion, reserve one of the Penthouse's cabana-like tables surrounded by sheer white curtains.

MAP 1: 1111 2nd St., 310/394-5454, www.thehuntleyhotel.com/penthouse; Sun.-Thurs. 7am-10pm, Fri.-Sat. 7am-11pm

CASUAL AMERICAN
Father's Office $

Featured on many of L.A.'s "must-eat" lists, the Father's Office gastropub keeps it simple, offering good beer, good company, and great burgers in a no-frills space…kind of like a restaurant your dad (or grandpa) might enjoy. Foodies come here for the Office Burger, a dry-aged chuck beef patty with sweet caramelized onions, apple-wood bacon confit, arugula, gruyere, and Maytag blue cheese. Beer snobs come here for the seasonally rotating selection of 36 craft beers on tap.

MAP 1: 1018 Montana Ave., 310/736-2224; Mon.-Wed. 5pm-1am, Fri. 4pm-2am, Sat. noon-2am, Sun. noon-midnight

SEAFOOD
Blue Plate Oysterette $$

Snag a sidewalk table under Blue Plate's blue-and-white-striped awning for fresh ocean breezes, a cold glass of

The Lobster

chardonnay, and, of course, very tasty seafood. This is a clean, classic seafood joint that knows how to deliver great food that's not coated with L.A. pretension (although you will pay L.A. prices). The oysters are a local favorite. And the lobster is great, too—try it steamed, in a roll, or taco-ed with truffle oil.

MAP 1: 1355 Ocean Ave., 310/576-3474, www.blueplateoysterette.com/home; Sun.-Thurs. 11:30am-10pm, Fri.-Sat. 11:30am-11pm

Santa Monica Seafood Cafe $$

Head to Santa Monica Seafood Cafe for a cold Corona and the freshest seafood in town. This casual café is housed in the big open space of the Santa Monica Seafood Market, a family-owned shop that has sold high-quality seafood since 1939. Its café is the perfect place for a no-frills, fresh-off-the-boat lunch—try the oysters, shrimp cocktail, or lobster roll. There's also a generous happy hour (2pm-5pm Mon.-Fri.) with beer and wine specials, $3 scallop tacos, and a scrumptious Pacific coast ceviche.

MAP 1: 1000 Wilshire Blvd., 310/393-5244, www.smseafoodmarket.com/cafe; Mon.-Sat. 11am-9pm, Sun. 11am-8pm

The Lobster $$$

Sitting right at the entrance to the Santa Monica Pier, The Lobster will bring you closer to the beach than any other restaurant in the area. As its name suggests, The Lobster specializes in upscale, tasty seafood. It has been popular for a long time and, happily, the quality of its food has stayed really high. The Lobster's menu is almost exclusively seafood, and the many lobster dishes (lobster rolls, lobster cocktail, California spiny lobster, etc.) are fan favorites. Call ahead to reserve a table with an ocean view.

MAP 1: 1602 Ocean Ave., 310/458-9294, www.thelobster.com; Mon.-Thurs. 11:30am-9:30pm, Fri.-Sat. 11:30am-10:30pm, Sun. 11am-9:30pm

THAI
Thai Vegan $

Thai Vegan is a humble shop right on Main Street that serves up delicious, animal-product-free Thai cuisine. The tofu satay with peanut sauce and the pineapple fried rice are especially tasty. Some customers come to Thai Vegan just for the beverages, which include a mean Thai iced tea, squeezed-to-order juices, and freshly blended smoothies. Order at the counter and then take a seat in the small but welcoming indoor dining area (there are only a few outdoor tables).

MAP 1: 2400 Main St., 310/581-4255, http://thaiveganism.com; daily 11am-midnight

ITALIAN
Bay Cities Italian Deli & Bakery $

Bay Cities is both a deli and a gourmet European food market. Its specialty sandwich is the Godmother, a crusty loaf of Italian bread packed with Genoa salami, prosciutto, mortadella, capocollo, ham, and provolone cheese; try it with "the works"—mayo, mustard, Italian dressing, onions, pickles, tomatoes, lettuce, and a zippy chopped pepper blend. Bay Cities market sells domestic and imported specialty foods, and also some housewares and gift baskets. There are a few outdoor tables here, but your best bet may be to grab a few sandwiches, some cheeses and olives, and take them to the beach for a picnic.

MAP 1: 1517 Lincoln Blvd., 310/395-8279, www.baycitiesitaliandeli.com; Tues.-Sun. 9am-6pm

Fritto Misto $$

Come to Fritto Misto for a laid-back plate of homemade pasta. There's nothing fancy about this place—its decor could use an update and there aren't any tablecloths—but you'll be hard-pressed to find tastier pasta and sauces in all of Santa Monica. My fave dish here is the homemade "pillows," globs of ricotta-filled pasta with just the right amount of chew. The black-and-white linguini is also delicious—order it with turkey sausage and pink sauce. Fritto Misto gets crowded around dinnertime, so arrive early to get a table.

MAP 1: 601 Colorado Ave., 310/458-2829, www.frittomistoitaliancafe.com; Mon.-Thurs. 11:30am-10pm, Fri.-Sat. 11:30am-10:30pm, Sun. 11:30am-9:30pm

MEXICAN
Mercado $$

The bustling Mercado is full of people with happy stomachs and a tasty margarita buzz. This restaurant adds new touches to traditional Mexican flavors. Take the chicken enchiladas, which combine pulled free-range chicken with Oaxacan mole, Mexican rice, *queso fresco*, red onions, sesame seeds, and *crema fresca*. Mercado has five locations across the city; this one is located right in the 3rd Street Promenade, making it a smart and delicious alternative to the big-name chains lining the outdoor mall.

MAP 1: 1416 4th St., 310/526-7121, www.cocinasycalaveras.com/mercado; Mon.-Wed. 5pm-10pm, Thurs.-Fri. 5pm-11pm, Sat. 4pm-11pm, Sun. 11am-3pm and 4pm-10pm

Venice   Map 2

CALIFORNIA CUISINE
Rose Café $$

Once you sit down at Rose Café, you won't want to leave. This adorable

Rose Café

street-side eatery is the perfect place to settle into for gourmet cocktails, thoughtful food, and casual people-watching. The roses painted on both interior and exterior walls, and the plants cascading to your table, will make you feel as if you're eating in a bohemian garden. For brunch, try the brioche French toast with crème fraîche; for dinner, try the smoked bucatini carbonara with poached egg. Truthfully, you can't go wrong with any of the dishes on the café's extensive menus. With two patios (one outside and one covered), a bar, and its own bakery, Rose Café has become one of Venice's favorite local restaurants.

MAP 2: 220 Rose Ave., 301/399-0711, www.rosecafevenice.com; Mon.-Thurs. 7am-10pm, Fri. 7am-11pm, Sat. 8am-11pm, Sun. 8am-10pm

Café Gratitude $$

A mecca for healthy eaters, Café Gratitude is practically a Los Angeles institution. One of three Café Gratitudes, this Venice location is bright, open, and airy, with reggae music blowing on the breeze and both indoor and outdoor seating. The food here is 100 percent organic and plant-based (vegan); it's also creative, inventive, and delicious. Try the Indian curry bowl or the pad thai kelp noodles. And there's a full bar, too. If you don't want to sit down, get a superpowered beverage to go, like iced Ayurvedic milk, collagen rose beauty water, or a goji-citrus smoothie. On weekends, make reservations.

MAP 2: 512 Rose Ave., 424/231-8000, www.cafegratitude.com; daily 8am-10pm

Sunny Spot $$

Aptly named, this down-to-earth café offers indoor, outdoor, and bar seating, with colorful flower bouquets on each table. Sunny Spot sits right at the end of Abbot Kinney Boulevard, so it's a great place to chillax after a day of shopping. Choose from a list of tantalizing cocktails, including one called Death in the D.R.—a mix of Dominican rum, lime, honey, absinthe, and champagne. Sunny Spot serves fresh, Caribbean-inspired food, and offers bottomless adult beverages for brunch, with your choice of mimosas, Bloody Marys, or sunny rum punch. Need I say more?

MAP 2: 822 Washington Blvd., 301/448-8884 www.sunnyspotvenice.com; Mon.-Thurs. 11am-10pm, Fri. 11am-1am, Sat. 9:30am-1am, Sun. 9:10am-10pm

Café Gratitude

Nighthawk $$

Breakfast for dinner! Nighthawk is a swanky, day-and-night breakfast bar, and its owners have clearly had fun creating their menu. Get your party started with a milky cocktail filled with Cinnamon Toast Crunch, Honey Nut Cheerios, or Cocoa Puffs (they're delicious!). The food menu has lots of exciting treats, like an espresso cinnamon bun, Benedict fries, and a gourmet breakfast sandwich on a pretzel bun. Weekends are crowded, so make a reservation and come hungry.

MAP 2: 417 Washington Blvd., 424/835-4556, www.nighthawkrestaurants.com; Tues.-Thurs. 6pm-midnight, Fri. 11am-1am, Sat. 10am-1am, Sun. 10am-midnight

Lemonade

Lemonade $$

This L.A.-born institution is the perfect place for a casual lunch on the go. Lemonade offers high-quality, local food at affordable prices, served cafeteria-style so you can choose your own seasonal entrées and sides. The salads are fresh, and the mac-n-cheese is particularly tasty. The namesake lemonade is made with love—choose from a variety of creative flavors like watermelon rosemary, peach ginger, and blueberry mint. This Venice location is one of over a dozen Lemonades scattered across California.

MAP 2: 1661 Abbot Kinney Blvd., 301/452-6200, www.lemonadela.com; daily 11am-9:05pm

Gjelina $$$

Did someone say rustic-chic? Gjelina is overpriced, but it's also Venice's place to see and be seen. Bring your trendiest sunglasses and prepare to see Abbot Kinney fashion at its finest. This is a nice shopping pit stop, and it's also a good place for brunch if you're willing to wait awhile for a table. There's a lot on the menu, and the meats and wood-fired pizzas are particularly good. There are also generous charcuterie boards and a nice selection of raw oysters. Portions are a bit small, and Gjelina includes 20 percent gratuity in every bill. Make a reservation online to avoid long wait times.

MAP 2: 1429 Abbot Kinney Blvd., 301/450-1429, www.gjelina.com; daily 11am-midnight

CASUAL AMERICAN
Abbot's Pizza Company $

This place smells like authentic New York pizza. It's unpretentious and super-casual, yet also takes its food quite seriously. In addition to pizza, the menu offers calzones and salads (all dressings made in-house!), and even gluten-free dough upon request. You can order pizza by the slice, which is ready within minutes, or create your own full-size pizza, which will take longer to cook. Celebrating something special? Pay three bucks extra for your very own heart-shaped pizza pie. And while you're at it, grab a few homemade chocolate chip cookies. The place is small and there are no tables, only counter seating.

MAP 2: 1407 Abbot Kinney Blvd., 301/396-7334, www.abbotspizzaco.com; Sun.-Thurs. 11am-11pm, Fri.-Sat. 11am-midnight

MEXICAN
Cerveteca $$

If you're looking for a satisfying meal in a hip setting that doesn't break the bank, look no further. Cerveteca serves up some of the best authentic tacos in Venice. The juicy beef tacos are particularly flavorful—it tastes like the meat has marinated all night long. Be sure to top off your taco with homemade salsa and guacamole and grab a beer or a glass of wine (no hard alcohol). You can watch the chefs working in the open kitchen, or just enjoy the people-watching on Rose Avenue. There's another location in Culver City.

MAP 2: 523 Rose Avenue, 301/310-8937, www.cervetecala.com; Mon.-Thurs. 11:30am-11pm, Fri. 11:30am-midnight, Sat. 10am-noon, Sun. 10am-11pm

ASIAN FUSION
Komodo $

This inventive, order-at-the-counter eatery will leave you both satisfied and wanting more. Komodo's food is a street-inspired fusion of Mexican, Asian, and Californian flavors. Executive chef Erwin Tjahyadi is an Indonesian-born, East L.A.-bred Le Cordon Bleu alumni who can make a mean taco. Favorite tacos (which can also be made as bowls or burritos) include the Loco Moco (Hawaiian seared Angus ground beef patty, green onions, pineapple teriyaki sauce, white rice, and sunny-side-up egg) and the Komodo 2.0 (seared sirloin steak, jalapeño aioli, and Southwest corn salad).

Order tater tots for your side, topped with steak and spicy aioli.

MAP 2: 235 Main St., 301/255-6742, http://komodofood.com; Sun.-Thurs. 11am-9pm, Fri.-Sat. 11am-10pm

JAPANESE
Hama Sushi $$

Hama is a welcoming spot that has been open since 1979 and has managed to stay un-trendy despite its ever-growing popularity. Come here for no-nonsense, low-frills sushi. There are a number of vegetarian dishes to choose from and, of course, your choice of fresh fish and seafood. Hama's house specialty roll is the Lobster Dynamite, "served to the brim with succulent lobster and mushrooms." You can find Hama a few blocks from the boardwalk on the Windward Circle traffic roundabout.

MAP 2: 213 Windward Ave., 301/396-8783, www.hamasushi.com; Mon.-Thurs. noon-10:30pm, Fri. noon-11pm, Sat. 4pm-11pm, Sun. 4pm-10:30pm

COFFEE
✪ Deus Ex Machina $

Start your day with a buzz at Deus Ex Machina, where you can sip coffee and nibble pastries on a sunny patio among motorcycles, surfboards, and California-inspired art. While there isn't a full breakfast menu, there are plenty of panini and pastries to fill you up. If you're into the biker look, browse the adjoining retail shop. This is one of Deus Ex Machina's seven flagship stores, and the only one in the United States. It's a great place to get some work done on your laptop.

MAP 2: 1001 Venice Blvd., 888/515-3387, http://deuscustoms.com/flagships/emporium-of-postmodern-activities; daily 7am-7pm

Blue Star Donuts

DOUGHNUTS
✪ Blue Star Donuts $

This three-store chain prides itself on high-quality "small batch" doughnuts—a pride that you will taste in every decadent bite of brioche. There are so many good flavors, most of which are unique. The OG, flavored with *horchata* (a sweet, creamy Mexican beverage) and a cinnamon-sugar glaze, is the best-selling doughnut. Other fave flavors are green tea latte, blueberry bourbon basil, and apple cider. Vegans, they have doughnuts for you, too! If you go in the afternoon, there will be fewer flavors to choose from, as most batches sell out before the end of the day.

MAP 2: 1142 Abbot Kinney Blvd., 301/450-5630, www.bluestardonuts.com; daily 7am-8pm

Beverly Hills   Map 3

CASUAL AMERICAN
Nate'n Al Delicatessen $$

L.A. has its fair share of Jewish delis, and Nate'n Al is among the best. Opened on North Beverly Drive in 1945, Nate'n Al has seen Beverly Hills grow up around it, and has continued to keep Angelenos full with thick potato pancakes, massive sandwiches served on rye, and a very popular extra-long hot dog. There are also great homemade desserts, like chocolate mousse pudding and fresh-baked brownies. Nate'n Al is casual and low-key, making it a nice escape from the neighborhood's ubiquitous highfalutin restaurants.

MAP 3: 414 N. Beverly Dr., 310/274-0101, www.natenal.com; daily 7am-9pm

The Honor Bar $$

Come to escape the bustle of Rodeo Drive and stay for fresh-from-the-oven fries and a crisp martini on the rocks. The Honor Bar, which sits in the heart of Beverly Hills, is a cozy, hip spot that serves as a lunchtime watering hole and chic dinner destination. This place is really popular and doesn't take reservations, so you'll find the bar area packed starting at 7pm. The food is casual, but the dress code is semi-formal—no flip flops or tank tops.

MAP 3: 122 S. Beverly Dr., 310/550-0292, http://honorbar.com/locations/beverlyhills; Sun.-Thurs. 11:30am-11pm, Fri.-Sat. 11:30am-midnight

CALIFORNIA CUISINE
Maude $$$$

Famed chef Curtis Stone named this inventive restaurant after his grandma, and Maude does have the intimate feel of a grandmother's kitchen thanks to the antique trinkets sparkling around its small dining room. But this is not your grandmother's food. Every few months, executive chef Justin Hilbert plans a new, seasonal menu around the cuisine and wines of a single wine region, like roasted wild mushrooms paired with white wines from Rioja. Since opening in 2015, Maude has received considerable attention and accolades—make reservations well in advance.

MAP 3: 212 S. Beverly Dr., 310/859-3418, www.mauderestaurant.com; Tues.-Sat. 5:30pm-9:30pm

Spago Beverly Hills $$$$

You won't have to search far to find accolades for Spago, one of L.A.'s most iconic restaurants. In a city where dining ventures come and go, Spago has held steady as an elegant, California-casual restaurant that serves superbly tasteful food. Opened in 1982, Spago was the first restaurant founded by celebrity chef Wolfgang Puck. Dishes here are both refreshingly new and comfortingly familiar, such as a grilled veal chop with black garlic, parsnip purée, and jus with preserved lemon. There are a number of menus here; the California tasting menu highlights dishes and flavors unique to Southern California.

MAP 3: 176 N. Canon Dr., 310/385-0880, https://wolfgangpuck.com/dining/spago; Mon. 6pm-10pm, Tues.-Fri. noon-2:30pm and 6pm-10pm; Sat. noon-2:30pm and 5:30pm-10:30pm, Sun. 5:30pm-10pm

Spago Beverly Hills

Bedford & Burns $$$

Bedford & Burns is refreshingly straightforward—it serves traditional American surf and turf in a laid-back atmosphere. This is a smart lunch stop if you've worked up an appetite browsing the shops on Rodeo Drive. There are ample pizzas, salads, and seafood entrées. Happy hour (4pm-7pm Mon.-Sat.) is popular here—it features a respectable selection of both wine and beer, as wells as scrumptious bar bites like deviled eggs, cheddar biscuits, and yellowfin tuna tartare. Snag a table on the cute patio out front for some good people-watching.

MAP 3: 369 N. Bedford Dr., 310/273-8585, http://bedfordandburns.com; Mon.-Fri. 11:30am-9:30pm, Sat. 11:30am-10:30pm

Citizen $$$

Are you trendy enough for Citizen? There's only one way to find out—wrap up in a chic kaftan, throw on a pair of faux designer sunglasses, and head to this cooler-than-cool restaurant and bar. The best part about this 1960s throwback eatery might be its woven tapestry décor, not to be outdone by the charming indoor/outdoor patio that is open during warmer months. Make sure to order a side of cheddar biscuits with chive butter and smoked honey—they're delectable.

MAP 3: 184 N. Canon Dr., 310/402-5885, http://citizenbeverlyhills.com; Mon.-Fri. noon-10pm, Sat. 5pm-10pm

COFFEE

Nespresso Boutique & Café $

If you're looking for a shopping break, head to Nespresso's big, contemporary café/storefront. This is the brand's largest flagship in the US, and it can get quite busy. Be sure to order some sweet treats and maybe peruse the giant assortment of coffees they have for sale.

MAP 3: 320 N. Beverly Dr., 800/562-1465, www.nespresso.com; Sun.-Thurs. 9am-7pm, Fri.-Sat. 9am-8pm

Urth Caffé Beverly Hills $

Angelenos love their Urth Caffés. This a great people-watching spot, so throw your coolest shades on and grab a table on the front patio (if you can get one). The coffee is organic and delicious, and the extensive drink menu also offers teas, smoothies, and Boba drinks. This is also a great spot for breakfast or lunch; the long menu features a large range of yummy, fresh options, including oatmeals, pastries, sandwiches, and pizzas. There are five other locations around Los Angeles.

MAP 3: 267 S. Beverly Dr., 310/205-9311, www.urthcaffe.com; Sun.-Thurs. 6am-11pm, Fri.-Sat. 6am-midnight

STEAK HOUSES
CUT $$$$

Come to CUT by Wolfgang Puck for a truly exquisite and very expensive dining experience. This restaurant pays close attention to *every* detail of both its service and food, and makes sure that you have a memorable meal. As you might imagine, the menu offers various cuts of fine beef, as well as seafood and an extensive wine list. The bone marrow flan and the aged bone-in rib eye are two very popular dishes. CUT is located in the Beverly Wilshire Hotel, and caters to guests from around the world; it is a standout even among standout steak houses.

MAP 3: 9500 Wilshire Blvd., 310/276-8500, https://wolfgangpuck.com/dining/cut-beverly-hills; Mon.-Thurs. 6pm-10pm, Fri. 6pm-11pm, Sat. 5:30pm-11pm

✪ Mastro's $$$$

On any given night, Mastro's is hopping: a group of hip millennials are celebrating a birthday, a music mogul orders a round of martinis, and an Oscar-winning actress dines conspicuously in the corner. Mastro's food is classic—buttery and cheesy and delicious. You can't go wrong with its seafood tower, and the steaks and side dishes (like onion rings, truffle mac'n'cheese, and lobster mashed potatoes) are fantastic, too. The wine menu offers some solid mid-priced options and the dessert menu has a

JEWISH DELIS

Los Angeles is home to a relatively large Jewish population, which means that there are quite a few delis here serving incredibly satisfying Jewish-style comfort food. There's no real consensus on which deli is the best, probably because each respective deli has its own specialty foods.

- To eat a heaping bowl of matzo ball soup in a classic 1950s-style setting, head to **Canter's** (419 N. Fairfax Ave., 323/651-2030, www.cantersdeli.com; daily 24 hours) in Hollywood, and don't leave without a sweet treat from the in-house bakery.

- For the best challah bread in town, swing by **Got Kosher?** (8914 W. Pico Blvd., 310/858-3128, www.gotkosherinc.com; Sun.-Thurs. 9am-9pm, Fri. 8am-2:30pm) near Beverly Hills and grab a loaf with Belgian chocolate chunks, rosemary and kalamata olives, or the famous pretzel bread challah (the challah sells out on Fridays for Shabbat—call to reserve a loaf ahead of time).

- In Beverly Hills, check out **Nate'n Al Delicatessen** (414 N. Beverly Dr., 310/274-0101, www.natenal.com; daily 7am-9pm) for huge lox-and-bagel sandwiches, knishes, and kosher hot dogs. Nearby, **Factor's Famous Deli** (9420 W. Pico Blvd., 310/278-9175, www.factorsdeli.com; daily 7am-9pm) serves up sky-high pastrami, corned beef, and brisket sandwiches.

surprisingly good "signature" butter cake.

MAP 3: 246 N. Canon Dr., 310/888-8782, www.mastrosrestaurants.com/Locations/CA/31-Beverly-Hills-Main/Default.aspx; Sun.-Thurs. 5pm-11pm, Fri.-Sat. 5pm-midnight

ITALIAN
Il Pastaio $$$

Il Pastaio serves fresh, classic Italian food right in the middle of Beverly Hills. It has an extensive salad menu with 14 beautiful salads including artichoke salad, asparagus salad, and *panzanella*; vegetarians (and veggie lovers) will be happy here. As for pasta, one of Il Pastaio's most popular dishes is the *linguine con crostacei*, a delightful heap of linguine and crab meat in a slightly spicy sauce, accompanied by a half lobster. Il Pastaio is comforting and familiar—it doesn't try to be anything other than itself.

MAP 3: 400 N. Canon Dr., 3102/05-5444, www.giacominodrago.com/il-pastaio; Mon.-Thurs. 11:30am-11pm, Fri.-Sat. 11:30am-midnight, Sun. 11:30am-10pm

Mulberry Street Pizzeria $

Finally, some down-home food in the heart of 90210. If you're traveling with kids or looking for a casual Italian meal, consider Mulberry Street Pizzeria. Order by the slice or get a whole pie (gluten-free options available), and make sure to get a salad on the side—they're surprisingly fresh for a pizza parlor. Mulberry may not be in New York, but it does a darn good job of re-creating a New York City spirit, checkered tablecloths and all. Outdoor seating is available.

MAP 3: 240 S. Beverly Dr., 310/247-8100, http://mulberrypizzeria.com; 11am-11pm Sun.-Thurs., 11am-11:30pm Fri.-Sat.

FRENCH
Sweet Beverly $

Craving something sweet after all that shopping? Head to Sweet Beverly, a cute little café tucked in between North Beverly Drive and North Canon Drive along Beverly Cañon Gardens. Order something decadent (maybe the salted caramel crepe with homemade vanilla bean custard and bananas?)

and enjoy it on the café's patio, which overlooks the gardens. If you'd prefer something healthy, there are some yummy Mediterranean salads, soups, and wraps as well.

MAP 3: 240 N. Beverly Dr. #150, 310/896-4664, www.sweetbeverly.com; daily 8:30am-9:30pm

JAPANESE
Yazawa $$$

Yazawa is an upscale Japanese barbecue restaurant on the edge of Beverly Hills's commercial district. Here, the meat speaks for itself. There are some sushi, chicken, and pork options, but beef is the true star. Each cut of wagyu beef is flown directly from Japan to your table…and it tastes like it. Every table at Yazawa has its own fire grill, where you'll cook your meat to perfection. I recommend Yazawa for both a fun lunch experience and an adventurous night out.

MAP 3: 9669 S. Santa Monica Blvd., 310/275-2914, http://yazawameat.com; daily 5pm-11pm

Hollywood   Map 4

CALIFORNIA CUISINE
Animal $$$

Animal is one of many successful restaurants from famed chefs Vinny Dotolo and Jon Shook. Here you can eat parts of animals that you've never tried before—like bone marrow, veal brain, and pig's ear, all tastefully prepared. Animal has enjoyed steady popularity since its opening in 2008. In fact, this place is so cool that there's no sign outside; look for a small, dark building with large windows in front and a line out the door. Reservations are recommended.

MAP 4: 435 N Fairfax Ave., 323/782-9225, www.animalrestaurant.com; Mon.-Thurs. 6pm-10pm, Fri. 6pm-11pm, Sat. 10:30am-2:30pm and 6pm-11pm; Sun. 10:30am-2:30pm and 6pm-10pm

The Golden State $

A great pit stop while shopping on Melrose, Golden State offers fresh Cali cuisine, including elevated burgers, hot dogs, and salads. It's also worth indulging in the fries, floats, and thoughtful selection of draft beers. Order at the counter and your food will come quickly—this is fast gourmet at its finest, located on Fairfax Avenue on one of L.A.'s trendiest shopping strips.

MAP 4: 426 N. Fairfax Ave., 323/782-8331, www.thegoldenstatecafe.com; Tues.-Sat. noon-10pm, Sun.-Mon. noon-9pm

Gwen $$$$

Step into Gwen and be transported to a bright, airy Hollywood, filled with light and flowers and crystalline possibility—and great food. Gwen is the progeny of fine-dining chef Curtis Stone and his brother, John. The space, while formal, has a warm and welcoming vibe. You'll want to try the meat here (steak if possible). The dining room menu is prix fixe, with options for three- ($55), five- ($85), and ten-course ($185) meals. If you're sitting at the bar or patio, you can order a la carte; try the house-made charcuterie, handmade pasta, or wagyu steaks.

MAP 4: 6600 Sunset Blvd., 323/946-7500, www.gwenla.com; Tues.-Sat. 10am-midnight

Jon & Vinny's $$

At $17 a pizza, Jon & Vinny's is over-priced for casual Italian fare, but its trendy, modern space and buzzing ambience might make it a worth-while dining experience. And the food *is* pretty darn good. Try the bruschetta with ricotta and orange blossom honey, salad with Calabrian chili dressing, and spicy fusilli pasta. Reservations are recommended, as there are a limited number of tables and they fill up quickly. Check out the porcelain light fixtures with dinosaurs, butterflies, and other hipster-inspired patterns. Pretty cool.

MAP 4: 412 N. Fairfax Ave., 323/334-3369, www.jonandvinnys.com; daily 8am-10am

CASUAL AMERICAN

Roscoe's House of Chicken & Waffles $

Roscoe's offers succulent soul food that sticks to your belly. Whether it's 9am or 2am, the signature chicken and waffles are always appropriate fare. Other options—like creamy mac'n'cheese—are good, too. Operating since 1975, Roscoe's has become a beloved local institution. On Friday and Saturday nights, it's the after-club hangout, so expect a bawdy party into the wee hours of the morning.

MAP 4: 1514 N. Gower St., 323/466-7453, www.roscoeschickenandwaffles. com; Mon.-Thurs. 8:30am-midnight, Fri. 8:30am-4am, Sat. 8am-4am, Sun. 8am-midnight

Canter's $$

If you're in the mood for home-style Jewish cooking, look no further. Open 24/7, Canter's has served some of the best matzo ball soup and pastrami sandwiches in town since 1931. Yes, it will feel like you're back in the 1950s when you walk inside the dimly lit dining room, but that's part of the fun. Stop by the bakery on your way out to grab a freshly baked brownie or moon cookie for the road.

MAP 4: 419 N. Fairfax Ave., 323/651-2030, www.cantersdeli.com; daily 24 hours; validated parking lot

SEAFOOD
Providence $$$$

Providence is not just a restaurant, it's an experience. The service here is fantastic, the space is beautiful, and the food is sublime—this is upscale seafood at its finest. Choose from a few different tasting menus, all of which highlight a wide variety of seafood, with exciting options like abalone and live sea scallops. There are also delicious meat options. Providence has been around for over a decade, and with handfuls of accolades (including two Michelin stars), it just might be the best seafood restaurant in Los Angeles.

MAP 4: 5955 Melrose Ave., 323/460-4170, http://providencela.com; Mon.-Thurs. 6pm-10pm, Fri. noon-2pm and 6pm-10pm, Sat. 5:30pm-9pm

Hungry Cat

COFFEEHOUSE CULTURE

As a writer, L.A. coffeehouses are very important to me. It's fun to order a latte, settle into a table, and be inspired while listening to people creating scripts, casting movies, and pitching television shows all around you. (Coffee has surely fueled some of the greatest books, movies, and TV shows of our time.) The best coffee shops take real pride in not just the drinks and food, but also the atmosphere, so each of these places has a feel and personality of its own.

Ask Angelenos for their favorite coffee shop and you'll get a lot of different answers—mostly because there are so many great ones to choose from—but here are some popular picks:

- In Venice, check out **Deus Ex Machina** (1001 Venice Blvd., 888/515-3387, http://deus-customs.com/flagships/emporium-of-postmodern-activities; daily 7am-7pm), a combination bike shop and coffee hub.

- In multiple locations throughout the city, **Urth Caffé** serves up some of the best brews (and food, too). It also has wide patios with generous outdoor seating. A particularly great place to people-watch is in Beverly Hills (267 S. Beverly Dr., 310/205-9311, www.urthcaffe.com; Sun.-Thurs. 6am-11pm, Fri.-Sat. 6am-midnight).

- If you take your brews very seriously, head to **Intelligentsia** (3922 Sunset Blvd., 323/663-6173, www.intelligentsiacoffee.com/silver-lake-coffeebar; Sun.-Wed. 6am-8pm, Thurs.-Sat. 6am-10pm) in Silver Lake. There's some great people-watching (i.e., hipster-watching) to be had here.

- In West Hollywood, check out **Alfred Coffee** (8428 Melrose Pl., 323/944-0811, https://alfredcoffee.com; daily 7am-8pm) for Stumptown brews, and take an Instagram picture of their wall painted with the phrase, "But first, coffee."

Hungry Cat $$

Hungry Cat is a big, bright restaurant with great seafood at reasonable prices. The restaurant creates house-smoked meats and seafood, does its own curing and pickling, and features rotating seasonal beers. The oysters and cocktails are particularly delicious, as is the Maine lobster roll. Come for the generous happy hour (3pm-6pm Mon.-Fri.).
MAP 4: 1535 Vine St., 323/462-2155, www.thehungrycat.com; noon-10pm Mon.-Thurs., noon-11pm Fri., 11am-11pm Sat., 11am-3pm and 4pm-10pm Sun.

DESSERT
Milk $

If you're in the mood for incredible ice cream (or cake or cookies), look no further. This small shop is known for its inventive ice cream sandwiches, and favorite flavors include Thai iced tea, Froot Loops, and red velvet. But you also can't go wrong with the chewy cookies or gooey cakes (including coconut, chocolate, and blue velvet). There's usually a line out the door, but it moves quickly. Limited indoor/outdoor seating is available.
MAP 4: 7290 Beverly Blvd., 323/939-6455, www.themilkshop.com; Sun.-Thurs. noon-11pm, Fri.-Sat. noon-midnight

The Pie Hole $

As you can guess, this is where to go for a slice of pie heaven. Some slices, like the Mexican chocolate pie, offer traditional takes with a twist; others, like the Froot Loop pie, are downright creative (and delicious). There's also a handful of savory food options, like shepherd's pie, mac'n'cheese, and a veggie-kale hand pie. Pie Hole prides itself not only on pies, but also on good coffee and tea drinks—there's cold-brew coffee on tap. It's right on the

Milk

Walk of Fame, which makes it a fun place to stop as you stroll Hollywood Boulevard. Order at the counter.

MAP 4: 6314 Hollywood Blvd., 323/963-5174, www.thepieholela.com, daily 7am-11pm

West Hollywood   Map 5

CALIFORNIA CUISINE
Joan's on 3rd $

Often bustling with writers, actors, and Hollywood hustlers, Joan's on 3rd is worth braving the crowd. For your meal, order anything from classic buttermilk pancakes to a juicy turkey meat loaf or a colorful Southwest salad. Decadent desserts include cupcakes, flourless chocolate cake, and raspberry crumb squares. All food here is made fresh, and the coffee is superb. Order at the counter and sit inside the restaurant's pretty, white-tiled space, or choose an outdoor table for great 3rd Street people-watching.

MAP 5: 8350 W. 3rd St., 323/655-2285, www.joansonthird.com; Mon.-Sat. 8am-8pm, Sun. 8am-7pm

Au Fudge $

Finally, a cool restaurant in Beverly Hills where it's okay to bring the kids. In fact, movie star Jessica Biel opened this California-casual eatery in 2015 specifically for parents. The dining room has an adjoining playroom with $15/hour adult supervision, so you can enjoy a moment of relative quiet with your meal. Au Fudge has quick-and-tasty fare (with lots of gluten-free and vegan options), and daily "camp" activities for kiddos who want to play for a few hours at a time.

MAP 5: 9010 Melrose Ave., 424/204-9228, www.aufudge.com; Mon. 11am-3pm, Tues.-Thurs. 11am-8pm, Fri. 11am-9pm, Sat. 10am-9pm, Sun. 10am-8pm

CASUAL AMERICAN
Irv's Burgers $

Irv's Burgers is unassuming—just the way we like it. A West Hollywood staple since 1950, Irv's serves delicious, greasy burgers at a fraction of the price of its fancier neighbors. Walk in, order at the counter, pay cash, and sit down at a small table to wait for your classic burger and salty fries, served on paper plates with personalized doodles. Family owned and operated, Irv's will make you feel like a welcomed friend.

MAP 5: 7998 Santa Monica Blvd., 323/650-2456, https://irvsburgers.com; Mon.-Sat. 9am-7pm

Hamburger Mary's $

Don't go to Hamburger Mary's for the food—go for the scene. And by "scene" I mean Sunday-evening brunch. Every Sunday, Mary's hosts a raucous drag queen bingo tournament starting at 6pm. Come for bottomless mimosas and greasy pancakes, and stick around for what's probably America's most boisterous bingo tournament. Hamburger Mary's is not known for being a nightlife spot, but on Sunday nights this is the place to be in West Hollywood. Arrive early to secure a table—the place gets packed.

MAP 5: 8288 Santa Monica Blvd., 323/654-3800, www.hamburgermarys. com/weho; Sun.-Thurs. 11am-1am, Fri.-Sat. 11am-2am

MEXICAN
Gracias Madre $$

Gracias Madre is an adorably welcoming nuevo-Mexican joint that serves raw, vegan takes on Mexican classics. What sets the cuisine at Gracias Madre apart from other vegan fare is that it tastes fantastic—each bite pops in your mouth with layers of rich flavor. Sit on the patio, shaded by olive trees, for great people-watching accompanied by gentle breezes, the humming bass of an indie music track, and entertainment industry chatter. It's hard to find a better spot to spend a West Hollywood afternoon.

MAP 5: 8905 Melrose Ave., 323/978-2170, http://graciasmadreweho.com; Mon.-Fri. 11am-11pm, Sat.-Sun. 10am-11pm

MEDITERRANEAN
Lucques $$$

Irresistibly simple, yet definitely not basic, Lucques is a beloved West Hollywood hot spot founded by Suzanne Goin, a James Beard Award-winning chef, author, and restaurateur. What's nice about Lucques is that its understated approach to décor and service allows you to really focus on its French-inspired, California-ish food. And while Lucques' dining room and airy outdoor patio may be humble, its food certainly is not—meats and veggies and cheeses burst with flavor, and each day's freshly baked bread (served with butter, olives, and almonds) is to die for.

Gracias Madre

MAP 5: 8474 Melrose Ave., 323/655-6277, www.lucques.com; Mon. 6pm-9:30pm, Tues. noon-2:30pm and 6pm-9:30pm, Wed.-Thurs. noon-2:30pm and 6pm-10pm, Fri.-Sat. noon-2:30pm and 6pm-10:30pm, Sun. 5pm-9:30pm

Tagine $$$

Step into Tagine and you're transported to a dark, sexy Moroccan café. Although Tagine's atmosphere is chill, you can tell that chef Ben takes his food seriously. Each plate served in this 10-table restaurant is filled with delicate, intricate flavors, as well as lots of love. You can order a la carte or choose from one of three tasting menus—chef's tasting, vegetarian, or pescatarian. The lamb tagine with couscous and tiger shrimp with co-conut gets rave reviews. Oh, and you may spot actor Ryan Gosling here—he's one of Tagine's owners.

MAP 5: 132 N. Robertson Blvd., 310/360-7535, www.taginebeverlyhills.com; daily 6pm-10:30pm

✪ The Little Door $$$

With stringed lights twinkling over-head, a dinner at The Little Door will make you feel like you've spent an evening in Marrakesh. Long touted as one of the most romantic restau-rants in Los Angeles (and indeed the world), The Little Door serves French-Moroccan cuisine in a candlelit gar-den setting. Its dishes—duck foie gras, grilled rib eye steak with *sel de guer-ande*, and couscous lamb stew—are rich, colorful, and flavorful. The Little Door is a beautiful place to celebrate an anniversary or birthday, or enjoy a charming night with someone special.

MAP 5: 8164 W. 3rd St., 323/951-1210, http://thelittledoor.com/west-hollywood; Mon.-Thurs. 6pm-midnight, Fri.-Sat. 6pm-1am, Sun. 6pm-11pm

JAPANESE

✪ Matsuhisa $$$

Matsuhisa's flagship restaurant was the beginning of the now-global empire of chef and restaurateur Matsuhisa Nobu. Food here is special, still made with the same attention to detail that Matsuhisa brought when he opened the restaurant in 1987. There are a few noodle and steak dishes on the menu, but seafood is the star, with dozens of dishes and sushi rolls to choose from. You may want to order the rock shrimp tempura or miso black cod—or splurge on the chef's choice menu and let the kitchen sur-prise you.

MAP 5: 129 N. La Cienega Blvd., 310/659-9639, https://matsuhisabeverlyhills. com; Mon.-Fri. 11:45am-2:15pm and 5:45pm-10:15pm, Sat.-Sun. 5:45pm-10:15pm

Sushi Park $$$$

This place took me by surprise. It's set on the 2nd floor of a West Hollywood strip mall, alongside a sunglass store and a burger chain. But don't let the humble exterior fool you—Sushi Park serves top-quality sushi, the kind that melts in your mouth, and tastes like it was alive just moments before you bit into it. You'll pay top price for this low-frills sushi experience—about $200 per person for the chef's tasting menu, which is the only thing served. A sign outside Sushi Park states that it this is not "trendy sushi." It's the real deal. It's closed on weekends.

MAP 5: 8539 Sunset Blvd. #20, 310/652-0523; Mon.-Fri. noon-1:45pm and 6pm-9pm

Aburiya Raku $$$

Aburiya Raku brings izakaya (pub)-style Japanese dining to L.A., complete with homemade tofu, lots of Kobe beef, and extensive sake offerings. Opened

The Little Door

in 2016, this is the first California outpost of the incredibly popular Las Vegas dining spot. Food here is mostly traditional Japanese, and the atmosphere is bubbly West Hollywood. Somehow the combination works, and as your meal stretches on, with lots of little side plates coming and going, you'll end up quite satiated. Save room for the green tea crème brûlée.
MAP 5: 521 N. La Cienega Blvd., 213/308-9393, https://aburiyarakula.wixsite.com/weho; Mon.-Thurs. noon-2:30pm and 6pm-11pm, Fri. noon-2:30pm and 6pm-midnight, Sat. 6pm-midnight

COFFEE
Alfred Coffee $

Alfred is in the middle of Melrose Place, a little enclave of high-end shops and restaurants in West Hollywood. This cute multilevel coffee shop is filled to the brim with Angelenos getting their latte fix, writing movie reviews, and catching up with old friends over iced tea. Its drinks are excellent, if overpriced. Music is loud and poppy, and seating is close, so head elsewhere for intimate conversation.
MAP 5: 8428 Melrose Pl., 323/944-0811, https://alfredcoffee.com; daily 7am-8pm

Verve Coffee Roasters $

Verve has one of the best outdoor patios in the city—its turquoise tiled floor, comfy couches, and leafy trees make it an excellent place to hang out for a few hours (plus, West Hollywood people-watching is fantastic). Verve's coffee is top-notch, and the food items—avocado toast, fresh-squeezed juice, Rice Krispies Treats cookies—are also popular. While you're here, buy a fancy brewing kit to help re-create your Verve experience back home.
MAP 5: 8925 Melrose Ave., 310/385-9605, www.vervecoffee.com/pages/locations-melrose-avenue; daily 7am-8pm

DESSERT
Duff's Cakemix $$

Kids of all ages come to Duff's to make their own cakes that are so beautiful they could be sold in bakeries. Patrons get super-creative here, making, for instance, underwater-, unicorn-, and flower-themed cakes that are exploding with color. This DIY cake shop accepts both reservations and walk-ins; I recommend making a reservation on Saturdays and Sundays. Most people like to go to Duff's and create their own creamy cakes in its sunlit baking studio, but you can also pick up a cake-making kit to go.

MAP 5: 8302 Melrose Ave., 323/650-5555, http://duffscakemix.com; Mon.-Thurs. 12:30pm-7:30pm, Fri. 12:30pm-8pm, Sat. 10am-8pm, Sun. 10am-6:30pm

Echo Park, Los Feliz, and Silver Lake   Map 6

CALIFORNIA CUISINE
Alcove $$
True to its name, this ivy-covered eatery feels like a secret getaway. There's some indoor seating and a bar, but the real find is the luxiouriously large outdoor patio. At night, trees light up with stringed lanterns, and glowing heat lamps warm the colder evenings. The food is fresh and tasty, with lots of vegetarian and health-conscious options. Breakfast is served until 5pm, and any time is the right time for a slice of house-made cake or pie (the carrot cake is my favorite). Order at the counter.

MAP 6: 1929 Hillhurst Ave., 323/644-0100, www.alcovecafe.com; Sun.-Thurs. 6am-midnight, Fri.-Sat. 6am-1am

Cliff's Edge $$
Cliff's Edge feels like an enchanted garden hidden right on Sunset Boulevard. You'll be seated on the wide patio that surrounds a sacred tree, with big arms reaching across the whole restaurant. Created by famed interior designer Dana Hollister, Cliff's Edge has been a neighborhood favorite for Saturday and Sunday brunch since 2004. Try the fried chicken, which comes on a waffle with maple butter and bourbon syrup. Feeling celebratory? Top off your brunch with a grapefruit mimosa.

MAP 6: 3626 W. Sunset Blvd., 323/666-6116, www.cliffsedgecafe.com; dinner Mon.-Thurs. 6pm-10pm and Fri.-Sat. 6pm-11pm, brunch Sat.-Sun. 11am-3pm

CASUAL AMERICAN
Masa $$
Masa is one of L.A.'s best places for deep-dish pizza. The crust is flaky and doughy, its red sauce fresh and tangy. Each pizza is made fresh and takes about 45 minutes to make; if you're feeling especially organized you can call ahead of your arrival to put in your pizza order and lessen the wait. In addition to pizza, Masa offers pastas, sandwiches, and salads, with all dressings and sauces made from scratch. If you're not too full to move after your meal, take a two-block walk to Echo Park Lake.

MAP 6: 1800 Sunset Blvd., 213/989-1558, www.masaofechopark.com; Sun.-Thurs. 11am-11pm, Fri.-Sat. 11am-midnight

Brite Spot Diner $

Need some *chilaquiles* (breakfast nachos) to soak up that booze in your belly? Swing by Brite Spot, a casually ironic, 1960s-style diner that has been satisfying L.A.'s east-siders for years. The food here is hearty; go for the gold and order the gravy-smothered buttermilk biscuit sandwich with fried chicken and bacon. Vegetarians can order the tofu hash or huevos rancheros. Everyone should save room for a slice of seasonal pie. After your meal, walk two blocks to hang out at Echo Park Lake.

MAP 6: 1918 Sunset Blvd., 213/484-9800, www.britespotdiner.com; daily 8am-3pm

MEXICAN
✪ Guisado's $

Head to Guisado's for a chill vibe and some of L.A.'s best tacos. You'll order tacos at the counter with your choice of fillings, including shredded beef, grilled mushrooms, and spicy chorizo. While you wait, sip a creamy *horchata* or tangy hibiscus tea. Your tacos arrive shortly, hot off the grill. They are spongy and dense, perhaps not the style you're used to, but just the way the Guisado brothers' *abuela* made them in Mexico. Guisado's is a great place to grab a bite either before or after a Dodgers game; the stadium is about a mile away.

MAP 6: 1261 Sunset Blvd., 213/250-7600, www.guisados.co; Mon.-Thurs. 10:30am-10pm, Fri. 10:30am-11pm, Sat. 9:30am-11pm, Sun. 9am-5pm

Tacos Tu Madre $

As you might infer from its playful name (translated as "Tacos Your Mom"), this Los Feliz taco spot has fun with its food. The menu is filled with fusion specialties that you can order in the form of a taco, burrito, or bowl. Patron favorites include the

Guisado's

MEXICAN CUISINE

L.A. sits about 150 miles north of the Mexican border; you can hear this proximity in the languages being spoken, see it in art galleries and shops, and, of course, taste it at the hundreds of Mexican restaurants gracing L.A. street corners.

One of the best things about the Mexican food scene here is its incredible diversity. You can sit down in an upscale restaurant or on a sidewalk with grease dripping down your hands; you can nosh on vegan tacos or sample decadent Oaxacan moles.

To get a sense of what Mexican food is all about here, try one of these acclaimed restaurants:

- Some of the city's most progressive Mexican food is at **Broken Spanish** (page 116), a Downtown eatery serving delicious, fresh takes on traditional Mexican cuisine.

- In Koreatown, **Guelaguetza** (3014 W. Olympic Blvd., 213/427-0608, www.ilovemole. com; 9am-10pm Mon.-Thurs., 9am-11pm Fri., 8am-11pm Sat., 8am-9pm Sun.) has the best Oaxacan (southern Mexican) cuisine in the city. Mole is a specialty in Oaxaca, so don't skip it here. There are several delicious ones to try, with varying spice levels. The atmosphere is as bold as the flavors, with bright pink walls and festive live music every day of the week.

- If you're not a meat-eater, not to worry—**Gracias Madre** (page 103) is a popular WeHo spot serving flavorful vegan takes on Mexican classics.

And let's not forget about L.A.'s favorite part of Mexican cuisine. As much a part of the city as sunshine and traffic delays, tacos have long been a critical fixture in L.A.'s culinary

Fried Chicken taco (buttermilk fried chicken, poblano-ranch slaw, fermented chili, cilantro, honey sriracha) and the Korean BBQ taco (marinated roasted pork belly, kimchi, fermented chili, cilantro). There are also more traditional choices like grilled shrimp and *queso chorizo* (cheesy sausage). Order at the counter, and save room for red velvet churros with cream cheese frosting.
MAP 6: 1824 N. Vermont Ave., 323/522-3651, http://tacostumadre.com; Mon.-Thurs. 11am-midnight, Fri.-Sun. 10am-midnight

HomeState $

Did someone say breakfast tacos? HomeState has become more and more popular over the past few years; on any given morning you'll find its sidewalk seats jam-packed with happy humans chomping away at tortilla chips smothered with eggs, beans, spicy meats, and gooey cheese. This tiny restaurant, where Mexican *chilaquiles* (breakfast tacos) get new life, is located right on the border of Los Feliz and Silver Lake and offers *strong* coffee. It's a perfect place to start your day.
MAP 6: 4624 Hollywood Blvd., 323/906-1122, www.myhomestate.com; daily 8am-3pm

JAPANESE
Silver Lake Ramen $

There are many tasty ramen spots in Los Angeles, and Silver Lake Ramen stands out as an Angeleno favorite. What's special about this ramen? The broth. It's thick and flavorful, clearly made with love and care. Choose from pork, chicken, seafood, or veggie broth, and add your choice of noodles, protein, and veggies. The salad, rice bowls, and sushi rolls are decent, and landscape. Today, the tacos here aren't just like *abuela* made them—they are farm-to-table, Korean fusion, truffle-infused, and so much more...But don't worry, you'll find plenty of authentic versions, too.

A popular way to indulge in these delicious morsels is via taco truck. Finding a good one is part research, part luck, and part smartphone scavenger hunt. The best way to ensure a good meal is to choose your desired truck ahead of time, then use that truck's website and/or Twitter page to get its daily schedule. Get in line, order three to five tacos, pay with cash, and take a sidewalk seat to enjoy your very Angeleno treat. Here are a few adored trucks:

- **Guerilla Tacos** (323/388-5340, www.guerillatacos.com): fresh, farm-to-table

- **Ricky's Fish Tacos** (323/395-6233, http://rickyfishtacos.juisyfood.com): traditional, fried fish

- **Leo's Tacos Truck** (323/346-2001, www.leostacostruck.com): spit-fire meat at its finest

Eating tacos in a restaurant can be just as yummy and a lot more convenient. You can't go wrong with these options:

- **Guisado's,** West Hollywood and Echo Park (page 107): doughy and spicy

- **Tacos Tu Madre,** Los Feliz (page 107): playful fusion tacos

- **B.S. Taqueria,** Downtown (page 116): fancy gourmet tacos

there are a handful of sake choices. Silver Lake Ramen is small, so expect a wait if you come during peak hours.
MAP 6: 2927 Sunset Blvd., 323/660-8100, www.silverlakeramen.com; Sun.-Thurs. 11:30am-11pm, Fri.-Sat. 11:30am-2pm

THAI
Night + Market Song $$

Critically-acclaimed Night + Market Song offers traditional northern Thai food that is sweet, sour, and *spicy* in every bite. Most dishes will light up your taste buds, make your eyes water, and leave you asking for more sticky rice to cool the fire on your tongue. Come with friends and order a bunch of items to share, because you'll want to try everything on this menu, from the fatty pork shoulder in coconut milk and turmeric to the popular pad thai. Night + Market Song has enjoyed considerable popularity for a while

and doesn't take reservations, so expect a wait on weekends.

There's a second location in West Hollywood on the Sunset Strip, **Night + Market WeHo** (9043 Sunset Blvd., 310/275-9724; Tues.-Thurs. 11:30am-2:30pm and 5pm-10:30pm, Fri.-Sun. 5pm-10:30pm).
MAP 6: 3322 Sunset Blvd., 323/665-5899, www.nightmarketsong.com; Mon.-Thurs. noon-3pm and 5pm-10:30pm, Fri. noon-3pm and 5pm-11pm, Sat. 5pm-11pm

ITALIAN
Farfalla $$

Farfalla offers thoughtful, high-quality northern Italian food in a relatively unpretentious setting. The pizzas and house-made pastas are dynamite; try the *rigatoni ai tre funghi* (tube pasta with champignon, shiitake, and porcini mushrooms in a light pink sauce). Farfalla's menu is full of authentic

FRUIT STANDS

On a hot summer day, there may be nothing better than a Styrofoam box filled with cold, freshly cut fruit, topped with salt, chili, and lime. A quintessential Los Angeles experience, the fruit stands serving these treats started in predominately Mexican and South American neighborhoods and slowly grew in popularity throughout the city.

As you're exploring the city in the warmer months, you will likely come across a bright, rainbow-colored umbrella covering a portable metal fruit stand. It's hard to know where the fruit stands will be on any given day, so your best bet is to simply keep your eyes peeled as you pass populated corners around Downtown, Hollywood, and the Eastside (Los Feliz, Silver Lake, and Echo Park). Make sure you have cash on hand.

Once you find one, you can order from your choice of fresh-cut fruit, including coconut, pineapple, mango, melon, cucumber, and watermelon. Most stands also have jicama, which can add a nice texture to your combo. Then you can choose toppings like salt, chili flakes, and lime (I recommended all three). Pay in cash and leave a nice tip—these vendors work hard to give us delicious and healthy treats!

Italian specialties, and there are even gluten-free pasta and pizza options. If you're not too full to move following your meal, you can mosey around the cute shops on Hillhurst Avenue.

MAP 6: 1978 Hillhurst Ave., 323/661-7365, http://trattoriafarfalla.com; Mon.-Fri. 11:30am-2:30pm and 4:30pm-10:30pm, Sat. 4pm-11pm, Sun. 4pm-10pm

TAIWANESE
Pine & Crane $

Pine & Crane is a tasteful, minimalist Taiwanese-Chinese eatery in the heart of Silver Lake. Order at the counter and start with some scrumptious hot plates, such as layered pork pancakes, daikon pot stickers, or spicy shrimp wontons. Then have your choice of vegetable, noodle, or rice dishes. There are delicious vegan options, and most of the vegetables come from Pine & Crane's own local vegetable farm. For drinks, enjoy wine, beer, or some of Pine & Crane's many hot and iced teas. This is fast-casual at its finest.

MAP 6: 1521 Griffith Park Blvd., 323/668-1128, www.pineandcrane.com; Wed.-Mon. noon-10pm

SEAFOOD
L & E Oyster Bar $$

Fresh oysters, considered some of the best in the city, are shipped daily to this cozy and casual dining spot on Silver Lake Boulevard. L & E has an extensive wine menu and a perfect upstairs patio, so it's a nice place for a tasteful dinner with someone special. Or, check out L & E's happy hour (5pm-7pm Mon.-Fri.) to get a dozen oysters and a draft IPA from a local brewery for about $30. L & E is a smaller space, and one of the most popular east-side seafood spots, so expect a wait on weekends.

MAP 6: 1637 Silver Lake Blvd., 323/660-2255, http://leoysterbar.com; Mon.-Thurs. 5pm-10pm, Fri. 5pm-11pm, Sat. 10am-2pm and 5pm-11pm, Sun. 10am-2pm and 5pm-9pm

FUSION
Button Mash $

Have you ever wanted to simultaneously play pinball, drink craft beer, and nosh on Asian noodles? Look no further than Button Mash, a vibrant arcade turned bar turned fusion restaurant. The menu is filled with fun goodies like a braised Coca-Cola jackfruit sandwich, galangal chicken fried rice, and lychee fruit fritters.

Vegetarian, vegan, and gluten-free options abound. Eat your meal, grab a beer, and stay awhile—this place will keep you entertained. Button Mash is all-ages until 9pm every night, when it becomes 21 and over; they start carding upon entry at 8:15pm.

MAP 6: 1391 Sunset Blvd., 213/250-9903, www.buttonmashla.com; Tues.-Thurs. 5pm-midnight, Fri. 5pm-2am, Sat. 4pm-2am, Sun. 4pm-midnight

Bowery Bungalow $$

Don't let Bowery Bungalow's humble, cottage-like exterior fool you: the food here is exquisite. Its menu pays homage to the Afro-Mediterranean foods it founder, restaurateur George Abou-Daoud, grew up eating. The flavors are exotic and unique, the meats and veggies uber-fresh. Go with a group so you can order a number of vegetable and meat dishes to share, such as the molasses-roasted squash (with lebneh, hazelnuts, and pomegranate) or the heirloom tomato bruschetta. For entrées, both the cast iron chicken and baby back ribs will melt in your mouth. Weekends feature a Mediterranean-style brunch.

MAP 6: 156 Santa Monica Blvd., 323/663-1500, www.bowerybungalow.com; Tues.-Thurs. 6pm-10pm, Fri. 6pm-1am, Sat. 11am-3pm and 6pm-1am, Sun. 11am-3pm and 6pm-10pm

COFFEE
Intelligentsia $

There are a handful of Intelligentsia locations across the United States, and this one is particularly great. Each latte, espresso, and cup of tea is brewed to order, and its pastries are perfectly decadent. But what makes this east-side hangout special is its setting. At pretty much any time of day, people are posted up at Intelligentsia,

sipping brews on the large patio, reading scripts at the counter, and catching up with old friends in line for a drink. Intelligentsia clearly takes pride not only in its coffee, but also in the fact that it has created a Silver Lake community space for more than 10 years.

MAP 6: 3922 Sunset Blvd., 323/663-6173, www.intelligentsiacoffee.com/silver-lake-coffeebar; Sun.-Wed. 6am-8pm, Thurs.-Sat. 6am-10pm

Blue Bottle $

Blue Bottle in Echo Park is a gorgeous open space, offering plenty of seating and, of course, its famed coffee. Blue Bottle was born in Chicago and has expanded to select cities across the country; this location is housed in the Jensen Community Center building, one of L.A.'s designated Historic-Cultural Monuments. My favorite drink here is the affogato—an espresso shot poured over a scoop of high-quality ice cream. Eat it with a spoon on a hot day, and you'll be in heaven. Come to Blue Bottle either before or after your walk around Echo Park Lake, a few blocks away.

MAP 6: 1712 W. Sunset Blvd., 510/653-3394, https://bluebottlecoffee. com/cafes/echo-park; Mon.-Fri. 6:30am-6pm, Sat.-Sun. 7am-7pm

JUICE AND SMOOTHIES
The Punchbowl $

As you're eating your way through Los Angeles, you may come to a point when your body is craving aclease. The Punchbowl has you covered. Come here for raw, organic, vegan juices and smoothies that taste great and make you feel good. For a green infusion, try the Meadow Greens juice (made with dandelion, grapefruit, tarragon, cucumber, spinach, and pear).

KOREATOWN

Los Angeles is home to the largest Korean community in the United States. It's been a hub for Korean immigrants since the 1960s, but for the past decade it's been growing in popularity with all Angelinos. Today it's a trendy place to eat, drink, and soak in a Korean spa.

EAT

• **POT CaFe** (3515 Wilshire Blvd., 213/368-3030, www.eatatpot.com; daily 6am-6pm; $5-15) is a trendy Korean fusion restaurant from famed chef Roy Choi. It provides a casual dining experience inside the uber-cool LINE hotel. POT's menu pays playful homage to diverse L.A. staples with Korean twists, including ramen, *empanadas,* and fruit-loaded tapioca pudding.

• You'll feel like you're entering one of Seoul's dark-cornered restaurants when you walk into **Dan Sung Sa** (3317 W. 6th St., 213/487-9100; Mon.-Sat. 6pm-1am, Sun. 6pm-midnight; $5-20). This late-night establishment has tightly-packed tables and serves skewers of marinated meat, strong *soju,* and, my personal favorite, cheese corn. Dan Sung Sa is a great place to hit up after the bars.

• Among throngs of Korean BBQ joints, ✪ **Gwang Yang BBQ** (3435 Wilshire Blvd. #123, 213/385-5600, www.gybbq.com; Mon.-Sat. 11am-11pm, Sun. 11am-10pm; $5-20) stands out for its upscale ambience, quality meats, and superior flavors. Order the famous Gangnam-style *bulgogi* and the pork belly, then cook these mouth-watering meats right at your table. This is traditional Korean BBQ at its finest. Gwang Yang accepts reservation—a refreshing alternative to waiting for hours, as you will at some other Koreatown spots.

• Anthony Bordain loves L.A.'s Koreatown, and one of his favorite snacks to eat here is *bingsoo,* a bowl of shaved ice loaded with sugary toppings like sesame, strawberries, red beans, and taro. **Sul & Beans** (621 S. Western Ave. #208, 213/385-5510, www.sulandbeans.com; Mon.-Sat. noon-11pm, Sun. noon-10pm; $5-15) is one of the best spots in town for this sweet-toothed treat.

DRINK

• From the outside, **Lock & Key** (239 S. Vermont Ave., 213/389-5625, http://lockandkey.la; Tues.-Sat. 7pm-2am, Sun. 5pm-midnight) doesn't look like much, but once you tell the bouncer the password (any made-up password will do—it's just for fun), you'll enter a sleek bar run by mixologists. Grab a drink and head to the open-air patio featuring a DJ, hanging lights, and lots of pretty people.

For smoothies, try the Golden Idol, a mix of mango, turmeric, coconut water, coconut butter, coconut nectar, cayenne, and lime. And yes, this is Los Angeles, so you'll spend over $10 for juice...When in Rome, right?
MAP 6: 4645 Melbourne Ave., 323/666-1123, http://lapunchbowl.tumblr.com; Mon.-Fri. 8am-7pm, Sat. 9am-7pm, Sun. 10am-7pm

DESSERT
Magpie's Softserve $

Magpie's is a local favorite for softserve goodness. Every flavor at this ice cream shop is made from scratch. Favorites include the *horchata* (a sweet Mexican drink), the *cortadito* (a sweetened Cuban espresso), and yuzu honey (a traditional Korean tea). There are lots of vegan flavors here, and homemade vegan toppings like chocolate-covered honeycomb and toasted maple coconut chips. Find Magpie's in a little

- Ready to take a shot of *soju* and step up to the mic for your best rendition of "Living on a Prayer"? No night in Koreatown is complete without karaoke, and **R Bar** (3331 W. 8th St., 213/387-7227; Mon.-Tues. 8pm-2am, Wed.-Fri. 5pm-2am, Sat.-Sun. 11am-2am) is dark enough that no one will see you blush when you miss the high note. This dive-y spot also has regular live music.

- **Beer Belly** (532 S. Western Ave., 213/387-2337, www.beerbellyla.com; Mon.-Tues. 5pm-11pm, Wed.-Thurs. 11:30am-midnight, Fri.-Sat. 11:30am-1am, Sun. 11:30am-11pm) is a chill hangout for foodies and beer-lovers alike. There are plenty of craft beers on tap and tasty finger foods on the menu—try the fried Oreos with ice cream and Nutella.

SOAK

- **Wi Spa** (2700 Wilshire Blvd., 213/487-2700, www.wispausa.com; open 24 hours daily) provides a place of respite for busy Angelinos. This huge complex has hot baths, dry saunas, a respectable Korean restaurant, and a sunny rooftop deck for lounging. Families are welcome.

- For women only, **Olympic Day Spa** (3915 W. Olympic Blvd., 323/857-0666, www.olympicspala.com; daily 9am-10pm) is a refuge that offers deep rejuvenation through traditional Korean practices. Soak in mugwort tea, receive a deep tissue massage, and experience a traditional Akasuri body scrub.

strip mall off busy Hyperion Avenue; it's the perfect pit stop after a stroll around Silver Lake Reservoir.
MAP 6: 2660 Griffith Park Blvd., 323/486-7094, www.magpiessoftserve.com; Sun.-Thurs. 11am-9pm, Fri.-Sat. 11am-10pm

✪ Jeni's Splendid Ice Creams $
Oh my gosh, is this ice cream good. Strawberry buttermilk is my favorite flavor, but the rest (like brambleberry crisp and mocha black cherry) are also delectable. Made with all-local, all-natural ingredients, this ice cream is filled with high-quality goodness, and you can taste the love in every sweet, drippy bite. Like any good artisan eatery, Jeni's rotates its flavors with the seasons. Sample a few to choose your favorite, and perhaps take your cone on a stroll down Hillhurst Avenue.
MAP 6: 1954 Hillhurst Ave., 323/928-2668, https://jenis.com; daily 11am-11pm

MARKETS
✪ Grand Central Market $

Grand Central Market may be the best place in L.A. for a casual lunch. It's surely the most exuberant. This big, warehouse-like space has over 30 vendors serving up flavors from countries including Thailand, China, Mexico, Germany, Japan, and Guatemala. There's also vegan food, a bar with craft beer, and G&B, which serves what is arguably L.A.'s best espresso. Two highlights of this culinary smorgasbord are Eggslut for breakfast sandwiches and McConnell's for California-style ice cream. Grand Central Market has an artsy light display now, and many more hipster-inspired shops than before, but thankfully some *abuelos* still lunch at its counters, and the smell of *mole* still wafts through the warm air.

MAP 7: 317 S. Broadway, 213/624-2378, www.grandcentralmarket.com; daily 8am-10pm

CALIFORNIA CUISINE
Redbird $$$

Set in the former rectory of a cathedral-turned-event venue, Redbird occupies a uniquely beautiful, glass-ceilinged space and exudes an effortless elegance. Its food, like its ambience, is creative and thoughtful. Try the chicken-fried sweetbreads with radish salad, preserved lemon, and black garlic, or the much-praised barbecue smoked tofu (relax, meat eaters—there's also a bone-in rib eye for two). You can order a bunch of small

Grand Central Market

plates and also bigger dishes for the table to share.

MAP 7: 114 E. 2nd St., 213/788-1191, http:// redbird.la; Mon.-Thurs. 5pm-10pm, Fri. 5pm-11pm, Sat. 10am-2pm and 5pm-11pm, Sun. 10am-2pm and 5pm-10pm

CASUAL AMERICAN
Cole's $

Cole's claims to be the originator of the French dip sandwich. It has also been called one of the best bars in America by *Rolling Stone* magazine. It's small, dark, and narrow, reminiscent of the days when it first opened in 1907. The space has been updated over the years, but has purposefully retained its original glass lighting, penny-tile floors, and historical photos. What's more, the food is delish. Try one of the five French dips with a side of tater tots.

MAP 7: 118 E. 6th St., 213/622-4090, http://213hospitality.com/project/coles; Mon.-Wed. noon-10pm, Thurs. noon-11pm, Fri. noon-1am, Sat. 11am-1am, Sun. 11am-10pm

The Original Pantry Cafe

The Original Pantry Cafe $

If it's 4am and you need some thick pancakes, come to the Original Pantry Cafe. This is the place to get huge breakfast portions for decent prices at any hour. The Original Pantry Cafe has been serving up meatballs and apple pie since 1924, and it has become somewhat of a neighborhood icon. Expect a line, great people-watching, and super-fast service during peak brunch hours. Cash only.

MAP 7: 877 S. Figueroa St., 213/972-9279, www.pantrycafe.com; daily 24 hours

✪ Eggslut $

There's a reason that people wait more than an hour to order at the Eggslut counter in Grand Central Market. Their breakfast sandwiches are just that good—definitely the best in L.A., and a contender for best in the country. Eggslut pays special attention to each and every component of your sandwich: the brioche bun is grilled just right, the cheese the right amount of melty, and the yolk perfectly runny. Pro tip: If you're famished, grab a snack from a nearby vendor before getting in the Eggslut line, which is at its longest 8am-11am on weekends. There are a few other locations around L.A., the second most popular being in Venice (1611 Pacific Ave., 424/387-8183; daily 8am-4pm).

MAP 7: 317 S. Broadway, 213/625-0292, www.eggslut.com; daily 8am-4pm

MEXICAN
Bar Ama $$

With its hip-hop soundtrack and lively crowd, Bar Ama feels like *the* place to be Downtown. Start your meal with some chips and creamy queso; for your main course, order a decadent mole to warm your soul or the slow-cooked beef short rib chalupa, both made with love. Save room for a tasty cocktail made with one of Bar Ama's many tequila and mezcal offerings.

MAP 7: 118 W. 4th St., 213/687-8002, www.bar-ama.com; Mon.-Thurs. 11:30am-2:30pm and 5:30pm-11pm, Fri. 11:30am-3pm and

5:30pm-midnight, Sat. 11:30am-midnight, Sun. 11:30am-10pm

Broken Spanish $$$

Broken Spanish offers the most sophisticated Mexican fare in L.A. Popular local chef Ray Garcia serves rustic comfort food with gastronomic flair at this small, bright spot near the Staples Center. The menu features bold flavors, unique meats, and local, seasonal ingredients. It's a great happy hour spot, too—order the fried chicken necks and a "second generation" cocktail (mezcal and caramelized pineapple, yum).

MAP 7: 1050 S. Flower St., 213/749-1460, http://brokenspanish.com; 5:30pm-10pm Sun.-Thurs., 5:30pm-11pm Fri.-Sat.

B.S. Taqueria $$

B.S. Taqueria is the cooler, more casual sibling of Broken Spanish, both run by innovative chef Ray Garcia. The menu here is cheaper but still modern and fresh, with favorites like clam and lardo tacos and cauliflower al pastor. The décor is natural-meets-urban, with wooden benches, big vibrant murals, and lush plants hanging from the ceiling.

MAP 7: 514 W. 7th St., 213/622-3744, http://bstaqueria.com; 11:30am-10pm Mon.-Thurs., 11:30am-11pm Fri., 5pm-11pm Sat., 5pm-10pm Sun.

JAPANESE
Sushi Gen $$

On Saturdays at 4:30pm, a line starts forming outside of Sushi Gen, anticipating its five o'clock opening. L.A. has lots of sushi restaurants, so the fact that people wait to eat here shows just how fantastic this sushi is—and believe me, it's that good. Sushi Gen serves high-quality cuts of fish both *omakase* (chef's choice) style and in affordable smaller platters. Don't come here expecting lounge music or dimmed lights—come for an authentic sushi experience—meaning generous and artistically plated cuts of super fresh fish.

MAP 7: 422 E. 2nd St., 213/617-0552, www.sushigen-dtla.com; Tues.-Fri. 11:15am-2pm and 5:30pm-9:30pm, Sat. 5pm-9:30pm

✪ Marugame Monzo $

Come to Marugame Monzo for brothy soups filled with traditionally made, hand-pulled udon noodles. Its open-air kitchen allows you to watch chefs pulling your thick and chewy noodles and topping them with an assortment of scrumptious meats. If you're feeling adventurous, try the udon with sea urchin—it's a local fave. Marugame Monzo is small and located in the popular Japanese Village, so expect a wait during peak lunch and dinner hours.

MAP 7: 329 E. 1st St., 213/346-9762, www.monzola.com; daily 11:30am-2:30pm and 5pm-10pm

VIETNAMESE
Gigo's Café $

Gigo's Café is a tiny, unassuming eatery doling out delicious Vietnamese meals amid the roasting ducks of Chinatown (a beautiful example of L.A.'s rich cultural overlaps). If you're looking for some steaming fresh pho or spring rolls at unbeatable prices (served in an unpretentious atmosphere), head to Gigo's. Just make sure not to tell too many people about your delicious meal: Gigo's hasn't gotten too popular yet, so maybe we can keep it that way.

MAP 7: 853 N. Broadway, 213/229-8889, www.gigoscafe.com; daily 9am-7pm

ITALIAN

Bottega Louie $$

Make any meal a special occasion with a trip to the elegant Bottega Louie. Its marble floors, high white ceilings, and floor-to-ceiling windows onto Downtown's busy streets make Bottega Louie's buzzy dining room feel like the place to be pretty much any time of day. Salads and pizzas are simple and tasteful, and the decadent desserts are worth saving room for. Rainbow-colored macarons, packaged in adorable pink boxes, are an especially enticing to-go treat.

MAP 7: 700 S. Grand Ave., 213/802-1470, www.bottegalouie.com; Mon.-Thurs. 8am-10pm, Fri. 8am-11pm, Sat. 9am-11pm, Sun. 9am-10pm

✪ Bestia $$$

Bestia is one of L.A.'s favorite restaurants, and it deserves its outstanding reputation. Ever since it opened in 2012, Bestia has been recognized by both locals and international critics for its raw, industrial-meets-homey atmosphere and its superb food. Bestia's menu changes seasonally, but usually includes a roasted bone marrow dish that is a fan favorite. You can also try an appetizer of house-cured meats, a variety of pastas with lamb or pork ragu, or braised oxtail. Don't expect a white tablecloth—this is fine dining with exposed ceilings, metal patio chairs, and a whole lotta character.

MAP 7: 2121 E. 7th Pl., 213/514-5724, http://bestiala.com; Sun.-Thurs. 5pm-11pm, Fri.-Sat. 5pm-midnight

Maccheroni Republic $$

Maccheroni Republic is a sweet spot to spend a balmy evening. Its pasta is handmade organic, its sauces rich and tangy. There are many fine Italian restaurants in Los Angeles, but few are this affordable with such a great patio. Year-round, you can sit at a comfortable outdoor table surrounded by plants, flowers, and gentle jazz. Tasteful but not pretentious, Maccheroni Republic is an excellent place to get some fresh pasta love. No reservations are accepted.

MAP 7: 332 S. Broadway, 213/346-9725, http://maccheronirepublic.com; Mon.-Tues. 11am-2pm and 5pm-9:30pm, Wed.-Thurs. 11am-2pm and 5pm-10pm, Fri.-Sat. 11am-10:30pm, Sun. 11am-9pm

FRENCH

Church & State $$$

Dim dangling lights, redbrick floors, and flickering candles make Church & State a beautiful place to spend a Parisian-inspired evening, but the real draw is the food. As you begin your meal with some house-made burrata or tender escargot, you'll get the feeling that Church & State takes deep pride in its food. Meats and cheeses, in particular, are fantastic—try the traditional French cassoulet, made with braised lamb shoulder, duck confit, and pork sausage. And don't worry, the atmosphere isn't *too* French: music from James Brown or another funky crooner will likely be the backdrop to your meal.

MAP 7: 1850 Industrial St., 213/405-1434, http://churchandstatebistro.com; Mon.-Thurs. 11:30am-2:30pm and 6pm-10pm, Fri. 11:30am-2:30pm and 6pm-11pm, Sat. 5pm-11pm, Sun. 5pm-9pm

FUSION

Baco Mercat $$$

Baco Mercat has gotten considerable attention for its playful fusion of eastern Mediterranean, northern Africa, southern European, and

Church & State

Asian cuisines. Once you move past its bustling patio and intense cool factor, you'll get to a sublime, small-plate, nuevo-Mediterranean meal. Baco sandwiches are the signature dish; these are doughy, fresh-from-the-oven flatbreads wrapped around a juicy meat of your choice. The Toron sandwich with oxtail hash and cheddar potatoes is to die for.

MAP 7: 408 S. Main St., 213/687-8808, www.bacomercat.com; Mon.-Thurs. 11:30am-2:30pm and 5:30pm-11pm, Fri.-Sat. 11:30am-3pm and 5:30pm-midnight, Sun. 11:30am-3pm and 5pm-10pm

Orsa & Winston $$$$

Walk by Orsa & Winston on a weekend night and you'll be beckoned into its small, candlelit dining room with wooden tables, metal chairs, and buzzy chatter. But don't be fooled by this minimalist décor—Orsa & Winston's dishes, which are mostly small plates, are complex and flavorful, blending Japanese and Italian cooking styles to create something new and different. You can order your own items for lunch, but dinner has just one option: a six-course tasting menu that changes daily.

MAP 7: 122 W. 4th St., 213/687-0300, www.orsaandwinston.com/home; Tues.-Fri. noon-2pm and 6pm-11pm, Sat. 6pm-11pm

DESSERT
Café Dulce $

Café Dulce is one of the best places in the city to get doughnuts, and the flavors here are like none other. (The custard-filled green tea and sugar-dusted red bean donuts are probably the tastiest of all.) This friendly cafe sits in the heart of Little Tokyo, and its sweets and drinks are a mix of Japan sensible and L.A. cool. Check out the impressive offering of hot and iced tea lattes—favorites include the Masala Chai and Hong Kong Milk Tea.

MAP 7: 134 Japanese Village Plaza, 213/346-9910, http://cafedulce.co; daily 8am-10pm

VEGAN AND VEGETARIAN

Au Lac $$

Au Lac offers dozens of tasty plant-based options for hungry travelers. One hundred percent vegan, Au Lac takes a creative approach to its Asian-inspired fare. You can start your meal with some kelp noodles and macadamia "cheese," nosh on sweet-and-spicy tempeh, and finish with Rainbow in the Sky, a fruity dessert featuring chilled layers of blueberry, raspberry, mango, coconut, pecan, and dates. Au Lac's atmosphere is pleasant, and there's live jazz on weekends.

MAP 7: 710 W. 1st St., 213/617-2533, www.aulac.com; Mon.-Thurs. noon-10pm, Fri.-Sun. noon-11pm

NIGHTLIFE

Nights in L.A. are electric and reflect the city's diversity; there are deep house discos, festive salsa clubs, '90s dance parties, blues dives, and so much more.

The Club Bar at the Peninsula

Hollywood is the place to go for see-and-be-seen clubs. After-dark options include exclusive lounges where celebrities have VIP status, speakeasy-style bars with live music, and raucous dance clubs along Hollywood Boulevard and the Walk of Fame.

West Hollywood is famous for its nightlife along the Sunset Strip, where you'll find a mix of tourist trap bars, upscale lounges where celebrities hang out on weeknights, and legendary clubs and music venues. WeHo is also L.A.'s epicenter of gay partying. Every Friday and Saturday night the one-mile strip of Santa Monica Boulevard is thumping with bass, beckoning partiers from around the world to partake in its *joie de vive.* Expect rainbow lights, heavy pours, and barely dressed go-go dancers.

Downtown is known for its hip, young crowd and rooftop bars—like Upstairs at the Ace Hotel and Rooftop at the Standard. Santa Monica and Venice both have a few bars that serve cocktails with an ocean view. And Echo Park, Los Feliz, and Silver Lake provide more causal nightlife options, like local wine bars and indie dance clubs.

Save money for taxis or ride shares, as venues can be spread out across the city. You'll also want to check to see if a bar or club charges a ticket price or cover fee (many do). Unlike New York City, which apparently never sleeps, L.A. tends to go to bed around 2am—at least that's when most bars close.

HIGHLIGHTS

✪ **BEST BEACHY VIBE:** Head to **The Bungalow** in Santa Monica to guzzle beers on a generous outdoor deck with Pacific views (page 122).

✪ **BEST DIRTY MARTINI:** Pregame in 1930s style at **Musso & Frank Grill,** a Hollywood institution with the best blue-cheese-filled olives in town (page 128).

✪ **BEST DANCE CLUB AND CIGAR LOUNGE:** Dance the night away at **La Descarga,** which has amazing beats, a slick cigar lounge, and a strict dress code to keep it classy (page 129).

✪ **BEST PLACE TO SPOT A REAL HOUSEWIFE:** WeHo bar **Pump**— owned by *Real Housewives of Beverly Hills* star Lisa Vanderpump—has appeared on a number of reality TV shows. It's also a surprisingly beautiful place to have a cocktail (page 130).

✪ **BEST POOLSIDE CHIC:** Bass pumps, champagne fizzes, and stilettos clink at **Skybar,** a pool lounge on top of the Mondrian Los Angeles (page 130).

✪ **BEST LGBTQ SCENE:** Bring your most seductive dance moves to **The Abbey,** a WeHo beacon where everyone can let loose (page 131).

✪ **BEST TIKI KITSCH:** Order from almost 100 tropical-themed cocktails at the tiny, beloved **Tiki-Ti** in Los Feliz (page 132).

✪ **BEST LIVE INDIE MUSIC:** In Silver Lake, **The Satellite** features great indie music in an intimate, divey venue (page 134).

✪ **BEST ROOFTOP BAR:** Whether you choose the effortlessly cool **Upstairs Bar at the Ace Hotel** or the ever-bumpin' **Rooftop at the Standard,** you'll be in the middle of Downtown's hip nightlife (page 135).

✪ **BEST REPURPOSED SPACE:** Enjoy delicious cocktails and 1920s tunes at **The Edison,** housed in one of L.A.'s first electric power plants (page 136).

Santa Monica

Map 1

ROOFTOP BARS

Onyx Rooftop Bar

Widely regarded as one of the finest rooftop bars in Santa Monica, the Onyx Rooftop Bar at the Hotel Shangri-La is *the* place to go in the area for boozy bluff-top views. Celebrate anniversaries, birthdays, or just plain anything with a glass of champagne and regularly stunning sunsets. Most people head to Onyx for the views, the scene, the pretty people, and the drinks—my recommendation is to come here for happy hour and make dinner reservations elsewhere.

MAP 1: 1301 Ocean Ave., 310/394-2791, www.shangrila-hotel.com/dining-en.html; Mon.-Wed. 4pm-midnight, Thurs. 4pm-2am, Fri. 3pm-2am, Sat. noon-2am, Sun. noon-midnight

BARS

✪ The Bungalow

Think of the Bungalow as an upscale, beachy cocktail bar, the kind of place you'd wear your jeweled flip-flops that are too nice to actually wear to the beach. The Bungalow is housed in the Fairmont Miramar Hotel, a grand beachside compound that feels very much the place to be on weekends. Order a potent margarita at the bar, and then head outside to lounge by the fire pits, play beer pong, or watch the sun set over the Pacific. There may be a line to get into the Bungalow on weekends.

MAP 1: 101 Wilshire Blvd., 310/899-8530, www.thebungalow.com/sm; Mon.-Fri. 5pm-2am, Sat. noon-2am, Sun. noon-10pm

Chez Jay's

Chez Jay's has the rare distinction of being both a dive bar and a designated historical landmark. Walk into Chez Jay's, and you'll probably recognize its dim lighting, wooden bar, and big round booths from at least one movie or TV show. This is not a fancy or big space—order a stiff cocktail (or a cheap beer), get close with other visitors, and relax into its casual-classic vibe. Oh, and Chez Jay's proudly serves peanuts at the bar, a large number of which end up on the floor.

MAP 1: 1657 Ocean Ave., 310/395-1741, www.chezjays.com; Mon. 2pm-midnight, Tues.-Fri. 11:30am-2am, Sat. 9am-2am, Sun. 9am-midnight

PUBS

Library Alehouse

Come here and choose from the "library" of beers. On any given day, Library Alehouse offers about 30 carefully selected craft beers on tap (I recommend anything from the Lost Coast Brewery in Northern California). The beers here are cold and the patio is friendly, making Library Alehouse a great post-beach hangout. During happy hour (Mon.-Fri. 3pm-6pm), Library Alehouse is bustling—and with $4 beers and $3 bar food, why not? The bar food is good, but it's best to head elsewhere for a full dinner.

MAP 1: 2911 Main St., 310/314-4855, http://libraryalehouse.com; Mon.-Thurs. 11:30am-11pm, Fri. 11:30am-11:30pm, Sat. 11am-11:30pm, Sun. 11am-11pm

POOL PARTIES

L.A. is filled with pulsing pool parties throughout the spring and summer. Expect DJs, neon bikinis, strong cocktails, and at least one inflatable swan. Some pool parties are more exclusive than others, so call ahead and check online to figure out the rules for entry. One sure way to guarantee access is to stay as a guest at that hotel. At some hotels, you can reserve bottle service in advance of the party to hold your space.

- In Hollywood, the **The Hollywood Roosevelt Hotel** (7000 Hollywood Blvd., 323/892-8835, www.thehollywoodroosevelt.com) has both day and night pool parties, and its palm-filled pool deck is very much a place to see and be seen. Check online for a calendar of events.

- In West Hollywood, head to **Skybar** (8440 Sunset Blvd., 323/848-6025, www.morgan-shotelgroup.com/mondrian) at the Mondrian Los Angeles for beautiful pool parties with sweeping views of Los Angeles. Check online for a calendar of events.

- In Beverly Hills, the glamorous **Altitude Pool** at the SLS Hotel (465 S. La Cienega Blvd.; 310/247-0400, www.slshotels.com) is also surrounded by spectacular views of Los Angeles. DJs play on weekends from 2pm-6pm in the warmer months. There's poolside service, featuring cocktails and light fare by Chef José Andrés. Reserve a cabana online if you're with a party of three or more.

- In Downtown, check out the very popular, hip scene at **The Rooftop at the Standard** (550 S. Flower St., 213/892-8080, www.standardhotels.com/la/features/rooftop), surrounded by skyscrapers. The pool parties are themed and happen every Sunday; be sure to RSVP online or by phone ahead of time.

Ye Olde King's Head

I've never been to England, but I hear that this is the most authentic British pub around. Ye Olde King's Head is open all day, so start here with a traditional English breakfast (fried bread, eggs, bacon, sausage, sautéed mushrooms, English baked beans, and grilled tomato) and stay to watch American football and soccer games throughout the day. In the afternoon, grab a few pints and finish off a platter of fish-and-chips with friends. Expect a lively crowd—this popular pub has a prime location near the 3rd Street Promenade and the Santa Monica Pier.

MAP 1: 116 Santa Monica Blvd., 310/451-1402, www.yeoldekingshead. com; Mon.-Wed. 9am-10pm, Thurs.-Fri. 9am-11pm, Sat. 8am-11pm, Sun. 8am-10pm

LIVE MUSIC
Harvelle's Blues Club

Harvelle's is one of the only places to catch live music in Santa Monica, and it offers a lively show almost every night. Yes, this classic and endearing venue has some old-school blues performances, but there are also shows in many other genres, including rock'n'roll, R&B, and a burlesque show every Sunday night (see online calendar for details). Harvelle's is a small and intimate venue, so you may want to go early to ensure a table or a seat at the bar.

MAP 1: 1432 4th St., 310/395-1676, http://santamonica.harvelles.com; doors open 7pm or 8pm, see online calendar for details

ROOFTOP BARS

High at Hotel Erwin

The view! After a long day of sight-seeing, head up to High for a swanky sunset cocktail. The perfect escape from the fervor of the Venice board-walk, High will give you a new per-spective on Venice Beach...literally. On a breezy night, wrap yourself in a blanket, cozy up on a comfy couch, and take in views of the Venice murals, skate park, boardwalk, and the mag-nificent Pacific. DJs spin relaxed tunes day and night, and drinks are strong and tasty. High at Hotel Erwin offers light snacks that are reasonably priced during happy hour.

MAP 2: 1697 Pacific Ave., 424/214-1062, www.highvenice.com; Mon.-Thurs. 3pm-10pm, Fri. 3pm-midnight, Sat. noon-midnight, Sun. noon-10pm

BARS

The Otheroom

A fun place to either start or end your night, this popular bar is known for having a thoughtful selection of hard-to-find beers, including local, craft, and specialty beer, and rotating brews on tap. It opens with a lively happy hour at 5pm each day and fills up with both locals and visitors. While the menu is mostly focused on beer, there's also wine (but no liquor) and a few snacks. With its dimly lit space, exposed brick walls, and chic mini-malist vibes, the Otheroom is so cool that it doesn't even seem like it's trying.

MAP 2: 1201 Abbot Kinney Blvd., 310/396-6230, www.theotheroom.net; daily 5pm-2am

Wurstkuche

At the chill, modern Wurstkuche, you can have a good time without spend-ing a ton of money. The German-style beer hall even has a build-your-own hot dog bar. For the adventurous meat eater, there are rattlesnake and rabbit sausages; there are also delicious op-tions for the vegetarians. Just a warn-ing—it'll be hard to choose from the many delicious beers. Ask the friendly staff if you need help making a selec-tion; I recommend the draft Belgian IPA from Houblon Chouffee. Look for the big, red-and-white-striped doors out front.

MAP 2: 625 Lincoln Blvd., 213/687-4444, www.wurstkuche.com; daily 11am-midnight

Wurstkuche

LOUNGES

Vampire Lounge & Tasting Room

Looking for a side of vampire to accompany your elegant glass of merlot? Come to the Vampire Lounge, a seductive and charmingly kitschy spot to sip wine, relax, and enjoy some alluring live entertainment. On any given night, performances may include a magic show, tarot card reading, or burlesque performers. All of the Vampire Lounge's wine comes from Vampire Vineyards in central California; order some chocolates or charcuterie to pair with your "Trueblood Wine" or "Fangria Sangria."

MAP 3: 9865 Santa Monica Blvd., 310/826-7473, www.vampire.com/the-vampire-lounge; Sun.-Thurs. 5pm-midnight, Fri.-Sat. 5pm-2am

BARS

The Club Bar at the Peninsula

Pull up an upholstered stool at this swanky cocktail lounge and stay awhile. Located inside the Peninsula Hotel, the Club Bar's wood-paneled walls and carpeted floors give it an elegant, homey feel that will invite you to settle in for more than one glass of wine. There's also vintage malt scotch and a nice selection of high-end cognacs. If you're hungry, order highbrow bar food like caviar, truffled mac'n'cheese, and petite lobster rolls.

MAP 3: 9882 S. Santa Monica Blvd., 310/551-2888, http://beverlyhills.peninsula.com/en/fine-dining/the-club-bar; Mon.-Sat. 11am-1am, Sun. 11am-midnight

The Club Bar

CIGARS

Buena Vista Cigar Club

Buena Vista feels like a secret hideout. It's owned by the one and only Rigoberto Fernandez, a man who will make sure you have just the cigar and scotch you need. This has pretty much everything you'd want in a cigar bar—dim lighting, stiff drinks, and a muted TV showing today's most important baseball game. What's especially nice about Buena Vista is that it's a bit removed from Beverly Hills pretense—not quite Havana, but almost.

MAP 3: 9715 S. Santa Monica Blvd., 310/273-8100; Mon.-Tues. 4pm-2am, Wed. 4pm-midnight, Thurs. noon-2pm and 4pm-2am; Fri. 4pm-2am, Sat. 7pm-2am

Hollywood   Map 4

ROOFTOP BARS

Mama Shelter

This colorful rooftop restaurant and bar is a great place to view the Hollywood sign and catch a stunning sunset. With foosball tables, hanging lights, and brightly colored couches, you really can't go wrong with the ambience. The food gets mixed reviews, so you might want to go somewhere else for dinner, but the bar snacks are solid. The rooftop gets more crowded as you get further into the night, especially on Fridays and Saturdays.

MAP 4: 6500 Selma Ave., 323/785-6666, www.mamashelter.com/en/los-angeles/restaurants/rooftop; Mon.-Thurs. 7am-11pm, Fri.-Sun. 7am-midnight; no cover

BARS

Brickyard Pub

Brickyard feels like a neighborhood bar despite its popularity. Come for the huge beer selection, and stay for pool, darts, and shuffleboard. Or just stay at the bar and hang out with Brickyard's super-friendly bartenders. Brickyard feels removed from the chaos of the Hollywood strip, so the atmosphere is a bit more chill. Happy hour is seven days a week 7pm-9pm, with deals on drinks and the pool table.

MAP 4: 1810 Wilcox Ave., 323/465-6356, www.brickyardnoho.com; daily 7pm-2am; no cover

Snake Pit Alehouse

Snake Pit Alehouse

Snake Pit manages to stay divey while pouring great, strong drinks, serving high-quality food, and living right in the heart of Melrose's shopping district. It's sometimes rough around the edges (in both appearance and service), but locals think that's just part of its charm. And you can't complain when you can choose from over 100 types of whisky. The jukebox selection is also fantastic, with something for everyone, and happy hour is every day 3pm-8pm.

Bar Lubitsch

MAP 4: 7529 Melrose Ave., 323/653-2011, www.snakepitalehouse.com; Mon. 5pm-2am, Tues.-Fri. 1pm-2am, Sat.-Sun. noon-2am; no cover

No Vacancy

Stepping into No Vacancy feels like walking through a time warp that takes you right into the speakeasy glamour of the 1920s. One of the best things about this place is that it feels like a well-kept secret…but it's not! On any given night, this Victorian-age bar will be packed with locals, celebs, and tourists alike, all here for the strong drinks, live music, and occasional burlesque show. The drinks are delicious and the vibe is exclusive.

MAP 4: 1727 N. Hudson Ave., 323/465-1902, http://novacancyla.com; Tues.-Sat. 8am-2am; no cover

Bar Lubitsch

Named after filmmaker Ernst Lubitsch, the kitschy and fun Bar Lubitsch has been a place to be in Hollywood for decades. With over 200 types of vodka, this Russian-inspired bar won't let you go home without a buzz. A DJ plays on weekends, and there's a dance floor and indoor/outdoor seating. While you can always dress casually here, people tend to dress to impress on weekends.

MAP 4: 7702 Santa Monica Blvd., 323/654-1234, www.barlubitsch.com; Mon.-Fri. 7pm-2am, Sat.-Sun. 8pm-2am; no cover

PUBS
The Pikey

The Pikey is a British-style gastropub with farm-to-table food and a respectable beer selection, with a few beers on tap and many more in bottles. Although it's right in the middle of the ever-busy Sunset Boulevard, the Pikey manages to feel like a neighborhood pub—if your neighborhood is thousands of miles away in the UK. Go either for a lively happy hour (4pm-7pm every day) or for a filling weekend brunch; the English breakfast really can't be beat.

MAP 4: 7617 Sunset Blvd., 323/850-5400;
Mon.-Fri. 11:45am-2am, Sat.-Sun.
11:30am-2am; no cover

LOUNGES

✪ Musso & Frank Grill

Opened in 1919, Musso & Frank Grill
is a Hollywood institution. Sipping
on one of Musso & Frank's famous
dirty martinis (with blue cheese-
stuffed olives!), you can imagine all of
the movie ideas that have been born

Musso & Frank Grill

here over the past century. Truth be
told, people come here more for the
ambience than the food, but its classic Italian American fare is pretty decent. Musso & Frank's is right in the
center of Hollywood Boulevard, making this a good place to fill your belly
and drink a few strong cocktails before
starting your night out.

MAP 4: 6667 Hollywood Blvd.,
323/467-7788, www.mussoandfrank.com;
Tues.-Sat. 11am-11pm, Sun. 4pm-9pm

The Study

Right in the center of Hollywood
Boulevard, the Study is a unique homage to Hollywood's famed writers. The
whole place has a playful, old-school
feel, with walls filled with books and
typewriters. The high-vaulted ceilings
and antique décor make this a great
place to relax and look around, both
at the place and the people. There's occasional live music and great DJs, and
Monday nights are buzzing with open-
mic jam sessions.

MAP 4: 6356 Hollywood Blvd.,
323/469-0040; daily 8pm-2am; no cover

Next Door Lounge

This 1920s speakeasy-style lounge is
a great place to relive Old Hollywood
glamour. It's a smaller, more intimate
venue, with leather chairs, dark walls,
and sometimes live performances.

Cocktails are delicious and strong.
The food may leave something to be
desired, so post up here before or after
dinner.

MAP 4: 1154 Highland Ave., 323/465-5505,
www.nextdoorhollywood.com; Mon.-Thurs.
11:30am-3pm and 5pm-midnight, Fri.
11:30am-3pm and 5pm-2am, Sat. 7pm-2am;
no cover

Three Clubs

Housed in an unassuming mini-mall,
Three Clubs is a small, intimate venue
that eschews the flashing lights of
Hollywood Boulevard. Grab a table
and enjoy nightly entertainment, including live musical theater, caba-
ret, burlesque, and DJs. But don't be
fooled—this popular watering hole
can get rowdy later into the night. Stop
by earlier in the night, during happy
hour (daily 6pm-8pm).

MAP 4: 1123 Vine St., http://threeclubs.
com; daily 5pm-2am; no cover

CLUBS

Avalon Hollywood

Right in the epicenter of Hollywood,
Avalon offers epic parties every weekend (and some weekdays, too). DJs
keep the floors thumping, and an
elaborate lighting system enhances the
beats. Compared to other Hollywood
clubs, the dress code is pretty lax, and
almost everyone gets in by buying

tickets. People get *drunk* here, so the dance floor (as well as the bouncers) can get intense. If you leave Avalon late at night or early in the morning, be cautious and stay aware of your surroundings—late-night tourists on Hollywood Boulevard (especially drunk ones) are prime targets for theft. Some nights are just for dancing, others have a more formal concert setup; check the online calendar for details.

MAP 4: 1735 Vine St., 323/462-8900, http://avalonhollywood.com; nights vary; tickets starting at $15

Sound Nightclub

Bass is thumping, lights are pulsing, and people are whirring. What's cool about Sound is that, in addition to providing a few great parties each week, it also prides itself on supporting up-and-coming artists. The walls feature rotating displays from local artists, and the food menu changes regularly, featuring bites from local chefs. Nights of operation vary, so check the schedule on the venue's website ahead of time.

MAP 4: 642 N. Las Palmas Ave., 323/962-9000, http://soundnightclub.com; nights vary; tickets $20-50

✪ La Descarga

From the music to the people to the professional dancers, this place is hot. On weekends, wait in line for a bit, pay a small cover charge, and then get excited as you head downstairs to the throbbing dance floor. Drinks are strong and the beats are infectious, so don't be surprised if you find yourself dancing for hours. Once your feet are tired, you can head to the cigar lounge for a more low-key vibe. The dress code is strict—the club requires "upscale attire" for entry (see the venue's website for the long list of details). Reservations can be made online and are highly encouraged.

MAP 4: 1159 N. Western Ave., 323/466-1324, www.ladescargala.com; Tues.-Sat. 8pm-2am

West Hollywood   Map 5

BARS

Original Barney's Beanery

California native John "Barney" Anthony first opened Barney's in 1920. Since then, this restaurant and bar has watched Los Angeles grow up around it while maintaining its down-home feel, and serving many a beverage to incognito writers, actors, and directors. Barney's is a classic spot for a weekday happy hour or football on Sundays. Its walls are lined with colorful license plates, and the rest of the place doesn't seem to have changed much over the past few decades. Check out the almost 50 beers on tap, generously discounted during happy hour (Mon.-Fri. 4pm-7pm).

MAP 5: 8447 Santa Monica Blvd., 323/654-2287, https://barneysbeanery. com/location/west-hollywood; Mon.-Fri. 11am-2am, Sat.-Sun. 9am-2am

The Den on Sunset

Located in a cozy building that looks like a ski chalet, this hole-in-the-wall bar on Sunset Strip keeps it casual. There are ambient string lights and fire pits. There's no cover and the tequila shots are cheap, so it can get kind of fratty on the weekends.

MAP 5: 8226 W. Sunset Blvd., 323/656-0336, www.thedenonsunset.com; 5pm-2am Mon.-Fri., 3pm-2am Sat., 10am-2am Sun.

The Saddle Ranch Chop House

This popular bar and restaurant is touristy, cheesy, and western to its core—complete with a mechanical bull and campfire pits. It became a favorite on the Strip after opening in 1999 and has since been featured on shows including *American Idol, Sex and the City,* and *Desperate Housewives.* The food isn't half bad, but skip brunch.

MAP 5: 8371 Sunset Blvd., 323/656-2007, www.thesaddleranch.com; 11am-2am Mon.-Fri., 10am-2am Sat.-Sun.

Rainbow Bar & Grill

The Rainbow Bar & Grill, with its iconic rainbow sign, opened in 1972 with a party for Elton John. It became known as a hangout for rock musicians from Neil Diamond to Guns N' Roses. Today, you'll find fabulous people-watching, a great jukebox, decent beer, and possibly Ron Jeremy or Lenny from Motorhead, both of whom hang out there.

MAP 5: 9105 Sunset Blvd., 310/278-4232, www.rainbowbarandgrill.com; lunch 11am-4pm Mon.-Fri., cocktails 11am-2am daily, dinner served until 2am daily

LOUNGES

✪ Pump

Founded and operated by *Real Housewives of Beverly Hills* star Lisa Vanderpump, this dimly lit restaurant and bar is the setting for the reality TV show *Vanderpump Rules.* Even if you don't like reality TV, Pump's garden-like patio is still a beautiful place to enjoy a few cocktails. House music lightly thumps in the background, glittering chandeliers dangle from low-hanging trees, and everywhere you look are subtle hints of pink, Lisa Vanderpump's favorite color. Start your West Hollywood evening at Pump, and then head next door to The Abbey to dance the night away.

MAP 5: 8948 Santa Monica Blvd., 310/657-7867, http://pumprestaurant.com; Mon.-Fri. 5pm-2am, Sat.-Sun. 11:30am-2am

✪ Skybar

Skybar at the Mondrian Los Angeles has everything you might expect of one of L.A. favorite rooftop bars: a glimmering pool, cushy lounge chairs, fantastic city views, and DJs spinning buzzing beats. It also has very pricey cocktails, served with an I'm-cooler-than-you vibe. You can pay for bottle service and sit at one of Skybar's coveted tables, or sip your cocktail standing up. Either way, Skybar is a posh place to spend a balmy evening. There's usually a line for entry on weekends.

MAP 5: 8440 Sunset Blvd., 323/848-6025, www.morganshotelgroup.com/mondrian; Mon.-Fri. 11am-2am, Sat.-Sun. 10am-2am

Pearl's Liquor Bar

Pearl's has three bars and a rooftop patio complete with swings. This Sunset strip staple has a fun 1920s atmosphere, with ivy-laden ceilings and a fireplace. The cocktail menu and beer lists are also great, and the happy hour menu is solid, starting at $5. This is a great all-day hangout spot on the weekends—you can even make your own mimosas during brunch service.

MAP 5: 8909 W. Sunset Blvd., 310/360-6800, www.pearlssunset.

A NIGHT ON THE SUNSET STRIP

Whisky a Go Go

For the quintessential late-night experience in L.A., look no further than the Sunset Strip in West Hollywood. This ever-growing section of Sunset Boulevard—stretching between Crescent Heights Boulevard and Sierra Alta Way—has all the flashing lights, pricey cocktails, and grungy bars you would expect from a legendary nightlife scene.

Take a taxi or rideshare to get to the western side of the strip (even if you have a designated driver—parking is very limited along Sunset Boulevard). Start your night with some delicious, spicy Thai food at the popular **Night + Market WeHo** (page 109).

After dinner, get in the mood with some live music: For gritty rock, head to the **Viper Room** (page 150); for an intimate show in a historic venue, go to **The Roxy Theatre** (page 150) or **Whisky a Go Go** (page 150). Be sure to check the website of whatever venue you choose in advance for event and ticket information.

After the show, it's time to start your bar crawl. Nearby you'll find the infamous **Rainbow Bar & Grill** (page 130), which has a crazy rock 'n' roll history as well as a small but bumpin' dance floor. After your first drink or two, make your way east up Sunset Boulevard. You'll walk past bright lights and various businesses for about twenty minutes until you hit **The Saddle Ranch Chop House** (page 130), a classic tourist trap—complete with a mechanical bull—that is surprisingly fun. After you've fallen off one too many times, continue down the street to **The Den on Sunset** (page 129), a cozy, brick-walled bar with an outdoor patio that's ripe for celebrity spotting.

For a more sophisticated evening, opt for the upscale rooftops of **Pearl's Liquor Bar** (page 130) and poolside **Skybar** (page 130) at the Mondrian Hotel, which has a dress code (i.e. men should wear collared shirts and leave the sneakers behind).

Did someone say drunchies? Top off your night with a late-night snack—either hot dogs from **Carney's** (8351 Sunset Blvd., 323/654-8300, www.carneytrain.com; 11am-midnight Mon.-Thurs., 11am-3am Fri.-Sat.), located inside a vintage yellow railcar, or tacos from **Pinches Tacos** (8200 W. Sunset Blvd., 323/650-0614, www.pinchestacos.com; 9am-midnight Mon.-Wed., 9am-3am Thurs.-Sat., 9am-10pm Sun.), which has a bright pink exterior. Both of these eateries are quite fun and open until midnight on weekdays and 3am on weekends.

com, Mon.-Thurs. 5pm-midnight, Fri. 11:30am-1:45am, Sat. 11am-1:45am, Sun. 11am-midnight

LGBTQ
✪ The Abbey

There's something irresistible about The Abbey. Perhaps it's the scantily clad men, happily dancing on elevated stages, or the booming remix of Cher's "I Believe in Life After Love." Or maybe it's the rich history of this venue that is part of the bedrock of West Hollywood's gay community.

Whatever the reason, the Bravo TV network took notice of The Abbey and in 2017 started a reality show that takes place in its expansive indoor/outdoor club space. We locals have always noticed The Abbey—we come here for boozy brunch on Sundays and dance parties on Thursdays. Expect a line for entry on Thursday, Friday, and Saturday nights.

MAP 5: 92 N. Robertson Blvd., 310/289-8410, www.theabbeyweho.com; Mon.-Thurs. 11am-2am, Fri. 9am-2am, Sat. 6am-2am, Sun. 9am-2am

Rage

Rage promises a party and never disappoints. This thumping gay club is right on Santa Monica Boulevard in the center of West Hollywood's epic nightlife. After dark, you can't miss Rage—people are streaming in and out, and music is booming (it might be show tunes, hip-hop, or Latin, depending on that day's theme). Saturdays and Sundays here are daylong dance parties, and every Thursday night boasts a fabulous drag show.

The Abbey

MAP 5: 8911 Santa Monica Blvd., 310/652-7055, www.ragenightclub.com; Mon. 6pm-2am, Tues.-Sun. 1pm-2am

The Bayou

If you're looking for deep bass, rowdy crowds, and inebriated joy, head to The Bayou any night of the week. Weeknights feature themed fun like trivia, 1980s music, and stand-up comedy, while weekends bring partiers of all types, packing this popular bar for affordable drinks, bumping music, and happy hour discounts. Some may call The Bayou divey, but locals don't care—we love getting loose at The Bayou, especially during L.A. Pride.

MAP 5: 8939 Santa Monica Blvd., 310/273-3303, www.thebayouweho.com/home.html; Mon.-Sat. 4pm-2am, Sun. 2pm-2am

Echo Park, Los Feliz, and Silver Lake
Map 6

BARS

Bar Covell

Do you take your wine and beer seriously? Want to be around other people who do, too? Come to Bar Covell. This small, dimly lit watering hole has earned a reputation both locally and internationally for its curated choice of 150 wines by the glass and eight rotating beers on tap. The bartenders here are friendly and knowledgeable, ready to help you make an informed selection. Light food is available to complement the drinks—try the charcuterie.

MAP 6: 4628 Hollywood Blvd., 323/660-4400, www.barcovell.com; Sun.-Thurs. 5pm-midnight, Fri.-Sat. 5pm-2am

✪ Tiki-Ti

Serving up almost 100 tropical-themed cocktails, Tiki-Ti is a small and mighty old-school tiki bar that has been a Los Angeles favorite since 1964 (*before* the east side was uber-cool). It's tiny in here—there are only 12 barstools—but what Tiki-Ti lacks in size it makes up for in character. Its walls are decorated with Polynesian and other indigenous décor, and its friendly bartenders are ready and willing to make you a sweet and strong tropical cocktail (or two or

DANCE PARTIES

The nice thing about a city as big as Los Angeles is that there's something for just about everyone—dance parties included. Every week, there are a considerable number of themed dance gatherings around town, all of them featuring talented DJs. All of these dance gatherings post and update their schedules online, so the best place to find up-to-date info is on their websites. Some happen in the same location each week, and others change venue for each event. Have fun, get loose, and wear comfy shoes!

- Looking for pulsating bangers? Check out **Avalon Hollywood** (1735 Vine St., 323/462-8900, http://avalonhollywood.com; nights vary; tickets starting at $15), which offers epic dance parties complete with big-name DJs and LED lights on Friday and Saturday nights.

- How about a more indie-dance vibe? Head to Dance Yourself Clean at **The Satellite** (1717 Silver Lake Blvd., www.thesatellitela.com; hours and prices vary) in Silver Lake. The casual party is held every Saturday in Silver Lake. It's usually cheap (if not free).

- If you have eclectic tastes, check out **Echo+Plex** (1154 Glendale Blvd., 213/413-8200, www.theecho.com; hours and prices vary), which offers a variety of dance parties. Come on Wednesdays for dub and on Saturdays for funk.

- And if you're not a night owl, don't worry: L.A. has a dance party for you, too. Try out the once-a-month **Daybreaker** festival (www.daybreaker.com; dates vary, check calendar online; $35), which starts with a yoga class from 5:30am to 6:15am followed by dancing from 6:30am to 8:30am (there's no booze, just juice).

three). Tiki-Ti is only becoming more popular, so there may be a line to get in the door on weekends; it's worth the wait.

MAP 6: 4427 Sunset Blvd., 323/669-9382, www.tiki-ti.com/pages/home.html; Wed.-Sat. 4pm-2am

Red Lion Tavern

Come to this German beer garden to kick back, eat some schnitzel, and down some frothy lager. I've never been to Germany, but I hear the Red Lion is pretty authentic, serving traditional German cuisine like spaetzle, potato pancakes, and bratwurst with sauerkraut. Founded in 1959, the Red Lion has always provided a den-like local hangout; in 2000 it expanded its popular second-floor patio, which is now filled with sunlight, colorful flags, and 10 hearty beers on tap.

MAP 6: 2366 Glendale Blvd., 323/662-5337, http://redliontavern.net; daily 11am-2am

1642

1642 is an understatedly cool wine and beer bar. Just a narrow room with exposed brick walls, 1642 has become an intimate hangout spot that offers a variety of live music, including DJs and acoustic artists. It's a great place to impress someone on a date without looking like you're trying too hard. Plus, if you show up between 6pm and 8pm on Thursday you'll get a free tamale with any beer as part of 1642's Tamale Happy Hour.

MAP 6: 1642 W. Temple St., 213/989-6836; Tues.-Sat. 6pm-2am, Sun. 6pm-midnight

Sunset Beer Company

This hybrid bar and liquor store sells pretty much any craft beer you could imagine—and you can drink them right in the store. Despite the super-small storefront tucked into a strip mall, there's a surprising amount of space to hang out, drink a few brews, and play some store-provided board games. A lot of people hang out here before Dodgers games, as the stadium is only a few miles away. There's no food, but the cold beer selection makes up for it.

MAP 6: 1498 Sunset Blvd., 213/481-2337, http://sunsetbeerco.com; Mon.-Thurs. noon-11pm, Fri.-Sat. noon-midnight, Sun. noon-10pm

LIVE MUSIC
INDIE
✪ The Satellite

The Satellite has become synonymous with live music on the east side. Its narrow stage has hosted dozens of well-known musicians over the past few decades, including the White Stripes and Death Cab for Cutie. This intimate venue is a great place to catch some live music, play a game of pool, and meet a diverse group of Silver Lake friends. What's more, The Satellite has maintained its cheap drinks and divey feel over the years, even as Silver Lake has grown up around it. Every Saturday night, The Satellite hosts a bumpin' indie-electronic dance party called "Dance Yourself Clean" (named after an LCD Soundsystem song). Admission for all shows is 21 and over.

MAP 6: 1717 Silver Lake Blvd., www.thesatellitela.com; hours and prices vary, check online for details

ECLECTIC
The Echo and Echoplex

The Echo and Echoplex = party. This club is actually two adjoining rooms—the Echo is a smaller concert venue, and the Echoplex is a big dance floor. Both provide pulsing, energetic shows many nights a week, as well as regular dance parties (funk on Saturdays, dub on Wednesdays).

Come here to get your groove on and see up-and-coming artists perform live before they make it big. There's a patio out back lit with hanging lights, a good place to catch your breath and rest your feet.

MAP 6: 1154 Glendale Blvd., 213/413-8200, www.theecho.com; hours and prices vary, check online for details

LOUNGE
The Dresden

The lounge at The Dresden offers live, jazzy music seven nights a week in a classic, old-school lounge setting. Marty and Elaine are The Dresden's in-house musical duo, performing five nights a week. The Dresden is proud of its cameo in the 1996 film *Swingers;* although many of its patrons enjoy the lounge in a slightly ironic way, this timeless establishment is as serious as ever about providing Angelenos with more than sixty years of live entertainment, night after night.

MAP 6: 1760 N. Vermont Ave., 323/665-4294, www.thedresden.com; Mon.-Sat. 5pm-11pm, Sun. 4:30pm-11pm

Akbar

LGBTQ

Akbar

Akbar loves to party, and all are welcome to join the fun. On weekends, expect to be packed into this dark bar with a thumping dance floor. There are new DJs every weekend, and on any given Saturday night you can dive into a themed dance party (think 1970s fly, disco ball and go-go dancer included).

On weeknights, Akbar's mood is a bit more laid-back, and there's always fantastic people-watching. Check out the Akbar website for its monthly schedule, which will list featured DJs *and* bingo and craft nights.

MAP 6: 4356 W. Sunset Blvd., 323/665-6810, www.akbarsilverlake.com; daily 4pm-2am; cover for dance floor on weekends

Downtown   Map 7

ROOFTOP BARS

Perch

Perch is a sweet little spot atop a classic Downtown office building. Its quieter vibe is a nice alternative to some of Downtown's more bumpin' rooftop bars. You'll take multiple elevators to get to Perch's 16th-floor rooftop deck, which has nice sunset views, two fireplaces, and a handful of fire pits to keep you warm during cooler nights. Choose from a selection of craft beers, cognacs, and French-inspired cocktails.

MAP 7: 448 Hill St., 213/802-1770, www.perchla.com; Mon.-Wed. 4pm-1am, Thurs.-Fri. 4pm-2am, Sat. 10am-2am, Sun. 10am-1am; no cover

✪ The Rooftop at the Standard

For as long as I've lived in the L.A., the rooftop at the Standard has been one of the most happening places to be on a Saturday night. You really can't go wrong with a heated pool, swaying DJs, twinkling city views, and, wait for it...waterbeds. Most nights, this is a great place to have some drinks and marvel at Downtown's silvery skyscrapers as the sun dips below the horizon. During the summer, the Standard hosts splashy pool parties every Sunday.

MAP 7: 550 S. Flower St., 213/892-8080, www.standardhotels.com/la/features/rooftop; daily noon-2am; $20 cover weekends after 7pm

✪ Upstairs Bar at the Ace Hotel

If you're an unfathomably cool, impossibly beautiful hipster in your 20s, this is the place for you. Seriously. Upstairs Bar has become the hippest place to hang out on a Downtown afternoon. There are DJs, live bands, and even a teeny-tiny pool. So pull up a tanned leather chair to a tree-trunk table, order one of the bar's creative cocktails, and post up for an elegant (and sometimes rowdy) evening of people-watching.

MAP 7: 929 S. Broadway, 213/623-3233, www.acehotel.com/losangeles/upstairs; daily 11am-2am; no cover

BARS

Arts District Brewing Company

No trip to the Arts District is complete without a stop at the Arts District Brewing Company. Where else in L.A. can you drink house-made beers, play Skee-Ball, and nosh on specialty hot

Arts District Brewing Company

dogs? This is a huge space with big tables, a chatty outdoor patio, and a game area to awaken your competitive spirit. I recommend starting your time here with a flight of beers—then you'll know what to order for the rest of the night!

MAP 7: 828 Traction Ave., 213/519-5887, http://213hospitality. com/artsdistrictbrewing; Mon.-Thurs. 3pm-midnight, Fri. 3pm-2am, Sat. noon-2am, Sun. noon-midnight; no cover

✪ The Edison

The Edison is an underground bar—literally. It's housed in what was one of L.A.'s first electric power plants, built in 1910. This is a dark, sexy space, filled with plush leather lounge chairs and well-dressed clientele. There's live music featuring 1920s tunes on weekdays and DJs on weekends. The Edison's menu is filled with a wide selection of cocktails and other libations; the Dead Man's Hand, for example, mixes double rye whisky, brown sugar, sarsaparilla, whisky-barrel bitters, and orange zest.

MAP 7: 108 W. 2nd St. #101, 213/613-0000, www.edisondowntown.com; Wed.-Thurs. 5pm-midnight, Fri.-Sat. 7pm-2am

Clifton's

Looking for beer with a side of quirkiness? Enter Clifton's, where weird meets cool. Some people come here for cafeteria-style lunches, but the real fun starts after dark, as Clifton's transforms into a nightclub turned hipster bar turned taxidermy museum. Did I mention the four-story redwood "tree" growing up through the middle of the bar? To know Clifton's, you must experience it—nooks, crannies, rushing waterfall, and all.

MAP 7: 648 S. Broadway, 213/627-1673, www.cliftonsla.com; Wed. 6pm-midnight, Thurs.-Fri. 11am-2am, Sat. 10am-2am, Sun. 10am-6pm, no cover

Preux & Proper

Once you walk into Preux & Proper's dining room, either stop at the bar for happy hour or head downstairs to a basement party that feels straight out of Mardi Gras. This New Orleans-inspired space serves outstanding cocktails and even slushies with an alcohol content that's akin to what you'd find on Bourbon Street. If you're looking for something dark, try the Sarsaparilla Smokeshow—cardamom-infused Ketel One, sassafras syrup, cinnamon ice, hickory smoke, and ginger air.

Preux & Proper

Clifton's

MAP 7: 840 S. Spring St., 213/896-0090, www.preuxandproper.com; Mon.-Thurs. 4pm-10pm, Fri.-Sat. 4pm-noon, Sun. noon-9pm

La Cita

La Cita appears to be a traditional Mexican bar—there are Mexican flags painted on its exterior and vintage leather booths inside—but evenings here are not traditional. Instead, they are pulsating with a fresh vibe created by some of the hottest DJs in town. The patio in back, which is surrounded by Downtown's high-rises, is a great place to chill and sip on a tasty *michelada* (a beer drink made with lime and traditional Mexican spices). It gets crowded here on weekends.

MAP 7: 336 Hill St., 213/687-7111, www. lacitabar.com; Mon.-Fri. 11am-2am, Sat.-Sun. 10am-2am; occasional $5-10 cover

LIVE MUSIC
Teragram Ballroom

Head to Teragram Ballroom if you want to catch an indie show in an intimate venue. This concert hall hosts a rocking show almost every night, and packs in a great crowd. It's standing room only and low-frills, an approach that has made Teragram a favorite place for locals to see a live show. Plus, Teragram is in Downtown, so there are lots of bars to spill into after your show—you never quite know where the night will take you after seeing a fantastic performance at Teragram.

MAP 7: 1234 W 7th St., 213/689-9100, www.teragramballroom.com; see online calendar for concert schedule; tickets $15-50

ARTS AND CULTURE

L.A. has this sort of wild creativity bubbling just below the surface. Downtown is fast becoming an incredible place for modern art, West Hollywood has world-class comedy shows, and there are live musical performance happening every night in exciting venues across town.

The Broad

Street art, upscale galleries, and world-renowned museums exist side by side in L.A. There's amazing art happening everywhere, but Downtown has become the epicenter of the art scene. Here you'll find The Broad and MOCA, as well as contemporary pop-up galleries and exquisite graffiti art. The Arts District on the east side is a good place to walk around on a sunny afternoon.

If you're bored by the mainstream film industry, check out L.A.'s exciting live theater scene. You'll see great theater at the Wallis Annenberg Center for the Performing Arts in Beverly Hills and at the Center Theater Group Downtown. But even more exciting are the comedy and improv clubs in Hollywood. Head to The Comedy Store for hilarious stand-up or Groundlings Theater for improv that will leave your mouth sore from smiling.

There's no better place in America to enjoy music outdoors. The Hollywood Bowl and Greek Theatre host huge musical acts in blissful outdoor settings. Summertime brings many fun outdoor concerts to the city, like Jazz Fridays at LACMA.

HIGHLIGHTS

✪ **BEST STREET ART:** You'll find some of the city's most creative and colorful street art at the **Venice Murals** and at **The Container Yard** Downtown (pages 141 and 155).

✪ **BEST ART GALLERIES:** Admire fine art from old masters at **Galerie Michael** in Beverly Hills and contemporary art from new masters at **Hauser & Wirth** Downtown (pages 143 and 155).

✪ **BEST BELLY LAUGHS:** The famous **Groundlings Theatre** offers the funniest improv, and **The Comedy Store** on the Sunset Strip has L.A.'s best standup comedians (pages 144 and 147).

✪ **BEST OUTDOOR CONCERTS:** The **Hollywood Bowl** and **The Greek Theatre** host the biggest musical acts in the country in beautiful outdoor spaces (pages 145 and 152).

✪ **BEST FILM SCREENINGS:** For an indoor experience and a chance to see a celeb on the red carpet, check out **ArcLight Cinema Hollywood.** For an outdoor experience attended by hundreds of dead celebrities, head to the Hollywood Forever Cemetery for a screening by **Cinespia** (pages 145 and 146).

✪ **BEST ART INSTALLATION:** The iconic *Urban Light* installation at the **Los Angeles County Museum of Art** features more than 200 restored streetlamps (page 148).

✪ **BEST PLACE TO HEAR ROCK 'N' ROLL:** The intimate, cool **The Troubadour** is one of the best rock venues in the world (page 150).

✪ **BEST CONTEMPORARY ART MUSEUM:** Wander around in awe of the groundbreaking art at **The Broad** museum Downtown (page 154).

✪ **BEST BEETHOVEN SYMPHONIES:** An architectural treasure, The **Walt Disney Concert Hall** has incredible acoustics that let the L.A. Philharmonic shine (page 157).

FREE-ENTRY MUSEUM DAYS

With the right planning, savvy travelers can visit a lot of L.A.'s favorite museums for free. These museums are **always free**:

• The Broad

• The Getty Center

• The Getty Villa

• The Paley Center for Media in Beverly Hills (with suggested donation)

• Fashion Institute of Design and Merchandising (FIDM)

• California Science Center

• Griffith Observatory

And these museums have **free-entry days** on either **Tuesdays** or **Thursdays**:

• LACMA: second Tuesday of every month

• Natural History Museum: first Tuesday of every month

• Autry Museum: second Tuesday of every month

• Page Museum at the La Brea Tar Pits: first Tuesday of every month

• Museum of Contemporary Art (MOCA) Grand Avenue: every Thursday 5pm-8pm

• Geffen Contemporary at MOCA: every Thursday all day

• Japanese Cultural Museum: every Thursday 5pm-8pm, and all day third Thursday every month

Santa Monica   Map 1

MUSEUMS

26th Street Art Center

If you're the creative type who doesn't mind turning down a few alleyways to find great art, make some time to wander around the 26th Street Art Center, formerly known as Bergamot Station. This gaggle of warehouses contain more than 20 art galleries, where you can view exquisite photography collections, purchase avant-garde paintings, and take some selfies in front of artfully spray-painted walls. Galleries here are often coming and going, but on any given day there are enough open to make a trip well worth your while.

MAP 1: 2525 Michigan Ave., 310/453-7535, http://bergamotstation.com; Tues.-Thurs. 10am-6pm, Sat. 11am-5:30pm; free

Axiom Contemporary

Founded in 2011, Axiom Contemporary has made a nice name for itself in both local and national art communities. This forward-facing gallery showcases pop, abstract, neo-street, and contemporary art in a number of mediums. It's a small gallery, so maybe not worth a specific visit, but if you find yourself wandering down Santa Monica's Main Street (which you should), it's a great place to pop in and look around and take in the boundary-pushing pieces.

MAP 1: 2801 Main St., 818/799-1110, http://axiomcontemporary.com; Mon.-Thurs. 11am-6pm, Fri.-Sun. 11am-7pm

Jadis

At Jadis, weird science rises to the level of art. Want to buy an antique flying bike, or a time-travel machine used in a recent film? Then come to Jadis, where you'll find that and so much more. Every cranny here is packed with rare finds—some used in science-fiction films and some that are authentic vintage scientific supplies. Jadis charges $1 for admission and is known to not stick to its posted hours of operation—apparently you can't rein in mad genius, though who would want to?

MAP 1: 2701 Main St., 310/396-3477, www.jadisprops.com; Thurs.-Sun. noon-5pm, $1 per person admission

CINEMA
Front Porch Cinema at the Pier

Friday nights in fall are for the Front Porch Cinema at the Santa Monica Pier. There's food, family, drinks, and, of course, fantastic films. Bring your own chair or blanket and spread out to enjoy classic family-friendly movies (think *Star Wars* and *Zootopia*), cool ocean breezes (bring layers), and even DJ music before and after the show. One of the many great things about Los Angeles is that our summers last long, so take advantage of our summertime-in-fall weather and enjoy a very Angeleno night under the stars.

MAP 1: Santa Monica Pier, 310/458-8901, http://santamonicapier.org/frontporchcinema; shows on select Fridays, see online schedule; free

Venice

Map 2

STREET AND PUBLIC ART
Venice Public Art Walls

The Venice Public Art Walls comprise multiple freestanding concrete walls where it's now legal for graffiti artists to work their magic. Sitting right on the sands next to the Venice Skate Park, these walls are always open to view, and on the weekends they're open for artists to use on a first-come, first-served basis, meaning you can watch the walls being remade in real time. Bring a camera—this place offers lots of colorful photo ops.

MAP 2: Ocean Front Walk

✪ Venice Murals

There are at least 20 unique public murals in Venice. If you're wandering around Abbot Kinney and the Venice Beach Boardwalk, you will definitely come by them naturally. To be more strategic, find a Venice mural map online and let it guide your adventure.

If you only check out one mural while you're in Venice, make it *Venice Reconstituted* by Rip Cronk; this giant painting reimagines Botticelli's *Birth of Venus* with a very meta, very Venice

Venice Reconstituted by Rip Cronk

vibe. Cronk, who created a number of other murals around Venice, painted the first version of *Venice Reconstituted* in 1980. You'll find the mural a block off the beach on the corner of Speedway and Windward Avenues. Head to Abbot Kinney for some more recently-created street art.

MAP 2: locations vary, www.visitveniceca. com or www.muralmapla.com

GALLERIES

L.A. Louver

L.A. Louver has been a Venice art community staple since 1975. Its humble exterior belies the fact that this small, two-story gallery hosts rotating collections of world-class art. The space itself is sparse and straightforward, which allows patrons to focus on the fascinating collections from contemporary American and European artists. L.A. Louver is conveniently located just off the Venice boardwalk, and it may just be the departure you

need after a long day of chaos and commercialism.

MAP 2: 45 N. Venice Blvd., 301/822-4955, www.lalouver.com; Tues.-Sat. 10am-6pm; free

C.A.V.E. Gallery

The Center for Audio and Visual Expression, known as C.A.V.E., started in 2001 as a series of traveling art events showcasing visual art, film, and music. It landed a permanent space in Venice in 2008 and has been acclaimed in the local art community ever since. C.A.V.E. features regularly rotating pop art, photos, and installations by both famous and up-and-coming artists from around the world. Just blocks from the Venice boardwalk, C.A.V.E. is the perfect pit stop for some culturally infused quiet time.

MAP 2: 55 N. Venice Blvd., 301/428-6387, http://cavegallery.net; Tues.-Fri. 11pm-6pm; free

PERFORMING ARTS
Wallis Annenberg Center for the Performing Arts

Affectionately referred to as "the Wallis," this community space provides local audiences with world-class dance, musical, and theater performances year-round. The building itself was constructed in 1933 as the original Beverly Hills post office and it's now listed in the National Register of Historic Places. It has been renovated and expanded and is a beautiful place to spend a Beverly Hills evening. There are two stages, both of which have a small and intimate feel.

MAP 3: 9390 N. Santa Monica Blvd., 310/246-3800, www.thewallis.org; showtimes vary; tickets free-$200

MUSEUMS
The Paley Center for Media

When in Beverly Hills, check out the Paley Center's extensive collection of TV and film memorabilia. The center showcases artifacts from one movie or TV show at a time, so when you visit, costumes from shows such as *Downton Abbey* or *American Horror Story* might be on display. Explore the Paley Center's three winding floors, set in a bright, modern space; you can even watch thousands of movies and television shows in its archival library. Located in the heart of Beverly Hills, the Paley Center makes for a good dose of culture in the midst of your shopping spree.

MAP 3: 465 N. Beverly Dr., 310/786-1000, https://media.paleycenter.org; Wed.-Sun. noon-5pm; free

GALLERIES
Mouche Gallery

This ultracontemporary art gallery with hip-hop booming in the background showcases intimate, larger-than-life portraits of celebrities like The Beatles and Marilyn Monroe. There are also graffiti portraits of stars like Frida Kahlo, Jackie O., and Bob Marley, some blowing gum bubbles. This is a vibrant and beautiful place to peruse colorful works of contemporary art, and perhaps purchase a big piece of art to take home. A few smaller works are also available for purchase.

MAP 3: 340 N. Beverly Dr., 310/858-8114, https://mouchegallery.com; Mon.-Thurs. 11am-7pm, Fri.-Sat. 11am-9pm, Sun. 11am-6pm

✪ Galerie Michael

Galerie Michael has just a little storefront on Two Rodeo Drive, but once you go inside and walk up the staircase, the second floor opens up to an expansive gallery showcasing works from the 17th through the 20th centuries from master artists including Picasso, Dalí, Chagall, Miró, and many more. Art lovers, plan to spend some time walking around this gallery wide-eyed. Galerie Michael prides itself on curatorial knowledge and expertise, so feel free to ask questions—staff are eager to discuss these breathtaking works of art.

MAP 3: 224 N. Rodeo Dr., 310/273-3377, www.galeriemichael.com; Mon.-Sat. 10am-7pm, Sun. 11am-5pm

Fredrick Weisman Foundation

How often is it that you get to tour the gorgeous home of an entrepreneurial art collector? Philanthropist Frederick Weisman passed away in 1994 with express instructions to maintain his entire art collection in his home in Beverly Hills and open the space for public viewing. Tour this Mediterranean-style villa to view hundreds of works of art, including paintings by Cezanne, Picasso, and de Kooning; pop art by Warhol and Lichtenstein; and sculptures by Hanson and De Andrea. Tours are by appointment only—call ahead to book. It's closed on weekends.

MAP 3: 265 N. Carolwood Dr., 310/277-5321, www.weismanfoundation.org; guided tours by appointment only, Mon.-Fri. at 10:30am and 2pm

Hollywood   Map 4

COMEDY CLUBS

✪ Groundlings Theatre

Born in 1974, Groundlings is the Los Angeles home of improv and sketch comedy. Not to brag, but famous alumni include Will Ferrell, Maya Rudolph, and Lisa Kudrow. The theater has one show almost every weeknight, and two shows per night on weekends. Buy tickets in advance, as they will often sell out. Prepare to laugh until you cry. There's a strict no-late-entry policy, so make sure to arrive early.

MAP 4: 7307 Melrose Ave., 323/934-4747, www.groundlings.com; evening shows 4-7 nights/week; tickets $18-20

Upright Citizens Brigade

This humble 92-seat theater tucked into a funky strip of Franklin Avenue belies the fact that the Upright Citizens Brigade (UCB) was founded by comedy royalty (including Amy Poehler) and is now one of the most respected comedy shops in the country. UCB prides itself on providing excellent comedy at affordable prices, seven nights a week. What kind of comedy does it offer? Improv, stand-up, sketch, talk/ variety, and, according to its website, "cool weird stuff that defies categorization." There are four UCB theaters nationwide—two in New York and two in Los Angeles (the second L.A. location is at 5419 W. Sunset Blvd.).

MAP 4: 5919 Franklin Ave., 323/908-8702, https://franklin.ucbtheatre.com; multiple shows every night; tickets $5-12

The Nerdist Showroom

The Nerdist Showroom feels like a well-kept comedy secret. Hidden in the back of Meltdown Comics, this self-proclaimed "DIY beating heart" of the Los Angeles comedy community has continually rotating shows with titles like "Hippie Sabotage," "Political Jerk," and "Smart, Funny & Black." There are a handful of free shows each month, and also some live-audience podcast recordings. This casual space is the home to the Comedy Central television series *The Meltdown with Jonah & Kumail.*

MAP 4: 7522 Sunset Blvd., 323/851-7223, http://nerdmeltla.com; shows most evenings; tickets $8-12

CONCERT VENUES

☼ Hollywood Bowl

Nestled into Hollywood's rolling hills, this outdoor concert venue hosts some of the world's greatest musical artists June-September each year. Genres range from hip-hop to jazz to classical to African beats. Patrons are encouraged to bring their own food and drinks, so make an evening of it and pack a picnic. Parking at the Hollywood Bowl is very limited, so it's best to use a rideshare service or park in one of the Bowl's public lots and use the Park & Ride bus.

MAP 4: 2301 N. Highland Ave., 323/850-2000, www.hollywoodbowl.com; June-September; tickets $35-$200

Hollywood Palladium

This big and beautiful art deco venue opened in 1940 and was added to the National Register of Historic Places in 2016. Thanks to extensive remodeling, the Palladium's sound quality is fantastic. There's standing (and dancing) room only, and the dance floor covers more than 11,000 square feet. Because of its relatively small size, the Palladium can feel like you're right up close to some of the biggest musical and comedic performers in the world. Buy tickets in advance, as popular shows sell out quickly.

MAP 4: 6215 Sunset Blvd., 323/962-7600, www.thehollywoodpalladium.com; concerts year-round; tickets $35-600

CINEMA

☼ ArcLight Cinema Hollywood

For the full ArcLight experience, grab tickets in advance to any movie playing in the Dome, a state-of-the-art theater with a domed, planetarium-like ceiling and plush seats. There's some cool film-related swag on display and for sale in the lobby, along with a small café. Lots of movies premiere here, so call ahead to ask about upcoming

Hollywood Bowl

FREE SUMMER CONCERTS

June through August, Los Angeles nights come alive with free-to-the-public music. While the days can be hot, evenings cool down, and rhythms from around the world fill public spaces across the city.

- One of L.A.'s most popular outdoor concert series is **Jazz at LACMA** (the Los Angeles County Museum of Art). Every Friday, Angelenos BYOB to the lawns of LACMA to listen to superb jazz-ish music as the sun sets on another beautiful day.

- In Santa Monica, the **Twilight Concert Series** takes place right on the beach every Thursday night and features well-known musical artists from a variety of genres, including reggae, dance, and indie rock.

- If you're Downtown, check out **Grand Performances in California Plaza,** where you'll gather around a sunken fountain surrounded by glowing skyscrapers and enjoy some funky grooves.

- For families, **The Grove in Hollywood** hosts free concerts every summer Friday. The Astroturf gets filled with dancing kids.

debuts—on these nights you can stand out front and catch some celebs walking the red carpet.

MAP 4: 6360 Sunset Blvd., 323/464-1478, www.arclightcinemas.com/locations/los-angeles/hollywood; showtimes daily starting at 10:30am; tickets $11-$15.95; validated garage parking

✪ Cinespia

This may be the only place in the world where you can watch a classic film on a giant outdoor screen surrounded by hundreds of deceased Hollywood stars. That's right—Cinespia takes place in the Hollywood Forever Cemetery, the final resting place of numerous celebrities and the filming location of dozens of movies and TV shows, including *Hot Shots* and *Dexter*. Cinespia screenings feature preshow DJs, themed photo booths, and occasional visits by actors, directors, and filmmakers. Movies play May-July each year. Buying tickets in advance is recommended.

MAP 4: 6000 Santa Monica Blvd., http://cinespia.org; weekends May-July; $12-16

El Capitan Theatre

El Capitan has been making movie magic since 1926. The theater is now a fully restored, truly gorgeous tribute to bygone days of Hollywood glamour. The theater exclusively plays Disney movies, so it's a great family-friendly adventure, but you'll also catch couples on dates here. This is a full movie-theater experience, complete with live preshow organ music and a glittering crystal movie curtain. After the film, stop by the Disney Studio Store and Ghirardelli Soda Fountain for sweet treats.

MAP 4: 6838 Hollywood Blvd., 818/845-3110, https://elcapitantheatre.com; shows daily, showtimes vary; $12-24

El Capitan Theatre

GALLERIES

M+B Gallery

M+B is a small, brightly lit art gallery that showcases unique modern art. Less is more in this minimalist space that showcases works from one contemporary artist at a time. Openings here are casually chic, with locals in flannel shirts sipping wine and rocking out to mariachi music. M+B is a cool space with a bit of a hipster vibe, and it's a worthwhile stop on your stroll around West Hollywood's Design District.

MAP 5: 612 N. Almont Dr., 310/550-0050, www.mbart.com; Tues.-Sat. 10am-6pm

M+B Gallery

Taschen

Even if you're not consciously aware of it, you've probably come across Taschen's sophisticated coffee-table books at some point; they're some of the most popular of their kind in the world. This gallery is Taschen's very own space to highlight the incredible and eclectic work of its artists at full scale (not just in book-sized images). The exhibits at Taschen rotate regularly, so you may find a collection of up-close-and-personal photographs of a recently deceased rock 'n' roll star, or original watercolor paintings from a Californian painter, or set design sketches from an Oscar-winning film. All art is for sale, and there are lots of books to buy too.

MAP 5: 8070 Beverly Blvd., 323/852-9098, www.taschen.com/pages/en/taschen_gallery/index.all_artists.htm; Tues.-Sat. 11am-7pm, Sun. noon-6pm

MUSEUMS

MOCA Pacific Design Center

L.A.'s Museum of Contemporary Art (MOCA) Grand Avenue, which occupies a huge building downtown, created this annex in West Hollywood as a complement to the adjacent Pacific Design Center. At this smaller MOCA, you can see rotating exhibitions that focus on architecture and design—think elegant concrete chairs, or couches made from leather and bone. There's also a very cool gift shop here, and a beautiful fountain right outside the doors.

MAP 5: 8687 Melrose Ave., 310/289-5223, www.moca.org/visit/pacific-design-center; Tues.-Fri. 11am-5pm, Sat.-Sun. 11am-6pm; free

COMEDY CLUBS

❂ The Comedy Store

Looking to laugh till your belly hurts? Head to The Comedy Store, the apex of comical genius here in Los Angeles. Located right on West Hollywood's Sunset Strip, The Comedy Store has three performance rooms and multiple shows per night from America's greatest comedians. The vibe here is infectious, with throngs of people lined up outside on any given night to have some drinks and see their favorite laugh-makers up close. Skip the food and save your money for the requisite drink order.

MIRACLE MILE

The Miracle Mile sits in what might be considered the center of Los Angeles. Its awesome museums and delectable Ethiopian restaurants make it a great place for curious travelers to spend a sunny afternoon.

MUSEUMS

- Art-lovers or even dabblers should not miss the ✪ **Los Angeles County Museum of Art** (5905 Wilshire Blvd., 323/857-6000, www.lacma.org; Mon.-Tues. and Thurs. 11am-5pm, Fri. 11am-8pm, Sat.-Sun. 10am-7pm; adults $25, seniors/students $21, ages 17 and under free, free for all after 3pm Mon.-Fri., parking $10). Spread over 20 urban acres, **LACMA** is a huge compound with multiple buildings housing over 135,000 pieces covering 6,000 years of art history, from ancient Greek sculptures and pre-Columbian artifacts to paintings from modern masters like Picasso and Warhol. Don't miss the cool installations here: *Levitated Mass* by Michael Heizer is a 340-ton boulder you can walk under, and *Urban Light* by Chris Burden features 202 restored streetlamps. There are also free jazz shows on Friday nights. Admission to the museum is free every second Tuesday of the month, plus Martin Luther King Day, President's Day, and Memorial Day.

- You may be surprised to find one of the world's most famous fossil sites in the middle of L.A.'s sprawling urban landscape, but that's what you'll get at the **Page Museum & La Brea Tar Pits** (5801 Wilshire Blvd., 213/763-3499, https://tarpits.org; daily 9:30am-5pm; adults $15, seniors/students $12, ages 3-12 $7). During the Ice Age, hot and sticky tar pits deep below Wilshire Boulevard bubbled up and caught hundreds of prehistoric animals, including mammoths, ground sloths, and saber-toothed tigers. The Page Museum tells the story of these animals through fossils and life-sized replicas. The grounds surrounding the museum and the tar pits themselves (which still bubble!) are free and open to the public.

- If you've never thought of cars as art, you need to check out the **Petersen Automotive Museum** (6060 Wilshire Blvd., 323/930-2277, https://petersen.org; daily 10am-6pm; adults $16, seniors/students $13, ages 3-12 $8, military free). You'll get up close to gorgeously crafted antique autos, learn about state-of-the-art car design, and become a simulated race car driver. The building's façade is a spectacle in and of itself, with long metal ribbons overlaying red walls and lit up by LEDs at night.

- The **Craft & Folk Art Museum** (5814 Wilshire Blvd., 323/937-4230, www.cafam. org; Tues.-Fri. 11am-5pm, Sat.-Sun. 11am-6pm, first Thurs. of every month 6:30pm-9:30pm; adults $7, seniors/students $5, military/ages 9 and under free) celebrates visionary takes on traditional art and craft forms, from quilting to ceramics and glass-blowing. This relatively small museum is a place to both view and create (check out the workshop schedule online). It also has one of the best gift shops in town.

RESTAURANTS

- At any time of day, **Republique**'s (624 S. La Brea Ave., 310/362-6115, http://republiquela.com; Sun.-Wed. 8am-3pm and 5:30pm-10pm, Thurs.-Sat. 8am-3pm and 5:30pm-11pm; $15-30) atmospheric interior is alive and bustling, full of patrons happy to have finally grabbed a table at this in-demand establishment. While all meals are good here, Republique has gained a reputation for its decadent brunch—think sweet rolls with bourbon and bacon. For dinner, try the organic rotisserie chicken and ask one of the expert sommeliers for a wine recommendation.

- At **Merkato** (1036 1/2 S. Fairfax Ave., 323/935-1775, http://merkatorestaurant.com; daily 11am-2am; $10-20), you'll eat a delicious Ethiopian meal surrounded by authentic art and animal hides. The food isn't fancy, but it's yummy, wholesome, and traditionally Ethiopian. After you eat, pick up some African trinkets at Merkato's adjoining shop.

- There are so many fantastic restaurants in Little Ethiopia that it's hard to choose just one to eat at, but when Angelenos must choose, they usually pick **Rahel Ethiopian Vegan Cuisine** (1047 S. Fairfax Ave., 323/937-8401, http://rahelvegancuisine.com; Sun.-Thurs. 11am-10pm, Fri.-Sat. 11am-11pm; $5-15). Rahel serves thick, spicy, heartwarming Ethiopian cuisine in a cute little space right on Fairfax Avenue.

NIGHTLIFE

- **Jazz Fridays at LACMA** (5905 Wilshire Blvd., 323/857-6000, www.lacma.org; Apr.-Nov. Fri. 6pm-8pm; admission free, parking $10) has one of the best twilight shows in town. During L.A.'s warmest months, you'll discover world-renowned jazz artists playing in front of the Urban Light installation at LACMA. Bring your own blanket and bubbly—and come early to secure your spot!

- The decadent art deco **El Rey Theatre** (5515 Wilshire Blvd., 323/936-6400, www. theelrey.com; showtimes and ticket prices vary) hosts a range of great musical acts, from smaller local talents to bigger artists such as Tame Impala, Jack White, and Sinead O"Connor. There are a few bars but the venue is all ages. There's street parking as well as a paid parking lot across the street.

MAP 5: 8433 Sunset Blvd., 323/650-6268, http://thecomedystore.com; daily 7pm-2am; tickets $5-$50

Laugh Factory

The Laugh Factory is in need of a renovation—its small, dank room feels like a flashback to comedy clubs of the 1980s. Luckily, its comedians are super-fresh, performing nightly shows that'll have you crying with laughter. Shows here are a treat because Los Angeles is filled with so many talented comedians and performers, many of whom perform regular live shows in order to test out new material and keep their comedic chops in shape. I recommend paying for priority seating—you'll be much more comfortable—and come prepared to meet the drink minimum.

MAP 5: 8001 Sunset Blvd., 323/656-1336, www.laughfactory.com/clubs/hollywood; daily 9:30am-11:30pm; tickets $25-$50

CONCERT VENUES
✪ The Troubadour

Angelenos love The Troubadour. Why? Because it's a small, intimate club with lots of history that, thankfully, hasn't changed much over the years. Since opening in 1947, The Troubadour has seen the starts of dozens of now-famous artists, including Elton John, Joni Mitchell, and Tom Waits. More recently, *Rolling Stone* magazine designated The Troubadour as the "second-best rock club in America." The Troubadour has a diverse concert lineup: You can catch huge stars like John Legend and Alicia Keys performing here, and you can also discover many up-and-coming artists.

MAP 5: 9081 N. Santa Monica Blvd., www.troubadour.com; see online calendar for performance times; tickets $10-$75

Whisky a Go Go

Opened in 1964, Whisky a Go Go was for many years the center of L.A.'s rock scene, and hosted shows by artists including the Doors, Janis Joplin, and Led Zeppelin. In fact, this nightclub was inducted into the Rock & Roll Hall of Fame in 2006. Today, you can come to Whisky a Go Go to grab cheap drinks and see spirited performances from up-and-coming artists in a no-nonsense concert space. It sits at the heart of West Hollywood's Sunset Strip and has stuck around as an original L.A. icon while the most of landscape around it has been graced by glitzy hotels and chichi sushi lounges.

MAP 5: 8901 Sunset Blvd., 310/652-4202, www.whiskyagogo.com; see online calendar for performance times; tickets $10-$30

The Roxy Theatre

The famous Roxy Theatre, open since 1973, has hosted everyone from Van Morrison to Prince. The original bar above the venue was also legendary, partied in by legends like John Lennon and Alice Cooper. Today, the intimate venue hosts much smaller events and acts, but most of them are pretty good. Some contemporary popular artists have included Ariana Grande and U2.

MAP 5: 9009 W. Sunset Blvd., www.theroxy.com; see online calendar for performance times

Viper Room

Viper Room is one of those classic Hollywood venues that makes you feel like you're back in the 1990s. It's the place where A-list celebrities used to rock out in dark corners, and where actor River Phoenix died of a drug overdose in 1993, its opening year.

Partially owned by actor Johnny Depp, Viper Room is still a good place to sip on cheap drinks and catch some great live rock'n'roll—concerts happen almost every night.

MAP 5: 8852 Sunset Blvd., 310/358-1881, www.viperroom.com; daily 8pm-2am; cover charge free-$25

Echo Park, Los Feliz, and Silver Lake
Map 6

MUSEUMS

Barnsdall Art Park

Barnsdall Art Park sits atop a rolling hill and offers 360-degree views of the east side of Los Angeles, including looks at the Griffith Observatory and the Hollywood sign. The park has two buildings that lovers of art and architecture will definitely want to visit: the **Hollyhock House** (Thurs.-Sun. 11am-4pm; $7 adults, kids 12 and under free) and the **L.A. Municipal Art Gallery** (Thurs.-Sun. noon-5pm; free). The Hollyhock House, the stunning structure that was the first to grace this hill, was designed by Frank Lloyd Wright between 1919 and 1921; it was home to oil heiress Aline Barnsdall in the early 20th century, and is now open to the public for jaw-dropping tours. Across the park, the LAMAG presents about six major visual art exhibits each year, often showcasing local artists. Barnsdall Art Park is relatively un-crowded, so pack a picnic and spread a blanket on the lawn to make a peaceful afternoon of your visit.
MAP 6: 4800 Hollywood Blvd., 323/644-6295, http://barnsdall.org; park daily 6am-10pm; free

La Luz de Jesus Art Gallery

Located inside the Soap Plant / Wacko complex, this very contemporary art gallery showcases up-and-coming, boundary-pushing artists via regularly rotating exhibits. You'll either love or hate the California-inspired post-pop narrative paintings and sculptures featured here. A new exhibit opens on the first Friday of each month, with a fun opening reception.
MAP 6: 4633 Hollywood Blvd., 323/666-7667, http://soapplant.com; Mon.-Wed. 11am-7pm, Thurs.-Sat. 11am-9pm, Sun. noon-6pm

mural on La Luz de Jesus Art Gallery (Brent Allen Spear)

MARQUEE ART MUSEUMS

You could spend a whole week just visiting the impressive art museums in L.A. If you don't have that kind of time, here's a helpful list of the top five and what they offer, from ancient pottery to progressive contemporary installations.

The Broad, the Getty Center, and the Getty Villa have free general admission; LACMA is free on the second Tuesday of every month, and MOCA is free every Thursday 5pm-8pm. Always purchase or reserve tickets in advance, and if you want to avoid crowds, try to visit on a weekday. If you're driving to any of these museums, expect to pay parking fees of $10-20. You can find more detailed information under each museum's listing.

THE BROAD (PAGE 154)

The Broad opened in 2016 and immediately became the place to see contemporary art in Los Angeles. Come here to marvel at bold architecture and see hundreds of over-the-top contemporary pieces. Don't miss the special exhibits, which have featured fun artists like Yayoi Kusama and Cindy Sherman.

LOS ANGELES COUNTY MUSEUM OF ART (PAGE 148)

LACMA is L.A.'s largest art museum, housing over 135,000 pieces spanning 6,000 years of art history. The collection is so vast that you really can't appreciate it all in one day, but try to get a balanced dose of pre-Columbian artifacts, Rembrandt masterpieces, and

CONCERT VENUES

✪ The Greek Theatre

Come to The Greek Theatre on a summer night to enjoy L.A.'s people, music, and natural beauty. What makes this amphitheater special is its location inside Griffith Park. Surrounded by trees, this open-air theater allows concertgoers to cheer for some of the world's biggest musical artists under the stars. The Greek has great sound quality and a capacity of just under 6,000 people, which makes it a bit cozier than the Hollywood Bowl (L.A.'s other major outdoor concert venue). The Greek often hosts artists who were once huge, so look at the online schedule to find out when your favorite 1990s icon is performing. **MAP 6:** 2700 N. Vermont Ave., 844/524-7335, www.greektheatrela.com; tickets $50-400

Downtown   Map 7

A fun way to check out downtown's galleries is through the **Downtown Los Angeles Art Walk** (www.downtown-artwalk.org), a self-guided walking tour that happens every 2nd Thursday of the month. It takes you to over 50 galleries and about a dozen food trucks.

MUSEUMS

Fashion Institute of Design & Merchandising (FIDM) Museum

FIDM is L.A.'s premier fashion school, and this attached museum has rotating exhibits of breathtaking costumes and fashion design. A great exhibit to catch is FIDM's annual Emmy show, which features costumes from television shows nominated that year. This is a contemporary installations—don't miss taking a selfie at the iconic streetlamp installation or strolling under the giant boulder on the north lawn.

MUSEUM OF CONTEMPORARY ART GRAND AVENUE (PAGE 154)

MOCA has been holding court in downtown ever since the 1980s, when it became an integral part of L.A.'s art scene. It continues to push boundaries with its rotating contemporary collections, usually showcasing some of the world's hottest visual artists. It's a cozy, underground museum conspicuously carved into Grand Avenue, which makes it easily accessible via public transportation.

GETTY CENTER (PAGE 84)

Perched in the Santa Monica Mountains, The Getty Center is a tranquil place with a wide variety of exhibits, from ancient Buddhist art to black and white photography from the 1970s. This is a great museum to visit even if you're not a huge art buff—there's interesting architecture, pretty gardens, and superb views. While you're here, enjoy a picnic lunch on the sprawling green lawn.

GETTY VILLA (PAGE 217)

A trip to the Getty Villa will transport you—to the luxurious Malibu hills and also to an ancient Grecian villa (okay, *replica* villa). If you're into ancient Greek and Roman art, or just like wandering around beautiful grounds with immaculate gardens and impressive sculptures, this is the place for you. There's also ancient Mediterranean pottery, jewelry, and tapestries.

small museum that many Angelenos don't know about, so it probably won't take you long to walk around. FIDM is only open for specific exhibits, so check online before you head over.

MAP 7: 919 S. Grand Ave., Suite 250, 213/623-5821, http://fidmmuseum.org; Tues.-Sat. 10am-5pm; free

Geffen Contemporary at MOCA

The Geffen is basically a big warehouse that's a blank canvas for ambitious art installations that rotate a few times annually. Expect the unexpected at Geffen—you'll find anything from massive neon light installations to dinosaur-filled bedrooms to tables covered with painted onions. Because each exhibit takes a while to install, the Geffen is sometimes closed for weeks at a time, so check exhibition dates in advance of your visit.

MAP 7: 152 N. Central Ave., 213/625-4390, www.moca.org/visit/geffen-contemporary; hours vary; free

The Grammy Museum

This is a great place for music lovers to spend a few hours. You can see blues artists' favorite guitars, read handwritten letters from rock'n'roll stars, and get up close to costumes pop icons wore for Grammy performances. The Grammy Museum has some fun interactive exhibits and even a sound booth for you to record your own song. It's part of the L.A. Live entertainment complex, so there are lots of shops and restaurants to check out once you leave.

MAP 7: 800 W. Olympic Blvd., 213/765-6800, www.grammymuseum. org; Mon.-Fri. 10:30am-6:30pm, Sat.-Sun. 10am-6:30pm; tickets $10-13

Japanese American National Museum

A good spot to learn about Japanese American history and culture, this museum has a few permanent exhibits and rotating collections that highlight of-the-moment Japanese arts and cultural phenomena (Hello Kitty, for example). The museum also focuses on the Japanese American experience during World War II, including incarceration. It's a kid-friendly space, smaller than other museums in the area, and located right across the street from the delicious restaurants and cute shops of Japanese Village Plaza.

MAP 7: 100 N. Central Ave., 213/625-0414, www.janm.org; Tues.-Wed. 11am-5pm, Thurs. noon-8pm, Fri.-Sun. 11am-5pm; tickets $6-12

Chinese American Museum

This museum educates its visitors on different aspects of the Chinese American experience in Southern California. It's located in the historic El Pueblo de Los Angeles pedestrian mall, and can be toured in less than an hour. For people unfamiliar with L.A.'s Chinese American history, a tour around the museum can provide a quick and interesting education, and thoughtful glimpses into what it was like for Chinese immigrants to come to America during the 18th and 19th centuries.

MAP 7: 425 N. Los Angeles St., 213/485-8567, http://camla.org; Tues.-Sun. 10am-3pm; tickets $2-3

✪ The Broad

Opened in 2016 to global fanfare, the Broad (rhymes with "road") is home to one of the world's greatest modern art collections. The collection comes from the museum's founder and namesake—philanthropic billionaire Eli Broad, who owns over 200,000 works of art. The 120,000-square-foot museum features a bold, contemporary façade, with a bright metallic perforated exterior that lets in a lot of light. The architecture is indicative of the art it houses—more than 2,000 works from the 20th and 21st centuries,

many of which defy traditional artistic conventions. The museum showcases hundreds of artistic masterpieces at a given time, from artists like Roy Lichtenstein, Jean-Michel Basquiat, and Andy Warhol. The vibe here is young and fresh—free of the stuffiness associated with most museums of this caliber.

You can walk up and wait in line for entry, but lines can get quite long, especially on weekends. It's a good idea to reserve tickets online in advance so you can skip the line. Occasionally there's a special exhibit that requires tickets to be purchased in advance. The special exhibits are usually worth it—past exhibits have included mirror installations from Yayoi Kusama and a comprehensive showcase of photographer Cindy Sherman.

MAP 7: 221 S. Grand Ave., 213/232-6200, www.thebroad.org; Tues.-Wed. 11am-5pm, Thurs.-Fri. 11am-8pm, Sat. 10am-8pm, Sun. 10am-6pm; free

The Broad

Museum of Contemporary Art (MOCA) Grand Avenue

MOCA is part of the bedrock of L.A.'s contemporary art scene. Since it established its first location here in 1979, MOCA has opened three additional galleries across the city. Come to the MOCA Grand Avenue to see works from 1940 on, some of which provide thought-provoking social and political commentary. MOCA Grand Avenue may not be as flashy as its neighbor, the Broad, but it still attracts exhibits from some of the world's most famous modern artists.

MAP 7: 250 S. Grand Ave., 213/626-6222, www.moca.org/visit/grand-ave; Mon. 11am-6pm, Wed. 11am-6pm, Thurs. 11am-8pm, Fri. 11am-6pm, Sat.-Sun. 11am-5pm; tickets $8-15

Zimmer Children's Museum

The Zimmer Children's Museum is a cute place to take kids for a few hours. They can become lots of things here—pilots, firefighters, chefs—or they can also just roll around in ball pit. On busy days, there's some guided craft time. Zimmer is often full of kids (some crying), and it seems a bit hard to keep clean. But kiddos ages 8 and under love it here, especially during L.A.'s rare rainy days.

MAP 7: 6505 Wilshire Blvd. #100, 323/761-8984, www.zimmermuseum.org; Mon.-Thurs. 10am-5pm, Fri. 10am-4pm, Sun. 12:30pm-4:30pm; tickets $7.50

GALLERIES
✪ Hauser & Wirth

This gallery is a must-see for lovers of contemporary and progressive art. Truth be told, Hauser & Wirth feels more like a compound than a gallery—it's an industrial complex with three separate spaces showcasing rotating collections and an open-air courtyard. The art here is bold, and the small gift shop has lots of special goodies like handmade blankets and body scrubs. What's special about Hauser & Wirth is that it simultaneously celebrates visionary art while also creating a unique and welcoming space in which to hang out. Did I mention there's a restaurant here, too?

MAP 7: 901 E. 3rd St., 213/943-1620, www.hauserwirthlosangeles.com; Wed.-Sun. 11am-6pm; free

STREET AND PUBLIC ART
✪ The Container Yard

At once a gallery, an event space, and an ever-changing street art exhibition, The Container Yard skips around different descriptors because it is a space unique unto itself. This sizable industrial venue—a collection of big brick warehouses—was once home to Japanese manufacturing company Mikawaya, whose founder invented mochi ice cream (there is a giant standalone mochi freezer building). Its brick walls have since been covered with colorful murals from emerging and established street artists. This creative hub houses various pop-up art shows, events, restaurants, and shops. BecauseTthe Container Yard prides itself on continually evolving, you'll never quite know what to expect here, which is all part of the fun (check the venue's Facebook page for the most current roster of events). It's worth visiting for the cool mural selfies alone.

MAP 7: 800 E. 4th St., https://thecontaineryard.com

PERFORMING ARTS
The Theatre at Ace Hotel

The Theatre at Ace Hotel is a special place to see a live show. It's a Spanish Gothic-style building, created in 1927 and recently revitalized. It may be haunted, but you'll be surrounded by about 1,500 people, so this shouldn't bother you too much. It's a spectacularly beautiful space, with grand vaulted ceilings and little mirrors that sparkle in the right light. No wonder more and more top comedians, podcasters, and musical artists are

ART BEYOND MUSEUMS

The museums in L.A. are incredible, but the art scene here goes far beyond those walls—**street and public art** are just as important. From walls of graffiti to huge public installations, the art is fresh and contemporary, with local and global artists venturing into new landscapes (literally and figuratively) of self-expression.

While pretty much indistinguishable, street art and public art are technically different. Street art is unsanctioned art created in public locations, whereas public art is officially commissioned by cities or property owners. Both are celebrated here in L.A.

You can discover most of this art by strolling around Venice, Downtown, or Hollywood. But if you prefer a more methodical approach, you can also take a self-guided tour via an **online map** (www.muralmapla.com), or take a graffiti/mural art tour with **L.A. Art Tours** (www.laarttours.com) or a "Neighba'hood Art Tour" by bike with **L.A. Cycle Tours** (www.lacycletours.com).

Urban Light at LACMA

- Venice is filled with particularly great street art. Locals use the concrete walls of the **Venice Public Arts Walls** (page 141) as a canvas for countless iterations of graffiti. The **Venice murals** (page 141) are also great—one of my favorites is *Venice on the Halfshell*, a play on Botticelli's Venus by famed mural artist Rip Cronk. It takes up the side of an entire building on Windward Avenue by the boardwalk (next to Jay's Rentals).

- The walls of many buildings in the **Downtown Arts District** are filled with a kaleidoscope of street art, making it a great place to walk around and take selfies. *Swing Girl*, a tongue-in-cheek description a girl on a swing, was created on the wall of a Downtown parking lot by world-famous street artist Banksy. There's also the giant sleeping rat (or bear??) at Jesse Street and Imperial Avenue, and a handful of gorgeous murals at **The Container Yard** (page 155).

- L.A.'s most notable public art installation is probably *Urban Light* by Chris Burden, a display of 202 streetlamps decorating the sidewalk in front of the LACMA building. It's one of the best places in the city to take pictures and play around like a kid. *Urban Light* is cool during the day but even better at night, when the lamps have a yellowish glow.

- Another notable piece of public art is the *Great Wall of Los Angeles*, located in the Tujunga Flood Control Channel of the San Fernando Valley. The huge mural takes up half a mile and depicts the history of ethnic peoples in California from prehistoric times to the 1950s. It was conceived by Judith Baca and completed by hundreds of community members, including youth from diverse backgrounds. There are plans to continue the mural to depict the remaining decades of the 20th century.

choosing to bring their performances here.

MAP 7: 933 S. Broadway, 213/235-9614, https://theatre.acehotel.com; see online calendar; tickets $25-1,000

Center Theatre Group

This is one of American's most respected nonprofit theater companies, and has been for over five decades. Not only does the Center Theatre Group produce award-winning shows, it also does youth engagement and arts education, so your ticket money will go toward a great cause. Center Theatre Group prides itself on attracting new artists and audiences, so expect to see groundbreaking plays from up-and-coming writers, performers, and directors. The group performs at the Ahmanson Theatre and the Mark Taper Forum Downtown, and at the Kirk Douglas Theatre in Culver City.

MAP 7: 601 W. Temple St., 213/628-2772, www.centertheatregroup.org; see online calendar; tickets $30-150

Orpheum

In the early and mid-20th century, the Orpheum was a huge part of Downtown L.A.'s rich performing arts scene; musical artists like Lena Horne, Ella Fitzgerald, Duke Ellington, Aretha Franklin, and Stevie Wonder all graced its stage. Today, this gorgeous 1920s-style theater is used as a filming location for movies and television shows, and it also hosts three or four concerts each week. It has seating for about 2,000 people, which feels nice and cozy compared with some of the huge venues in the neighborhood.

MAP 7: 842 S. Broadway, 877/677-4386, http://laorpheum.com; see online calendar; tickets $25-108

CONCERT VENUES

✪ Walt Disney Concert Hall

The Walt Disney Concert Hall towers over Downtown like a giant silver wave. Designed by acclaimed architect Frank Gehry, the concert hall is both an architectural landmark and a

Walt Disney Concert Hall

performance space with state-of-the-art acoustic design. This 3.6-acre complex is home to the L.A. Philharmonic Orchestra, and shows here are strictly classical. There are often world-famous musicians performing with the L.A. Phil, and the concert hall is usually open for either self-guided or docent-guided tours.

MAP 7: 111 S. Grand Ave., 323/850-2000, www.laphil.com/philpedia/about-walt-disney-concert-hall; see online calendar; tickets $70-300, tours free

The Novo

The Novo is an intimate-feeling concert space in the L.A. Live entertainment complex. Its capacity is 2,300, so it's not tiny, but it will get you much closer to big-name artists than most other venues in town. There's a standing-room space by the stage for dancing, and the Novo's state-of-the-art design makes for fantastic sound quality no matter where you sit or stand. Get dinner before your show at one of L.A. Live's many eateries.

MAP 7: 800 W. Olympic Blvd., 213/765-7015, www.thenovodtla.com; see online calendar; tickets $5-50

Microsoft Theater

You can't miss the big, bright Microsoft Theater, one of L.A.'s largest performance venues. It's located right in the L.A. Live entertainment complex, and hosts over 100 shows every year, including the Grammy and ESPY awards. Its 7,000-plus seats are nice and cushy, and if you have a seat way in the back or up on the balcony, two huge screens surrounding the massive stage will give you a clear picture of what's happening up front.

MAP 7: 777 Chick Hearn Ct., 213/763-6030, www.microsofttheater.com; see online calendar; tickets $40-500

ARTS AND CULTURE

MUSEUMS

Museum Of Tolerance

With a strong focus on social justice, his important museum educates on the history of the Jewish Holocaust with the goal of preventing prejudice and discrimination from continuing in our world today. The Museum of Tolerance highlights a number of civil rights issues, including immigration, segregation, genocide, and freedom of speech, and encourages collective accountability for the rights of others. There are interesting interactive exhibits, some of which use graphic images or recordings and might not be appropriate for younger kids.

MAP 8: 9786 W. Pico Blvd., 310/772-2505, www.museumoftolerance.com; Sun.-Thurs. 10am-5pm, Fri. 10am-3:30pm; $11.50-13.50

Annenberg Space for Photography

The Annenberg Space for Photography is a modern facility that showcases a handful of photography exhibits each year. This state-of-the-art museum allows visitors to experience both visual and digital art, including pieces created with 4-D technology. Its easy parking and lesser-known status make the museum relatively accessible, and it's a nice place to spend a quiet hour or two during your visit to Beverly Hills. Take note of the architectural design while you're there—it's inspired by the mechanics of a camera and its lens.

GREATER LOS ANGELES

MAP 8: 2000 Ave. of the Stars, 213/403-3000, www.annenbergphotospace.org; Wed.-Sun. 11am-6pm; free

Autry Museum of the American West

Autry Museum of the American West

Right across the street from the Los Angeles Zoo sits the Autry Museum of the American West, a great place for families to experience an inclusive history of the western United States. There's a wide variety of exhibits showcasing American Indian art, modern Southwestern artists, and golden guns from the days of the Wild West. Kids can try their hand at sifting for "gold," and everyone can have a nice meal at the Crossroads West Café. This is a big complex with multiple buildings, so you can spend a whole afternoon immersed in the past.

MAP 8: 4700 Western Heritage Way, 323/667-2000, https://theautry.org; Tues.-Fri. 10am-4pm, Sat.-Sun. 10am-5pm; adults $14, ages 3-12 $6, under 3 free

SPORTS AND ACTIVITIES

With 284 sunny days per year and luxuriously mild temperatures, Los Angeles is a city that begs you to get outside and play.

Santa Monica and Venice have recreational opportunities in and out of the water. Rent a surfboard and get in the water, or just jump right in. Most beaches have lifeguards May-September, when the water is just warm enough to be welcoming and just cold enough to be refreshing. Out of the water, The Strand is a 22-mile path that runs along the beach from Malibu to Venice. It's the perfect place to bike, blade, skate...or just take a long walk.

If you're in the mood for a real hike, head to Runyon Canyon in Hollywood or Griffith Park in Los Feliz. The trails will take your breath away with their uphill climbs and summit panoramas. Beverly Hills has some nice parks for a more subdued walk, and Echo Park Lake is a fun place to mosey around and rent a pedal boat.

With five professional sports teams, there are exciting games to attend year-round. I love a good Lakers game at the Staples Center (look courtside for celebs), or a Dodgers game on a mild evening (with a veggie hot dog on the side). The Kings hockey team and the Sparks and Clippers basketball teams also play at the Staples Center, which is adjacent area to the L.A. Live entertainment complex.

L.A. is a great city to bike around.

Finally, L.A. is the western yoga capitol of the world. It shows in the range and popularity of studios here, whether on the beach or in a hot, sweaty room (maybe even next to a sweaty celeb).

HIGHLIGHTS

✪ **BEST SURF SCHOOL:** Waves can get big here in Los Angeles. Keep yourself safe by learning from true professionals at **Learn to Surf L.A** (page 161).

✪ **BEST PARK WITH A VIEW: Palisades Park** in Santa Monica has a particularly charming glow during twilight. Meander its lazy paths and find a nice bench to watch the sun set over the ocean (page 161).

✪ **BEST BIKE RIDE:** No trip to Santa Monica is complete without a ride down **The Strand,** a 22-mile path running parallel to the Pacific (page 162).

✪ **BEST YOGA SETTING:** Yoga is generally relaxing, but hearing the sound of waves crashing when you're doing **Beach Yoga** takes relaxation to the next level (page 164).

✪ **BEST SKATEBOARDING TRICKS:** Whether you're skating yourself or just observing, you'll feel extreme at the **Venice Skate Park** (page 165).

✪ **BEST SPA FOR SPLURGING: Spa Montage** is luxe enough to make you feel like an A-lister but accessible enough to be within reach (page 166).

✪ **BEST HOLLYWOOD HIKE:** The multiple loops around **Runyon Canyon** will pump up your heart rate and provide selfie-worthy views of the city below (page 168).

✪ **BEST BOWLING SCENE:** Part bowling alley, part dance club, **Lucky Strike** will get you moving (page 169).

✪ **BEST PADDLE:** Take a stroll or rent a paddleboat to enjoy beautiful flowers and great views of L.A. at **Echo Park Lake & Boathouse** (page 171).

✪ **BEST BALLGAME:** Nothing beats a summer night watching the **Los Angeles Dodgers,** hot dog in hand (page 172).

✪ **BEST URBAN OASIS:** Head to **Griffith Park** for challenging hikes, trickling streams, and acres of leafy green (page 174).

BEACHES
Santa Monica State Beach

Santa Monica State Beach is one of L.A.'s most popular beaches, I think because there's plentiful parking that makes it pretty accessible. During summer, the beach area surrounding the Santa Monica Pier will be packed with tourists and locals alike. For a quieter beach scene, head a few hundred yards north or south of the pier to take a swim in the salty waves. From late May to early September there are lifeguards manning the whole beach, so during those months pretty much anywhere is safe to swim. During sunset and sunrise you'll be joined by pods of surfers, and perhaps even of dolphins.

MAP 1: Pacific Coast Hwy., www.smgov. net; daily 24 hours; free

Annenberg Community Beach House

The Annenberg Community Beach House is a great place to spend a full day, especially if you have kids. The Annenberg Foundation created this beachside space as a place for L.A. denizens to come together and enjoy our greatest asset—the Pacific Ocean.

Set on the sea a bit north of the Santa Monica Pier, this beach house has a big, glowing pool, art exhibits, a splash pad for kids, a game room, and, wait for it…free Wi-Fi! The pool is open all summer, with special nights reserved for adult swim and snacks. Check online for regular special events.

MAP 1: 415 Pacific Coast Hwy., 310/458-4904, www. annenbergbeachhouse.com; daily 8:30am-5:30pm; pool admission $10 adults, $4 children, $5 seniors

SURFING
✪ Learn to Surf L.A.

Don't trust your surf experience to just anyone—go to the experts at Learn to Surf L.A. This friendly surf shop offers group and private lessons for adults and kids of all ages and has been helping people catch their first waves since 2002. Their fun and low-pressure approach has earned them a good amount of acclaim over the years. If you'd rather paddle than surf your way around the sea, take a stand-up paddleboard (SUP) lesson instead.

MAP 1: 1750 Appian Way, 310/663-2479, www.learntosurfla.com; daily 8am-6pm; pricing depends on package, details online

PARKS
✪ Palisades Park

A lot of places in Los Angeles can be described as picturesque; Pacific Park is without a doubt among the most picture-worthy of them all. It's essentially a cliffside pathway that runs along the Pacific Coast Highway and Pacific Ocean beyond. Because it's elevated above the sea, Palisades Park offers breathtaking views of the entire

Palisades Park

Santa Monica Bay—from the Malibu Mountains in the north to Palos Verdes in the south. Palisades Park is in a very busy area of Santa Monica (right near the Santa Monica Pier), so it's usually quite lively. This is a great place to take a long walk, snap some pics, and watch the sun set with someone special.

MAP 1: Ocean Ave. between Colorado Ave. and Adelaide Dr., 310/458-8300, www.smgov.net; daily 24 hours; free

Tongva Park

A newer addition to the Santa Monica scene, Tongva Park is a state-of-the-art community space, complete with ocean views. Filled with native and sustainable plants, Tongva uses its space well and feels larger than its six square acres. The park is super-fun for kids, with a play area with a modern climbing wall and a splash pad with water to giggle in. There are walking paths and shaded picnic areas for adults, as well as beautiful fountains, public restrooms, and free Wi-Fi.

MAP 1: 1615 Ocean Ave., 310/458-8310, http://tongvapark.smgov.net; daily 6am-11pm; free

BIKING AND ROLLER SKATING
✪ The Strand

The Marvin Braude Bike Trail, affectionately known as The Strand, is a 22-mile paved path that runs along the Pacific Ocean from Malibu to Venice. It's a beautiful, palm-lined trail filled with colorful people on all sorts of wheeled vehicles: bikes, roller skates, skateboards, and so forth. With almost 300 sunny days annually, Santa Monica is pretty much the perfect place to ride a bike any time of year. Early mornings on The Strand are

cool and quiet, and sunsets are pretty great, too.

MAP 1: Runs along the beach; daily 24 hours; free

biking The Strand

Santa Monica Beach Bicycle Rentals

A professional and organized shop, Santa Monica Beach Bicycle Rentals will equip you with all the necessities (bike, helmet, lock, etc.) for an afternoon of cruising. Choose a basic beach cruiser or mountain bike, and take off along Santa Monica's 22-mile bike path, stretching up and down the coast. A bigger group can rent a four-person family surrey (with the fringe on top). Its reasonable prices and central location make Santa Monica Beach Bicycle Rentals the perfect place to start your oceanside adventure.

MAP 1: 1428 4th St., 310/428-5337, www.smbikerental.com; daily 9am-8:30pm

TRAPEZE ARTS
Trapeze School of New York

Want to fly through the air on one of the world's most famous piers? Come for a two-hour lesson at the Trapeze School of New York, right on the Santa Monica Pier. The instructors here are positive and supportive, and offer careful coaching that will help you feel comfortable way up in the air, no matter your experience level. Book

SCENIC DRIVES

L.A. is a driving city, which makes most people think of traffic, delays, and road rage. But it also means that there are some really fun roads to take around here. The following routes capture some of L.A.'s most scenic views.

- **Mullholland Drive** has a certain sort of allure—maybe because it winds around the homes of some of L.A.'s richest and most famous stars. You can start your drive at Mullholland's eastern end, near the Hollywood Bowl. The drive will take you past a number of impressive vistas, some of which have space to pull over and breathe in the view. If you're feeling ambitious, drive the entire length Mullholland all the way to the mountainy state parks in the west (or just drop down into Beverly Hills for happy hour).

- **Griffith Park**'s windy roady will take you up into the Hollywood hills and provide a few direct views of the white-lettered Hollywood sign. The Griffith Observatory is a nice destination for your afternoon drive—it provides panoramic city views and lets you peer down onto much of Hollywood. Griffith Park has a number of entrances, and good online maps that show different driving routes. Bring your long lens camera.

- **The Pacific Coast Highway (PCH)** runs for 655 miles up the California coast, but you don't need to drive the whole thing to get a taste of its beauty—a particularly scenic part of the celebrated highway runs from **Santa Monica to Malibu.** Start in Santa Monica by driving west on California Avenue, which will veer right and swoop downhill to become the PCH. As you drive north on the PCH, you'll pass Santa Monica State Beach and several smaller beaches interspersed with colorful oceanside homes. Pull over to enjoy one of these beaches or continue north into Malibu, where tall hills rise up alongside the sea. Finish your drive in Malibu with oceanside cocktails and grilled octopus at Moonshadows.

your class and make sure to bring sunscreen, a few layers of clothing, and comfy socks (that's what you'll wear during class). To check in, head to the small wooden shack toward the end of the pier. Kids are welcome, too!

MAP 1: 370 Santa Monica Pier, 310/394-5800, https://losangeles. trapezeschool.com; open daily, hours vary, see online schedule

YOGA AND MEDITATION

Bhakti Yoga Shala

Visit Bhakti Yoga Shala for a radical yoga experience. This special studio focuses on the *bhakti* (love and devotion) aspect of yoga, and has become a cornerstone of the Santa Monica yoga community. Bhakti Yoga Shala welcomes beginners, so go ahead and check it out, even if it's your first time. Music is an integral part of every class,

and there are a number of classes each week that include live music or *kirtan* (call-and-response chanting). Look at the online schedule for details.

MAP 1: 207 Arizona Ave., 310/804-9290, www.bhaktiyogashala.com; Mon.-Fri. 7am-10pm, Sat.-Sun. 8am-10pm

Santa Monica Power Yoga & Meditation

This wood-floored yoga space stays packed to the brim, and for good reason. The classes here are awesome—challenging, deep, and smart, all thanks to the expert teachers. In fact, Santa Monica Power Yoga has become so popular that it now offers subscription-based digital classes for practitioners around the world. Bryan Kest, its founder, has been practicing for over 30 years and still teaches regular classes here; if you can, take a class with him.

MAP 1: 1410 2nd St., 310/458-9510, https://poweryoga.com; hours vary, see online schedule

Kundalini by the Sea

Good vibes abound at Kundalini by the Sea, a bright little yoga studio just off of busy Colorado Avenue. Kundalini is a specific style of yoga that usually includes chanting and meditation. The studio welcomes newcomers, so be brave and give it a try! You'll enter the studio from a parking lot in back of the building; the front door can be hard to spot, so leave yourself some extra time to find the entrance, sign in, and get settled before class.

MAP 1: 605 Colorado Ave., 310/963-9811, www.kundaliniyogabythesea.com; hours vary, see online schedule

✪ Beach Yoga

What's better than feeling totally relaxed in Shavasana pose? Shavasana with the warm sun on your skin and the sound of crashing waves in the background. Yoga on the beach is an amazing experience, and L.A. is a great place to try it. You'll even venture into the water for some poses. The instructors are great and will give you one-on-one attention without being too pushy. It's a beginner's class, so all are welcome. Check the Facebook page for updated information.

MAP 1: near South Beach Park, 310/826-6958; Sat.-Sun. 10:30am-noon

Venice

Map 2

BEACHES
Venice Beach

The backdrop for so many films and TV shows, Venice Beach boasts a unique blend of human energy and pure natural beauty. Almost all parts of this beach are swimmable, and there are lifeguards from early morning to sundown every day during the summer. You can also swim during the winter, but there are no lifeguards and the water is cold (wet suit recommended). There are plenty of shops lining the beach where you can rent boogie boards, beach chairs, and other gear for the day. On sunny summer days, the beach will be packed with people. Stay close to your stuff—it may get snatched if you don't keep an eye on it. For great sunset views, walk down the Venice Pier, an old-school fishing spot.

MAP 2: 1800 Ocean Front Walk, 301/396-6794, www.laparks.org/venice

Venice Beach

SURFING
Zuma Surf & Swim Training

Founded by Kai Sanson, one of L.A.'s best surf instructors, Zuma will

Venice Skate Park

get you in the water, keep you safe, and hopefully help you catch some waves. Zuma offers both individual and group lessons for students of all shapes, sizes, ages, and ability levels. There are a number of surf schools to choose from in Los Angeles, and Zuma is among the best—the instructors are true teachers and surf lovers. Call ahead to schedule your lesson.

MAP 2: 301/455-6900, www.zumasurfandswim.com; about $100 per person per lesson, depending on group size

YOGA AND MEDITATION
The Yoga Collective

The Yoga Collective is a friendly, inviting yoga studio—and a great place to work up a sweat. Although quite popular, it still feels like a local neighborhood studio. Classes are inspired by Ashtanga and Iyengar yoga, but feature the unique expressions of the teachers here, who are all wise and accessible. The Yoga Collective sees a lot of travelers, and the staff is warm and welcoming to new students. The studio is relatively small, with one practice room and one bathroom.

MAP 2: 512 Rose Ave., 301/392-2000, http://venice.theyogacollective.com; daily, hours vary, see online schedule

BIKING AND ROLLER SKATING
Jay's Rentals

Jay's Rentals is located right on the boardwalk and can supply all of your biking and roller skating needs for cheap. If you plan on cruising down the boardwalk or The Strand, this is a great place to rent gear from. The friendly, surfer-type staff here are helpful and knowledgeable. Choose a three-hour rental and be prepared to leave your keys or identification card behind for collateral.

MAP 2: 1501 Ocean Front Walk, 301/392-7306, www.jaysrentalsvb.com; daily 7am-8pm

SKATEBOARDING
✪ Venice Skate Park

If you're around the boardwalk, stop by the Venice Skate Park for a quintessential SoCal experience. Marvel at boarders of all ages showing off their best moves in sunken concrete pools. Any day it's not raining (which is most days), the park will be filled with talented skaters from noon till sunset. You can join fellow spectators and cheer on the skaters, or rent a board from one of the skate shops lining the boardwalk ($8/hour, $30/day) and try out the park for yourself—it's free and open to all.

MAP 2: 1800 Ocean Front Walk

NEW AGE L.A.

YOGA AND MEDITATION

Los Angeles may very well be the western yoga capital of the world. Where Rishikesh, India has an ashram on every hilltop, Santa Monica has a yoga studio on every street corner. There are three great things about doing yoga in Los Angeles: 1) most studios are super welcoming to beginners and excited to support you through your first class, 2) there are so many types of yoga taught here that's there's bound to be a class for almost everyone, and 3) because yogis from around the world flock to live Los Angeles, there are world-class teachers all over the city.

Of course, Angelinos *do* have their favorite studios.

- **Hot 8 Yoga** (page 170) is an upscale studio with heated practice rooms.

- **The Yoga Collective** (page 165) in Venice is a more local operation with very friendly staff.

- In Santa Monica, **Bhakti Yoga Shala** (page 163) infuses music and chanting throughout its classes.

- For seaside yoga, check out **Beach Yoga** (page 164) on Saturday and Sunday mornings in Santa Monica.

- In Hollywood, head to **Wanderlust** (page 169) for trendy yoga or **The Den** (page 168) to meditate with master yogis.

Beverly Hills

Map 3

SPAS

✪ Spa Montage

Ask anyone for the best spa in Los Angeles outside of Koreatown, and most will choose the Spa Montage. This huge, 20,000-square-foot space is where celebrities come to rest and restore before red-carpet events. Spa Montage offers facial and body therapies, massage, couples experiences, organic treatments, men's treatments, and individual packages tailored to your unique wellness needs. The Spa Montage, which is housed in the Montage Beverly Hills hotel, has Turkish steam rooms, dry redwood saunas, lounges, and a mineralized wellness pool. There are also makeup and hair services for those looking to add extra glam.

MAP 3: 225 N. Canon Dr., 310/860-7840, www.montagehotels.com/spamontage/en/beverlyhills; daily 9am-9pm

Hotel Bel-Air Spa by La Prairie

Located in the Hotel Bel-Air and surrounded by 12 lush acres of gardens, this luxurious spa is the top of the line—and the price reflects it. This is where celebs and wealthy Angelenos go for privacy and relaxation. The treatments here focus on nature, taking a cue from the hotel's setting in the hills. Of course, there's a good bit of indulgence as well, like caviar

METAPHYSICAL SUPPLIES
From healing crystals to sage bundles, L.A. has you covered.

- Venice is probably L.A.'s best neighborhood for new-age shopping. Buy gemstone jewelry, chakra healing books, and much more at **Mystic Journey Bookstore** (page 182) on Abbott Kinney Boulevard. Down the street is **Made In Earth** (page 184), which sells an incredible collection of rare gemstones.

- In Santa Monica, check out the two-storied **Thunderbolt Spiritual Books** (page 179) for metaphysical tomes and gifts from around the world.

- And if you really love mystical goods, don't miss **House of Intuition** (page 188) in Silver Lake and West Hollywood, beloved by Kate Hudson, Bella Hadid, Miranda Kerr and Lena Dunham. This store offers an outstanding selection of everything your hippie self could want, including homemade incense, crystals, and Tibetan singing bowls.

ALTERNATIVE HEALING
L.A. probably has more alternative healing options than any other American city.

- One popular path is sound healing, which uses gongs, chimes, bowls, etc. to inspire healing at a cellular level. **The Den** (page 168) has a popular sound bath.

- In addition to offering a great selection of goods to buy, **House of Intuition** (page 188) also offers tarot card readings and reiki healing sessions.

- Or, if you're looking for an even more free spirited method of healing, check out the **Griffith Park drum circle** (4730 Crystal Springs Dr.), held every Sunday morning around 9am. The circle can get quite large, and the drumming lasts until late hours of the night sometimes. It's been ongoing for over 35 years.

facials and Pinot Noir infused scrubs. If you're not willing to shell out thousands for a face mask, however, there are some more reasonably priced services (basic facials and mani/pedis) that run around $200 and less. Book a treatment in advance online.
MAP 3: 701 Stone Canyon Rd., 310/472-1211, www.dorchestercollection.com/en/los-angeles/hotel-bel-air

TOURS
Beverly Hills Trolley
This green-and-yellow open-air trolley will take you from one end of the Beverly Hills commercial district (at the Beverly Hills Civic Center) to the other (at Beverly Drive and Dayton Way). The trolley provides a relaxing ride around most of Beverly Hills's main streets, but there is no narrated tour—just sightseeing from the comfort of your seat.

MAP 3: 445 N. Rexford Dr., 310/285-1128, http://beverlyhills.org/exploring/trolley; Jul. 5-Sept. 2 Tues.-Sun. 11am-5pm, rest of the year Sat.-Sun. only; free

PARKS
Coldwater Canyon Park
Coldwater Canyon Park has one of L.A.'s best playgrounds and a human-made brook for kids to wade in on hot days. It's less than a mile from Sunset Boulevard, which means you won't take too much time away from sightseeing in order to give your kids some time to run free. Adults can run here, too: The park has a soft, well-kept track that is lit at night.
MAP 3: 1100 N. Beverly Dr., 310/285-6820, www.beverlyhills.org/exploring/cityparks/coldwatercanyonpark; 24 hours daily; free

HIKING

✪ Runyon Canyon

On a clear day, the top of Runyon Canyon provides panoramic views of all of L.A., from Downtown to the Pacific Ocean. It's a fantastic place to raise your heart rate, take some pictures, and perhaps spot some celebs in workout gear. This busy urban park has two main hiking loops that are 1.65 miles and 3.25 miles long. Parts of each hike are unpaved and steep, so it's best to wear shoes with traction, and don't forget sunscreen! There's a donation-based yoga class every morning at 10:30am in the grassy knoll near the Fuller Avenue entrance.

MAP 4: 2000 N. Fuller Ave., 323/666-5046, www.laparks.org/park/runyon-canyon; daily sunrise-sunset; free

YOGA AND MEDITATION

Modo Yoga

This welcoming studio offers its own style of hot(ish) yoga and a variety of classes to choose from. You'll practice in an open, light-filled room with vaulted ceilings and wood floors. The last time I was here, there were paparazzi outside the front door, waiting to take pictures of a young actress after her yoga class...just saying. Expect to sweat and probably laugh. Discounts are available for first-timers.

MAP 4: 340 S. La Brea Ave., 323/938-5000, http://los-angeles.modoyoga.com; classes daily, hours vary; $25 drop-in

Liberation Yoga

Take a class in the garden patio with Christine, the studio owner, who is warm, kind, wise, and bubbly. The garden yoga space is a true urban oasis; surrounded by running water, ivy-covered walls, and hummingbirds, you may forget the churning helicopters and four lanes of traffic just outside the door. What's really special about Liberation is that it feels grassroots in an industry that has become largely commercialized here in Los Angeles.

MAP 4: 124 S. La Brea Ave., 323/964-5222, www.liberationyoga.com; Mon.-Fri. 8am-11pm, Sat.-Sun. 12:30pm-6:30pm; $17/class

The Den

Aptly named, The Den is a cozy meditation hideaway. It's tastefully designed, and the teachers are true experts in their field. Even if you've never meditated, The Den will help you feel comfortable giving it a try. The Den offers about 10 meditation classes per day, with some really enticing focuses, like "How to Get the Love You Really Want." There are even private classes if you're looking for one-on-one (or small group) guidance.

MAP 4: 360 S. La Brea Ave., 323/424-3444, https://denmeditation.com; classes all day, check online schedule; $23/class

Runyon Canyon

SIGHTSEEING TOURS

Los Angeles offers both general city tours and niche tours. Because the city is spread over so many miles, almost all tours include bus or van transportation. See the websites of individual tour companies for tour times and prices.

GENERAL TOURS

- **Starline Tours** (www.starlinetours.com) is a great general tour that runs double-decker buses across the whole city. You can choose when and where you want to hop off and explore, so plan your day ahead of time.

- **Esotouric Tours** (www.esotouric.com) and **TOURific Escapes** (www.tourificescapes.com) are two smaller tour companies that offer more nuanced perspectives on Los Angeles history, food, and culture.

SPECIALTY TOURS

- To explore Hollywood in all its gossipy glory, choose **TMZ Hollywood Tours** (www.tmztour.com) or **Legends of Hollywood Tours** (egendsofhollywoodtours.com), which give you all the details about celebrities and their haunts.

- For a tipsy tour, check out **LA Beer Hop** (www.labeerhop.com), which will escort you to some of L.A.'s favorite breweries and watering holes.

- There are also **Melting Pot Food Tours** (www.meltingpottours.com), **Architecture Tours L.A.** (www.architecturetoursla.com), and the **Dearly Departed Tours** (www.dearlydepartedtours.com), which will show you the "dark side" of Hollywood.

Wanderlust

The best things about Wanderlust are a) the teachers, b) the beautiful yoga rooms, and c) the yummy healthy snacks available at the studio's in-house café. The worst things about this large studio are a) the very expensive jewelry and yoga clothes in the shop, b) the pictures on the wall of fit people with body paint running through the woods, and c) the "I'm more flexible than you'll ever be" vibe. If you like yoga and want to get a feel for the L.A. yoga scene, take a class at Wanderlust. Just remember that your practice is perfect, no matter how it looks—what's important is how you feel.

MAP 4: 1357 Highland Ave., 323/967-8855, http://wanderlusthollywood.com; daily classes 6:45am-9pm; $20/class

BOWLING
✪ Lucky Strike

Lucky Strike is more than a bowling alley—it's a scene. Located at Hollywood & Highland, right in the middle of the Walk of Fame, this lively spot has become an ebullient place to eat, drink, bowl, and listen to live music. Lucky Strike Hollywood has a lounge, a dance floor, and delicious fried mac'n'cheese. During the day, this is a great place to bring kids; at night, Lucky Strike becomes more clubby, and admission is limited to people 21 and older.

MAP 4: 6801 Hollywood Blvd., 323/467-7776, www.bowlluckystrike.com/locations/hollywood; Mon.-Wed. noon-1am, Thurs.-Fri. noon-2am, Sat.-Sun. 11am-2am

TOURS

Legends of Hollywood

Continually recognized as one of the best Hollywood tours, Legends of Hollywood provides small-van rides around Downtown, Hollywood, and Beverly Hills. The tour vans are much nicer than those of most tours, complete with air-conditioning and a multimedia learning experience. You'll see lots of celebrity homes and hangouts and learn about the history of each neighborhood. Tours are 4-5 hours long, depending on your pickup location.

MAP 4: 323/928-2024, www. legendsofhollywoodtours.com/index.html; morning and afternoon tours, hours vary; $59-79

TMZ Tours

TMZ tour guides are entertainers in their own right. You may not see an actual star, but people seem to have fun on these tours whether or not there's a celeb sighting. This van tour will take you on a ride through all of Hollywood and Beverly Hills's celebrity hot spots, with great insider stories to boot. Pickup is from Hollywood Boulevard or the Grove and Farmers Market. Expect to be crowded into a van during peak tourist times.

MAP 4: 6801 Hollywood Blvd., 844/869-8687, www.tmz.com/tour; daily 9am-6pm; $41.50-51.50

West Hollywood   Map 5

YOGA AND MEDITATION

Aura Yoga

Aura is a small but mighty yoga studio. Its teachers, music, and sound system—which pumps a respectable level of bass—are all quite enjoyable. But the real draw is the studio's gorgeous light display that gives the impression of practicing in a rainbow-colored bubble. Aura has a variety of classes to choose from, and even a cost-free community yoga class. Give yourself a few extra minutes to find this studio—it's hidden in the bottom corner of the very posh Sunset Plaza.

MAP 5: 8608-A West Sunset Blvd., 323/570-0570, www.auraworkout.com/aurayoga; hours and costs vary—check online for details

Tantris

Tantris is hands-down the most luxurious yoga studio I've experienced. Celebrity music producer Russell Simmons founded Tantris in 2008, and his influence shows in the hip-hop inspired playlists thumping during classes. With valet parking, infrared-heated rooms, and waterfall showers, it's just as much of a spa as a yoga studio. But beneath all this glamour is something special—a deep commitment to the practice of yoga, with expert teachers, photos that pay homage to India, and bookshelves full of yogic wisdom.

MAP 5: 9200 Sunset Blvd., 213/894-9200, www.tantris.com; Mon.-Thurs. 6:30am-9pm, Fri. 6:30am-7pm, Sat.-Sun. 8am-7pm

Hot 8 Yoga

On the border of West Hollywood and Beverly Hills, you'll find Hot 8 Yoga; it's the kind of upscale yoga studio that supplies chilled, eucalyptus-oiled towels to cool you off during your practice. And you'll need that towel, because these classes are hot. There are three practice rooms, all of which are more than 100°F. There's a wide variety of classes here beyond traditional hot yoga, a good number of which are accompanied by pulsating indie-electronic music. Most yogis here are pretty, skinny, and wear brand-name yoga clothing, but don't let that stop you from getting an awesome, sweaty workout—what's important is how the yoga feels, not how it looks. There are locations in Santa Monica (1422 Second St.) and Downtown (3150 Wilshire Blvd., Suite 200) as well.

MAP 5: 8383 Wilshire Blvd. #75, 310/986-6420, http://hot8yoga.com/beverly-hills; daily 6am-8pm

BIKING
WeHo Pedals

You may notice bright green and yellow bicycles dotting West Hollywood sidewalks. These are WeHo's sharable bikes that are available for anyone to rent and ride. You can get a riding pass by quickly signing up for an online membership. Once you sign up, pick up your bike at any one of the 20-plus rental stations scattered across WeHo, mostly along Santa Monica Boulevard. Each bike has a cute basket that you can use to store your backpack and any goodies you pick up along your ride.

MAP 5: 323/900-0669, http://wehopedals.com; daily 24 hours; $7 per hour

TOURS
Out & About Tours

Out & About tours highlight Los Angeles's rich LGBTQ history. There are many different tours to choose from, including walking tours in Hollywood, West Hollywood, and Downtown. If you're looking for a bit more luxury, book a VIP tour, which will take you around the city in an air-conditioned van. Out & About's tour guides are welcoming and knowledge-able, and the tours themselves are fun for all—gay and straight, young and old, and everything in between. Tour locations vary; check the website and Facebook page for the most up-to-date calendar of events.

MAP 5: 844/429-8687, www.thelavendereffect.org/tours; see online calendar for tour times; tickets $45-65

Echo Park, Los Feliz, and Silver Lake   Map 6

PARKS
✪ Echo Park Lake & Boathouse

Head to Echo Park Lake for a relaxing urban stroll. During warmer months, the lake is filled with pink, yellow, and purple lotus flowers floating on lily pads. Each July, there's an annual Lotus Festival celebrating these beloved blooms with arts, music, and food. Year-round, there's a cute café on the lake and a boathouse that rents paddleboats by the hour. On clear days, the 0.8-mile walk around the lake provides beautiful views of the Downtown Los Angeles skyline. Since this is a human-made lake, you won't exactly feel like you're in wilderness, but it's definitely a nice space to stroll. If you're lucky, you may glimpse a rainbow in the mist of the mid-lake fountains.

MAP 6: 751 Echo Park Ave., 213/847-0929, www.laparks.org/aquatic/lake/echo-park-lake; park: daily 24 hours; free; paddleboats: 9am until around sunset, $5 per child, $10 per adult for one hour of boating

Silver Lake Reservoir

The Silver Lake Reservoir is one place where you'll notice Southern California's desert-like conditions—it's nearly empty for most of the year. But don't let that stop you from taking a lap around its two-mile perimeter. This walk is an excellent way to see some of Silver Lake's most beautiful hilltop houses. For a challenging workout, climb any one of the multiple flights of stairs on the steep inclines surrounding the lake. The staircases are listed online, but you'll probably find them just as easily by just keeping your eyes peeled toward the hills. On the northeast side of the reservoir is a flowery, grassy park that's a nice place for a picnic or yoga.

MAP 6: 1850 W. Silver Lake Dr.; 24 hours daily

SPECTATOR SPORTS
BASEBALL
✪ Los Angeles Dodgers

Opened in 1965, Dodger Stadium is the third-oldest continuously used park in Major League Baseball. Carved into a hillside overlooking the San Gabriel Mountains, it's also one of the most picturesque. Games start in late April and run through summer and into early fall. You can invest in some up-close tickets, or get nosebleed seats for a bargain—on a clear night you'll see a gorgeous sunset from any seat

Dodger Stadium

(and fireworks on Fridays!). The stadium is surrounded by a *huge* parking lot, so come early if you're parking your car and be prepared to walk a ways (and climb a few flights of stairs) to your seat.

MAP 6: 1000 Vin Scully Ave., 866/363-4377, www.mlb.com/dodgers; tickets $25-$1,050; check online for schedule

Downtown   Map 7

YOGA AND MEDITATION
Peace Yoga Gallery

Hidden amid Downtown's skyscrapers, Peace Yoga asks you to enter through its ivy-covered front door and travel down into its expansive basement studio, filled with new age knickknacks and psychedelic art. Classes at Peace Yoga are an experience—they'll start late, stretch you deeply, and fill you with love. The class offerings are varied, and include cool things like acro-yoga and LGTBQ yoga. If you can, take a class with Cheri Rae, the studio's founder—she's electric.

MAP 7: 903 S. Main St., 213/500-5007, www.peaceyogagallery.com; see online schedule; single class $16

TOURS
Los Angeles Times Tour

The Pulitzer Prize-winning *Los Angeles Times* is one of the world's most popular news sources, and its building in downtown L.A. is a work of art; it opened in 1935 and in 1937 won a gold medal for its architectural style at the Paris Exposition. There are two L.A. Times tours: one that will take you through this main headquarters where the content of the paper is created, and another that will show you where the physical papers

are printed. The days of printed papers may be numbered, so newspaper lovers may want to check out this tour while they still can.

MAP 7: 202 W. 1st St., 213/237-5757, www.latimes.com/about/la-building-tour-story.html; call for tour days/hours; free

PARKS
Grand Park

Grand Park provides 12 acres of fountains and grassy knolls that are perfect for afternoon lounging. Opened in 1966, Grand Park got a huge makeover in 2012 when it reopened after $56 million worth of updates, including the addition of more than 300 trees, 24 gardens, and 170 plant species. During the summer, you'll find kids running through Grand Park's fountains during the day and free weekend concerts at night. With accessible elevators and paths, this park welcomes all visitors; it's a great place to lie back and appreciate L.A.'s rich cultural and botanic diversity.

MAP 7: 200 N. Grand Ave., 213/972-8080, https://grandparkla.org; daily 24 hours; free

SPECTATOR SPORTS
BASKETBALL
Los Angeles Lakers, Clippers, and Sparks

L.A. has two professional men's basketball teams, the Lakers and the

Clippers, and the Staples Center is a super-fun place to watch either play. If you're looking for a bit more fanfare (and pricier tickets), check out a Lakers game; Clippers games tend to be more laid-back. The L.A. Sparks, our awesome women's basketball team, play here, too. The Staples Center is a beautiful arena, and the L.A. Live entertainment complex that surrounds it has a plethora of shops and restaurants for you to hang out pre- and postgame.

MAP 7: 1111 S. Figueroa St., 213/742-7100, www.staplescenter.com; see online calendar; tickets $40-500

HOCKEY
Los Angeles Kings

What's not to love about a night of ice hockey? Kings fans are intensely loyal, and you can feel their energy from blocks away as you approach the Staples Center on game night. Any seat in the house will provide great views of the action on the ice, which will likely include some goals and a good old-fashioned brawl. Make a night of it and start with dinner at one of several restaurants in the adjacent L.A. Live entertainment complex.

MAP 7: 1111 S. Figueroa St., 213/742-7100, www.staplescenter.com; see online calendar; tickets $40-500

ATTRACTIONS
Angels Flight Railway

For a fun little experience, take a trip on the world's shortest railway (only 298 feet long!). Two bright red-orange funicular cars take passengers between Hill Street and Grand Avenue and vice versa (California Plaza to Grand Central Market, basically). The railway has been open since 1901, having been dismantled, reconstructed, and renovated since. It's been featured in movies, art, video games, and literature.

MAP 7: 350 S. Grand Ave., 213/626-1901, https://angelsflight.org; 6:45am-10pm daily; $1 one way

Greater Los Angeles   Map 8

HIKING
✪ Griffith Park

Griffith Park feels worlds away from Hollywood Boulevard, the 405 freeway, and the rest of L.A.'s traffic-laden corridors. This is a place where you can lay a blanket, read a book, eat a picnic lunch, and hike trails across more than 4,000 acres. You'll come across hundreds of plant species that thrive in this arid climate, including oak, walnut, lilac, mountain mahogany, sage, and sumac. Within its boundaries are also the Los Angeles Zoo, the Autry Museum of the American West, the Griffith Observatory, and the Greek Theatre.

A popular hike that offers great views of the Hollywood Sign is Brush Canyon Trail, accessed from Canyon Drive or Griffith Observatory. It's a moderate but doable 5.7-mile out-and-back hike with 1161 feet of elevation gain. You'll end on Mount Hollywood, with a panoramic view behind the famous sign. Dogs must be kept on leash.

You can either plan your Griffith Park adventure ahead of time using its online maps, or just choose one of its many entrances and start exploring.

MAP 8: 4730 Crystal Springs Dr., 323/913-4688, www.laparks.org/griffithpark; 24 hours daily; free

hiking in Griffith Park

Topanga State Park

Part of the Santa Monica Mountains National Recreation Area, this beautiful park is filled with 76 miles of trails that are short and long, easy and hard. Most of these dusty paths lead to the kind of ocean views that make you go "ahhhhhhhhh." Paths are well-maintained (and shared with the occasional deer or rattlesnake). Embark early to beat the midday heat—many of Topanga's trails have full sun exposure and very little shade.

A popular hike is Temescal Canyon Trail, a moderate 2.9 mile loop with 875 feet of elevation gain. The trail is located near Pacific Palisades and features amazing views and a waterfall, depending on the season. The peak offers panoramic views of Santa Monica and Malibu. The trailhead starts at Temescal Canyon Road and Sunset Boulevard just off the PCH. There's a ranger station and a parking lot. To avoid the parking fee, park on Temescal Canyon Road.

MAP 8: 20828 Entrada Rd., 310/455-2465, www.parks.ca.gov; daily 8am-sunset; $10 parking

Will Rogers State Historical Park

When you need a break from L.A.'s clogged concrete arteries, head out west to Will Rogers State Historical Park in the Santa Monica Mountains for challenging hikes through dry canyons and expansive hilltops overlooking the mighty Pacific.

The most popular hike is Inspiration Point Trail, an easy 2.1-mile loop route with 324 feet of elevation gain and multiple vistas of the Los Angeles basin and Santa Monica Bay. On a clear day, you can see out to Catalina, Saddleback Peak, and the Chino Hills. The trailhead begins in the main parking lot (address below). Dogs must be kept on leash.

Alternatively, book a private horseback ride (310/662-3707, www.will-rogerstrailrides.com; ride times vary, tours last 50 minutes; $75 pp) with the park's official guides. You can call to book in advance or show up at the ranch near the main parking lot of the park.

Will Rogers State Historical Park is right off of the Pacific Coast Highway, so you won't have to travel too far out of the city to access it.

MAP 8: 1501 Will Rogers State Park Rd., 310/454-8212, www.parks.ca.gov; daily 6am-6pm; parking $12

SPECTATOR SPORTS
SOCCER
LA Galaxy

Head to the StubHub Center to cheer on the Los Angeles Galaxy, L.A.'s Major League Soccer (MLS) team that plays here March through October, with playoff games through November. Kids of all ages love Galaxy games, especially because of SoccerFest, an interactive area with games, food, and music. The L.A. Galaxy is one of the MLS' most decorated soccer teams, having won the MLS Cup five times since the league was founded in 1993.

MAP 8: 18400 S. Avalon Blvd,. 310/630-2000, www.stubhubcenter.com; $15-300

FOOTBALL
Los Angeles Rams

Angelinos are proud to have the Rams back from St. Louis. The Rams play in the historic Los Angeles Coliseum (where L.A. hosted the 1989 Olympic Games). In 2020 both of L.A.'s football teams will play home games at a brand new stadium in L.A.'s Inglewood neighborhood.

MAP 8: 3911 S. Figueroa St., www. lacoliseum.com; tickets $70-700

Los Angeles Chargers

Los Angeles is also excited to welcome the Chargers from San Diego. The Chargers currently play at the StubHub Center in Carson, but will be moving to a new stadium with the Rams in 2020.

MAP 8: 18400 S. Avalon Blvd., www. stubhubcenter.com; tickets $90-700

SHOPS

With famous stretches like Rodeo Drive and Melrose Avenue, L.A. is a shopping destination. If you're not ultra-wealthy, however, you're still in luck: L.A. shops cater to a broad range of budgets, tastes, and interests. From the chain stores along 3rd Street Promenade in Santa Monica to authentic Mexican arts and crafts on Olvera Street, one thing is certain—it's not hard to find fabulous, one-of-a-kind goods in this city.

For the latest high-end fashion and best window-shopping, head to Beverly Hills, where you'll see personal shoppers picking up designer dresses for celebrity clients. West Hollywood is also quite upscale; it's particularly notable for its gorgeous home goods and avant-garde clothing, jewelry, and accessories.

For vintage, look to Hollywood, where shops sell thousands of playfully used threads. Hollywood also has a bunch of street-savvy fashion shops lining Fairfax Avenue. If you're more into bohemian-chic, head to Venice, Silver Lake, or Los Feliz,

Hollywood & Highland

where you'll find lots of little shops selling hippie-inspired bags, dresses, candles, pottery, and more.

For some special California gifts, go shopping at Los Angeles County Store in Silver Lake, Mollusk Surf Shop in Venice, or Mindfulnest in Santa Monica. These charming shops sell only made-in-state goods.

HIGHLIGHTS

✪ **BEST MUSIC STORE:** Sip a cup of coffee on the house, tap some vintage bongos, and connect with true music lovers at **McCabe's Guitar Shop** in Santa Monica (page 179).

✪ **BEST CALIFORNIA-MADE GOODS:** Both **Mindfulnest** in Santa Monica and the **Los Angeles County Store** in Silver Lake sell unique jewelry, clothing, art, books, and other items made by local artisans (pages 181 and 194).

✪ **BEST SURFING GEAR: Mollusk Surf Shop** in Venice sells surfboards, gear, and clothing that are distinctly Californian (page 184).

✪ **BEST YOGA WEAR:** Celebrity-approved **Alo Yoga** has fresh-brewed kombucha, a bright studio, and a rooftop deck for lounging—oh, and yoga gear for sale (page 185).

✪ **BEST VINTAGE CLOTHING:** Don't get discouraged by Beverly Hills prices—**What Goes Around Comes Around** makes designer wear affordable and fun (page 185).

✪ **BEST UPSCALE FLEA MARKET:** Every Sunday morning the **Melrose Trading Post** attracts shoppers from across the city to peruse new and used local goods, scattered across the parking lot of the famous Fairfax High School (page 187).

✪ **BEST SKATE CULTURE:** The only store in America that has its own skate park, **Supreme** is where the cool kids shop (page 187).

✪ **BEST NEW-AGE SHOPPING:** Want to know where Gigi Hadid and Lena Dunham buy their healing crystals? Enter the **House of Intuition** (page 188).

✪ **BEST HOLLYWOOD SOUVENIR:** If you have space in your suitcase, you can take home a movie prop from **Nick Metropolis Collectible Furniture** (page 189).

✪ **BEST PLACE FOR CALI AESTHETIC:** West Hollywood's **Fred Segal** has an iconic style, with its laid-back yet luxe clothing, accessories, and home goods (page 191).

✪ **BEST INTERIOR DESIGN:** There are so many furniture and interior design shops to ogle at the **Pacific Design Center** (page 192).

✪ **BEST PLACE TO GET LOST IN A BOOK: The Last Bookstore** has walls of books—and even a tunnel to walk under (page 200).

Santa Monica

Map 1

SHOPS

SANTA MONICA

MALLS AND MARKETS
Santa Monica Farmers Markets
Santa Monica is home to the largest certified farmers market in California. With more than 70 vendors, this Wednesday farmers market in downtown Santa Monica is a favorite for local chefs; the quality and variety of produce here is superb and sold year-round.

There's a smaller market every Sunday (2640 Main St.), complete with live music, foods from local restaurants, and face painting; it's a great (albeit crowded) place for a family afternoon.

MAP 1: Arizona Ave. and 2nd St., 310/458-8712, www.smgov.net; Wed. 8:30am-1:30pm

Santa Monica Farmers Market

SURF SHOPS
ZJ Boarding house
ZJ has proudly served Santa Monica's skating and surfing communities since 1988. It's a locally owned surf shop located just two blocks from the beach amid a handful of chain surf stores. This shop keeps running because it's staffed by true surfing experts. Whether it's a wet suit made from environmentally friendly materials, a colorful skateboard, or a state-of-the-art surf watch, the guys here will help you find just what you're looking for. (I went here to buy my first wet suit and they were super-patient with my beginner questions.)

MAP 1: 2625 Main St., 310/392-5646, www.zjboardinghouse.com; Mon.-Sat. 10am-7pm, Sun. 10am-6pm

BOOKS
Thunderbolt Spiritual Books
Thunderbolt beckons with the smell of incense and an extensive collection of mystically minded literature. This two-story bookshop right in Santa Monica's commercial corridor has been expanding the minds of the spiritually inclined since 1999. Its welcoming staff are helpful and also give you space to peruse not just the books but also statues, jewelry, gemstones, tarot cards, mala beads, and more. Sift through the used book section, where there are usually some great finds.

MAP 1: 512 Santa Monica Blvd., 310/899-9279; daily 10am-10pm

MUSIC
✪ McCabe's Guitar Shop
McCabe's Guitar Shop reminds me of my best friend's garage in high school—the place where we would hang out, laugh, and play all different types of music. Since 1958, McCabe's has been a place to buy top-of-the-line instruments—not only guitars but also banjos, accordions, drums, and more—and also a place to gather. There's free coffee here all day long, and multiple live shows from talented musicians each week. Buy performance tickets ($10-$35) in advance

SHOPPING DISTRICTS

3RD STREET PROMENADE/MONTANA AVENUE IN SANTA MONICA

One of the great things about shopping in Santa Monica is how varied the shops are; you'll find everything from luxury sleepwear to authentic American Indian jewelry. For large chain stores, head to the Santa Monica Promenade. There are some upscale shops at Santa Monica Place, and adorable local boutiques on Main Street and Montana Avenue.

RODEO DRIVE IN BEVERLY HILLS

Come to Rodeo Drive to see the latest fashions from the world's most well-known designers, including Gucci, Channel, Louis Vuitton, and Saint Laurent. These designers have big and gorgeous shops on Rodeo Drive itself, begging for ooohs and ahhhs. The side streets off Rodeo Drive have smaller boutiques from a diverse range of designers. Beverly Boulevard also has some great local boutiques. No matter which store you land in, you are not likely to find bargain or discount items—even secondhand Chanel bags sell for thousands of dollars here.

FAIRFAX AVENUE IN HOLLYWOOD

Fairfax Avenue between Melrose Avenue and 3rd Street is one of my favorite shopping districts in the city. It has some classic stores (like the cool Supreme skate shop) and also a bunch of pop-up shops that creatively showcase the talents of up-and-coming artists and designers. The high-end Melrose Trading Post swap meet happens here every Sunday.

MELROSE AVENUE IN HOLLYWOOD AND WEST HOLLYWOOD

Melrose Avenue is where you'll find fashion with an edge, world-class furniture and interior décor stores, and more men's clothing than in other neighborhoods. You'll pay high-end prices while shopping on Melrose in WeHo, but the shops become more affordable as you move into Hollywood proper, where you'll find vintage shops, sneaker stores, Japanese fashion, and much more.

EL PUEBLO DE LOS ANGELES IN DOWNTOWN

Olvera Street in El Pueblo caters to tourists, selling Mexican hats, purses, dresses, paintings—pretty much any knick knack you might imagine. It's a fun place to experience L.A.'s cultural heritage and pick up some colorful gifts. The strip is only a quarter-mile long, so you won't need more than a couple of hours here.

---

on McCabe's website (www1.mccabes.com/concerts).

MAP 1: 3101 Pico Blvd., 310/828-4497, www1.mccabes.com; Mon.-Thurs. 10am-10pm, Fri.-Sat. 10am-6pm, Sun. noon-6pm

KIDS' STUFF

Puzzle Zoo

Yes, there are lots of cool jigsaw puzzles at Puzzle Zoo, but there's also much more, including action figures, board games, and educational dolls. This is a great place to pick up a gift for a kiddo back home or buy the little ones a treat during your Santa Monica adventure. Puzzle Zoo is a family-owned shop where staff are happy to help you find just the toy you're looking for. And don't be surprised if you find a gift for yourself here—Puzzle Zoo has plenty of goodies for adults, too.

MAP 1: 1411 3rd St. Promenade, 310/393-9201, www.puzzlezoo.com; Sun.-Thurs. 10am-1pm, Fri.-Sat. 10am-11pm

Peek Kids

See all those adorably dressed kids riding their bikes around Santa Monica? Chances are they got their duds from Peek Kids, a stylish (and pricey) clothing store in the Montana Avenue shopping district. You'll find adorable pieces here for children ages newborn to preteen. Peek Kids has clothing for casual playdates, everyday school wear, and also outfits for special events. All the patterns are fresh, most quite trendy. Peek Kids also sells books, plush toys, and educational games.

MAP 1: 1015 Montana Ave., 310/434-9700, https://peekkids.com/santa-monica; Mon.-Sat. 10am-7pm, Sun. 11am-6pm

FOOD
Co-Opportunity
This natural-foods store has been serving the local Santa Monica community since 1974. Co-Opportunity is both a grocery store and a deli where you'll find organic, local, non-GMO and natural foods (I recommend the hearty breakfast burritos). There's also earth-friendly shampoo, soap, and other self-care products for sale. This is a truly local operation that runs on member dues, but you don't have to be a member to come and grab a bag of healthy goodies for your day at the beach.

MAP 1: 1525 Broadway, 310/451-8902, www.coopportunity.com; daily 7am-10pm

Andrew's Cheese Shop
If you love cheese, it doesn't get much better than Andrew's Cheese Shop. In addition to a wide variety of artisan beer and cheese, Andrew's also sells gourmet chocolates, olives, and sandwiches. This small shop provides excellent service and a level of expertise that will satisfy even the most discerning fromagier. I recommend stopping here to pick up a mouthwatering sandwich to eat on the beach, or buying tickets online to Andrew's monthly

Grilled Cheese and Beer Night (http://andrewscheese.com/events/grilled-cheese-beer-night, $60 per person).

MAP 1: 728 Montana Ave., 310/393-3308, http://andrewscheese.com; Mon.-Fri. 11am-7pm, Sat. 10am-7pm, Sun. 10am-6pm

GIFTS
Taos Indian Trading Company
Taos Indian Trading Company proudly sells goods produced by dozens of American Indian tribes. Established in 1987 in downtown Santa Monica, Taos has a wide variety of stuff for sale, including masks, sculptures, woven rugs, and dream catchers. The beadwork items, such as moccasins and wall hangings, are particularly beautiful, as is the handmade sterling silver jewelry. Taos has supplied authentic American Indian artifacts to many a movie and TV show production—all in a day's work here in Los Angeles.

MAP 1: 403 Santa Monica Blvd., 310/395-3652, https://taostradingcompany.com; Mon.-Fri. 11am-6pm, Sat. 11am-4pm

✪ Mindfulnest
Come to Mindfulnest for a unique selection of artisan jewelry, clothing, and art. This is a proudly local shop where 70 percent of the goods are made by California-based artists. You'll notice its prices might be a bit higher than those in surrounding stores; what you're paying for is the extra time and love that goes into these hand-picked treats. There are only three Mindfulnest stores (the others are in Highland Park and Burbank). Even if you're not planning on buying gold hummingbird earrings or a handcrafted leather bracelet, come to Mindfulnest to appreciate some of L.A.'s best local ware.

MAP 1: 2711 Main St., 310/452-5409, www.mindfulnest.com; Sun.-Thurs. 11am-7pm, Fri.-Sat. 10:30am-9pm

CLOTHING AND ACCESSORIES
Kathmandu Boutique
If you're strolling down Santa Monica's busy Lincoln Boulevard, pop into Kathmandu Boutique for funky clothes, good vibes, and a powerful whiff of incense. This colorful shop sells clothing, accessories, and home goods from Tibet, Nepal, and India. It has that hippie-New Age vibe that's endemic to Southern California. There are many beautiful gifts here, such as a golden Ganesh statue, a rare emerald pendant, and embroidered cotton kaftans. Kathmandu Boutique even hosts monthly dinner with live music; check its website for dates.

MAP 1: 1844 Lincoln Blvd., 310/396-4036, www.kathmanduboutique.com; daily 11am-6:30pm

Lunya
Treat yourself to some luxurious sleepwear from Lunya, a boutique that makes nighties so comfy you won't want to take them off. What's the key to Lunya's uber-comfortable clothing? Its fabric and cut. Lunya uses high-quality cotton and hemp to create masterful shorts, jumpers, and other garments that are virtually seamless. Founded by entrepreneur Ashley Merrill in 2014, Lunya was created to help women feel beautiful in the bedroom. If you're looking for an intimate gift for a lady you love, you've found the right place.

MAP 1: 1032 Broadway, 310/395-2666, https://lunya.co; Mon.-Fri. 9:30am-6pm, Sat. 10am-4pm

Venice

Map 2

BOOKS
Mystic Journey Bookstore
With calming vibes and a wide selection of spiritually minded books, Mystic Journey lives up to its name. There are also vibrant crystals and gemstones for purchase, as well as a nice jewelry selection. Sign up for a private reading with one of the in-house "intuitive readers," who might help you with your journey in real life. Walk to the back of the store to relax on its big, sunny patio, which hosts multiple community events each week, such as "Open Mic of the Spirit," and "Connecting and Clearing with the Angels."

MAP 2: 1624 Abbot Kinney Blvd., 301/399-7070, https://mysticjourneybookstore.com; Mon.-Fri. 10am-9pm, Sat.-Sun. 10am-11pm

GIFTS
Strange Invisible Perfumes
Strange Invisible Perfumes sells perfume made like it was in the good old days—aged for six months with all-natural scents and a splash of cognac. This tiny Abbot Kinney Boulevard shop is a truly local operation, with all of its concoctions made in Venice by a botanical perfumer. The perfumes will make you swoon, and they can even be matched to your zodiac sign. The shop takes its scents quite seriously,

which you'll appreciate if you're going to spend $115 on a 15mL bottle.
MAP 2: 1138 Abbot Kinney Blvd., 301/314-1505, https://siperfumes.com; Mon.-Sat. 11am-7pm, Sun. noon-6pm

General Store
You could get lost in General Store's high-end, artsy-hipster goods. This is a great place to find a beautiful, unique gift, like a locally made ceramic pot, first-edition book, or artisanal bath product. There's also a lovely selection of women's clothing and jewelry, mostly in soft color palettes. A lot of love and careful curation goes into this store—and the prices reflect it. Save up if you plan on shopping here.
MAP 2: 1801 Lincoln Blvd., 301/751-6393, https://shop-generalstore.com; Mon.-Sat. 11am-7pm, Sun. noon-6pm

Burro
The Burro flagship store is truly a gift buyer's paradise. It's only a slight exaggeration to say that I want to buy everything in this store. There are tons of fun greeting cards, quirky decorations (including a snow globe filled with crystals), books, kitchen gear, and so much more. Burro also sells some beautiful rustic-looking jewelry and a rainbow of sexy and soft undies. Stuff here isn't cheap, but it also isn't so expensive that you'll feel duped. Check out Burro Kids right next door.
MAP 2: 1409 Abbot Kinney Blvd., 301/450-6288, https://burrogoods.com; daily 10am-7pm

CLOTHING AND ACCESSORIES
TOMS
More than a shoe shop, this TOMS flagship store is an experience. Eat and people-watch at the café, hang out with friends on the sunny patio, and, of course, browse the latest and coolest pairs of TOMS shoes and sunglasses. There are also other TOMS-brand goods, like clothing and coffee. And because TOMS has more than 100 give-back partnerships around the world, you can feel good about your socially conscious spending!
MAP 2: 1344 Abbot Kinney Blvd., 301/314-9700, www.toms.com/toms-stores; Mon.-Fri. 9am-9pm, Sat. 9am-9pm, Sun. 9am-8pm

Will Leather Goods
Founded by leather expert Will Adler, this friendly shop will meet all your high-quality cowhide needs (and wants). Leather products sold here include bags, laptop cases, purses, belts, bracelets, hats, pens, journals, flasks, backpacks, and more—even bow ties. All goods come with a lifetime guarantee, and can be personally embossed with words or initials right in front of you. This is a great place to buy a thoughtful gift, or just step in and smell the leather.
MAP 2: 1360 Abbot Kinney Blvd., 301/399-8700, https://willleathergoods.com; Mon.-Thurs. 11am-8pm, Fri.-Sat. 10am-8pm, Sun. 11am-7pm

Will Leather Goods

Made In Earth

If, like me, you're mildly obsessed with natural stones, you must pop into Made in Earth, a rock-solid gem store on Abbot Kinney Boulevard (pun intended). This magnetic shop has jewelry made from semiprecious gems like amethyst, ruby, and emerald, and some unique finds, like rocks from comets and gem necklaces created to help wearers with specific life challenges. This is one of four Made in Earth shops; the others are in San Diego, New York City, and St. Kilda, Australia.

MAP 2: 1506 Abbot Kinney Blvd., 310/396-3838, https://madeinearthus. com; Mon.-Tues. 11am-8pm, Wed.-Thurs. 11am-8:30pm, Fri.-Sat. 11am-9:30pm, Sun. 10:30am-8:30pm

SURF SHOPS
✪ Mollusk Surf Shop

Located in the heart of Venice and steps from the boardwalk, Mollusk is a casual, artsy shop that takes pride in its surfboards, gear, and clothing for men and women. A refreshing alternative to name-brand surf chains, Mollusk decorates with local art and sells its own brand of clothing and accessories. It's a good place to go if you're looking for a gift that's distinctly California. Even if don't purchase anything, it's a fun place to stop into and browse. There are only two other Mollusk locations on the planet: one in Silver Lake and the other in San Francisco.

MAP 2: 1600 Pacific Ave., 301/396-1969, https://mollusksurfshop.com; daily 10am-6:30pm

Beverly Hills　　　　Map 3

CLOTHING AND ACCESSORIES
Kyle | Alene Too

I think most people end up at Kyle | Alene Too in hopes of meeting Kyle Richards, a former child actor who now stars in the Real Housewives of Beverly Hills and owns this large boutique. Occupying a major corner in Beverly Hills's prime shopping district, Kyle | Alene Too sells a plethora of trendy, expensive clothing and accessories, all for women. And you just might get to take a proud picture with Kyle, who occasionally stops by the store.

MAP 3: 9647 Brighton Way, 310/278-6200, www.kylebyalenetoo.com; Mon.-Sat. 10am-6pm, Sun. noon-5pm

Beverly Hills Bikini Shop

Beverly Hills Bikini Shop has held court on Beverly Boulevard since 1966, offering a variety of women's beachwear, including bathing suits, sarongs, straw bags, and sandals. Most (but not all) of its swimwear is pretty skimpy, but you'll still pay Beverly Hills prices for an itty-bitty piece of fabric. The Beverly Hills Bikini Shop is an especially fun place to accessorize your swim look with brightly colored kaftans, playful towels, or jeweled jean cutoffs.

MAP 3: 245 S. Beverly Dr., 310/550-6331, www.thebeverlyhillsbikinishop.com; Mon.-Sat. 10am-7pm, Sun. 11am-6pm

The Lady & The Sailor

The Lady & The Sailor has an ivy-covered exterior and sits just outside of Beverly Hills's main commercial district. The shop's high-end casual women's pieces are "simple but necessary luxuries" according to the store's website; I'm not sure how necessary a $500 sweater is, but the clothes here are certifiably gorgeous. All of The Lady & The Sailor's clothing uses muted color palettes and high-quality, made-in-America textiles. It's no wonder these clothes are quickly gaining attention from women who love splurging on such decadent fabrics.

MAP 3: 9296 Civic Center Dr., 310/276-1015, https://theladyandthesailor.com; Mon.-Sat. 10am-6pm

✪ Alo Yoga

So much more than a yoga clothing store, the Alo Yoga flagship provides a full yoga and wellness experience. With fresh-brewed kombucha, a bright yoga studio, and a rooftop deck for lounging, this 8,000-square-foot store is a hub for all things yoga and wellness. Alo Yoga athletic apparel is for both men and women, and has been sported by numerous fitness gurus and celebs. Staff here are quite friendly, and will help you find just the right pair of stretchy pants.

MAP 3: 370 N. Canon Dr., (310) 295-1860, https://aloyoga.com/pages/yoga-classes; Mon.-Sat. 8am-7pm, Sun. 9am-7pm

SCHUTZ Shoes

This trendy shoe spot, an export from Brazil, opened its second U.S. store in Beverly Hills in 2016. Since then, it has gotten even more attention from celebrities and bloggers, and for good reason—the shoes here, which are all women's styles, are fashionable, trendy, colorful, and made with high-quality leather. Whether you're looking for a pair of tasseled yellow sandals or some baby-pink pumps, you'll find them here at Schutz. Prices are reasonable for Beverly Hills—most pairs cost $100-250.

MAP 3: 314 N. Beverly Dr., 310/435-9669, https://schutz-shoes.com; Mon.-Sat. 10am-8pm, Sun. 11pm-7pm

VINTAGE
✪ What Goes Around Comes Around

In 2016, this luxury vintage boutique opened to considerable celebrity fanfare, with actress Rashida Jones, stylist Rachel Zoe, and other stars attending its opening party. What Goes Around Comes Around claims to have the world's largest collection of vintage Chanel clothing and accessories—and it just might be possible, with dozens of earrings, pairs of shoes, and adorable clutches lining its walls. There's 4,000 square feet of clothing and accessories for both men and women; while the prices are discounted, they still reflect the fact that you're in Beverly Hills, just a stone's throw from Rodeo Drive.

MAP 3: 9520 Brighton Way, 310/858-0250, www.whatgoesaroundnyc.com; Mon.-Sat. 10am-7pm, Sun. noon-6pm

JEWELRY
Leon's of Beverly Hills

I'm not one for nostalgia, but shopping at Leon's feels like a throwback to a time when customers received more personalized service and attention. Leon, the store owner and jewelry maker, treats each customer with care, often creating unique handmade pieces to meet client needs. This small establishment, right in the heart of Beverly Hills, is a great place to buy a gift or a wedding ring, and a nice alternative to the big-name jewelry stores right down the street. This is high-end jewelry, all of which comes with a lifetime guarantee.

MAP 3: 9626 Brighton Way, 310/246-0277, http://leonsbeverlyhills.com; Mon.-Sat. 10am-6pm

XIV Karats

XIV Karats has jewelry that's hard not to lust over. There are both traditional pieces, such as diamond engagement rings, and more modern pieces, such as asymmetrical pearl earrings. The jewelry here is so shiny that it's worth stopping by even if you're not planning on making a major purchase. Given the store's wide range of price options—from dainty necklaces to multi-karat bracelets—it's no wonder that both famous and non-famous Angelenos cite XIV Karats as their favorite place to buy a sparkling gift.

MAP 3: 314 S. Beverly Dr., 310/551-1212, www.xivkarats.com; Mon.-Sat. 9:30am-5pm

KIDS' STUFF

Trico Field

The kids' clothing at Trico Field is on trend. If you have kids (or nieces or nephews), beware—you'll want to buy everything in here. There are Trico Field stores in Tokyo, New York, and Beverly Hills, all of which sell high-quality, high-comfort kids clothing with style. All of the clothing at Trico Field is from one of three popular Japanese brands and is designed to "bring out a child's inner glow."

MAP 3: 9460 Dayton Way, 310/786-8290, www.tricofield.net; Mon.-Sat. 10am-6pm, Sun. 11am-5pm

Hollywood

Map 4

MALLS AND MARKETS

The Grove

The Grove is L.A.'s favorite outdoor shopping mall. There are many high end chains to visit here, including Nordstrom, Madewell, and Coach. Take a break in front of the koi-filled fountain (with water shows set to music every hour). There are restaurants in the complex, but you should head next door to the Farmers Market for lunch instead.

MAP 4: 189 The Grove Dr., 323/900-8080, www.thegrovela.com; Mon.-Thurs. 10am-9pm, Fri.-Sat. 10am-10pm, Sun. 10am-8pm; validated parking in surrounding lots

The Original Farmer's Market

Fresh local produce at more than 50 restaurant stalls await at the Farmers Market, a go-to dining spot since 1934. Local food favorites include Indonesian food at the Banana Leaf and Brazilian at Pampas Grill. The eclectic shops of the Farmers Market are a good place to buy gifts to bring home.

MAP 4: 6333 W. 3rd St., 323/933-9211, www.farmersmarketla.com; Mon.-Fri. 9am-9pm, Sat. 9am-8pm, Sun. 10am-7pm; validated parking in surrounding lots

Hollywood & Highland

This three-story outdoor shopping complex at the center of the Walk of Fame was designed so that patrons on all levels have a great view

FARMERS MARKETS

L.A. is only 100 miles from some of America's most productive agricultural regions, so it makes sense that many Angelinos rely on local farmers markets as a main source of meat, dairy, and produce.

- For the most comprehensive market selections, head to the **Santa Monica Farmers Market** (Arizona Ave. and 2nd St., 310/458-8712, www.smgov.net; 8:30am-1:30pm Wed.). With hundreds of vendors from across the state, this is the biggest certified farmers market in California. A lot of L.A. chefs get their produce here each week. There's another Santa Monica market on Sunday (2640 Main St.). Go to that one if you have kids—there's entertainment and face-painting for the little ones.

- Beyond a place to get groceries, the **Hollywood Farmers' Market** (Ivar and Selma Ave., www.hollywoodfarmersmarket.net; Sun. 8am-1pm) is a community meeting spot where locals and visitors can connect with their neighbors, listen to live music, and nosh on delicious local fare.

- **The Original Farmer's Market** (6333 W. 3rd St., 323/933-9211, www.farmersmarketla.com; Mon.-Fri. 9am-9pm, Sat. 9am-8pm, Sun. 10am-7pm) in Hollywood started as a market in 1934 and has since become a permanent dining mecca with more than 50 food vendors from around the world. It can get crowded on weekends, but it's a great place for a weekday lunch.

of the Hollywood sign. It's filled with American chain stores like Sephora, Victoria's Secret, and Forever 21. There is also a handful of chain restaurants including California Pizza Kitchen and Hard Rock Café.

MAP 4: 6801 Hollywood Blvd., 323/467-6412, http://hollywoodandhighland.com; Mon.-Sat. 10am-10pm, Sun. 10am-7pm; validated garage parking

Hollywood & Highland

✪ Melrose Trading Post

Every Sunday, the parking lot of Fairfax High School becomes a huge swap meet full of antique furniture, new and vintage clothing, local art, and handcrafted goods like candles and deodorant. There's also a handful of food stands and live music. It's best to go early in the morning, as it can get hot and crowded in the afternoon. A bunch of celebs attended Fairfax High, including Demi Moore, Mila Kunis, and Lenny Kravitz.

MAP 4: 7850 Melrose Ave., 323/655-7679, www.melrosetradingpost.org; Sun. 9am-5pm

CLOTHING AND ACCESSORIES
✪ Supreme

This might be the only shop in the world that has its own skate park. Supreme's one-of-a-kind T-shirts, hats, and skateboards are definitely pricey, but they're also cool, creative, and cutting-edge. Even if you're not particularly interested in skateboard gear, it's worth going inside just to

peek. Every Thursday there will be a line of customers out the door waiting for a new Supreme product release.
MAP 4: 439 N. Fairfax Ave., 323/655-6205, www.supremenewyork.com/stores; Mon.-Sat. 11am-7pm, Sun. noon-6pm

Wasteland

With white vaulted ceilings and soothing indie music, Wasteland beckons sophisticated shoppers looking for designer goods at discount prices. This surprisingly big space offers gently used clothing, shoes, and accessories, mostly for women. High-end goods, like fringed Louis Vuitton moccasins, are locked behind glass, but still available for purchase.
MAP 4: 7428 Melrose Ave., 323/653-3028, www.shopwasteland.com/hollywood; Mon.-Sat.11am-8pm, Sun. noon-8pm

Anthem

If you love shoes, don't skip Anthem. This big shoe store, comfortably located in the Melrose shopping district, will have you drooling over many of the latest fashions as well as some understated ones. There are plenty of shoes in a variety of styles for both women and men. The store has a cool vibe, and the shoes rotate depending on the season, so you can buy colorful sandals in the summer or chic boots during winter.
MAP 4: 7660 Melrose Ave., 323/556-7694, Mon.-Sat. 10am-8pm, Sun. 11am-7pm

✪ House of Intuition

As this shop's exterior will tell you, "Your intuition brought you here." This new-agey paradise is replete with feathered dream catchers, crystals in all shapes and sizes, a wall of incense, and books about various topics related to spirituality. The best things to buy here are the goods that House of

Intuition creates itself—bubble bath, candles, and incense blends. Born in Los Angeles, there are two other locations in the city (5108 York Blvd. in Highland Park and 2237 W. Sunset Blvd. in Silver Lake).
MAP 4: 7449 Melrose Ave., 213/413-8300, www.houseofintuitionla.com; Mon.-Fri. noon-7pm, Sat. 10am-8pm, Sun. 10am-6pm

House of Intuition

Joyrich

Joyrich specializes in flashy, edgy, urban streetwear. It's super-popular in Hong Kong, Shanghai, and Japan, but this is its only store in the United States. There's clothing for both women and men, as well as lots of fun accessories. The store has a colorful exterior, perfect for social media photo ops. Before you go, check online for sales—the goods at Joyrich can be expensive, but there are regular sales of 40-60 percent off sticker price.
MAP 4: 7700 Melrose Ave., 323/944-0631, https://joyrich.com; daily noon-8pm

Flight Club

The place to go for rare sneakers (both new and resale), Flight Club is just one long room filled wall to wall (and floor to ceiling) with Nikes, Adidas, Vans, and more. Yes, you may experience sticker shock, but don't you think that pair of limited-release turquoise Air Jordans is worth it? This is one of two

Flight Club stores in the United States, the other being in New York City, and both are frequented by celebrities, particularly hip-hop stars.

MAP 4: 535 N. Fairfax Ave., 888/937-8020; Mon.-Sat. 11am-7pm, Sun. noon-6pm

VINTAGE AND ANTIQUES

✪ Nick Metropolis Collectible Furniture

Want to take home a Starbucks sign recently used in a blockbuster film? Or deck chairs that have been passed around indie flicks for decades? Or maybe life-size *Simpsons* characters? This is the place where movie props and furniture are resurrected for your using pleasure. If you're prepared to wade through piles of collectibles, you can make Hollywood a permanent part of your home for a reasonable price.

MAP 4: 100 S. La Brea Ave., 323/934-3700, https://nickmetropolis.com; Mon.-Sat. 10:30am-7pm, Sun. 11am-7pm

Jet Rag

Walk into Jet Rag and you're greeted with a rainbow of petticoats and feathered boas. Yes, it may smell a bit like your grandma's attic, but don't let that deter you from perusing everything from leather jackets to Hawaiian shirts and bridal dresses. Most of the clothing is used, and there's plenty of options for women, men, and gender-nonconforming individuals. There's a $1 sale every Sunday, where shoppers from across the city dig through piles of clothing in the parking lot—yes, anything you find is only $1.

MAP 4: 825 N. La Brea Ave., 323/939-0528; Mon.-Sat. 11am-7:30pm, Sun. 9am-5pm

Nick Metropolis Collectible Furniture

FURNITURE AND INTERIOR DECOR
Muji Hollywood

Muji is a tasteful respite in the midst of over-the-top Hollywood Boulevard; the lavender-scented mist blowing inside this minimalist Japanese chain will almost certainly feel like a breath of fresh air. There's a huge selection of understated home goods (including adult beanbags) and racks of monotone cotton clothing, all reasonably priced. You can't really see Muji from the street because it's tucked in back of the Hollywood Galaxy Plaza—walk straight back past the Subway to find it.

MAP 4: 7021 Hollywood Blvd., 323/785-2013; www.muji.com; daily 10am-9pm

MUSIC
Amoeba Music

Occupying an entire Hollywood block, this is the biggest of Amoeba's three locations (the other two are in Northern

Amoeba Music

California). Its two floors house thousands of constantly rotating new and used CDs, DVDs, and vinyl titles. There's also a bunch of cool concert gear, from vintage T-shirts to collectible posters. Amoeba regularly hosts small concerts showcasing lesser-known musical artists.

MAP 4: 6400 Sunset Blvd., 323/245-6400, www.amoeba.com; Mon.-Sat. 10:30am-11pm, Sun. 11am-10pm

West Hollywood   Map 5

MALLS
The Beverly Center

The Beverly Center is a pretty typical high-end American mall. It has standard department stores like Macy's and Bloomingdale's, and also lots of designer shops from brands including Fendi, Gucci, and Salvatore Ferragamo. The Beverly Center is a big, bright space with almost 100 stores, so if you've forgotten to pack anything—like your laptop charger, a tasseled bathing suit, or luxury skincare products—you'll likely find it here.

MAP 5: 8500 Beverly Blvd., 310/854-0070, www.beverlycenter.com; Mon.-Fri. 10am-9pm, Sat. 10am-8pm, Sun. 11am-6pm

CLOTHING AND ACCESSORIES
DASH

DASH is pretty much what you'd expect from a store created by reality TV stars Kim, Khloe, and Kourtney Kardashian. It's a small shop with super-trendy clothes that provide ample opportunity to show a whole lotta skin. Poke around to find a bunch of reasonably priced clothing—everything from workout gear to long dresses to lots of bodysuits—in fabrics studded, lacy, sheer, and more. If you're a serious Kardashian fan, you can pick up soaps wrapped with images of Kim's face, or Khloe's tell-all tome.

MAP 5: 8420 Melrose Ave., 323/782-6822, https://shopdashonline.com/pages/west-hollywood; Mon.-Sat. 11am-7pm, Sun. noon-6pm

Irene Neuwerth Jewelry

Irene Neuwerth is a Southern California native whose jewelry is sold in Barney's department store and boutiques around the world, and this West Hollywood shop is her only stand-alone store. It's a quaint space with gentle lighting that lets her ocean-inspired jewelry sparkle. Irene's pieces are at once earthy and ethereal—boldly colored gemstones pop against bright gold and baby-sized diamonds. Her earrings are particularly popular; they've been worn by many a celebrity on many a red carpet.

MAP 5: 8458 Melrose Pl., 323/285-2000, http://ireneneuwirth.com/stores/our-store; Mon.-Sat. 10am-6pm

✪ Fred Segal

Buyer beware—you may want to purchase everything in Fred Segal's flagship store…at least I do. This iconic California retailer first opened in 1961, and ever since has offered clothing, accessories, and home goods in a style it calls "Southern California laid-back luxe." Some of the stuff here is from the Fred Segal brand, while other goods are curated from a host of international designers and creators. You can't miss the huge, ivy-covered building on Melrose Avenue—there's even a café inside where you can sit and recuperate from all that shopping.

Fred Segal opened a massive new store in 2017 in another part of West Hollywood, on the Sunset Strip (8500 Sunset Blvd.); this bold space has a café, floral shop, salon, and pop-up shop featuring rotating designers.

MAP 5: 8100 Melrose Ave., 323/651-4129, www.fredsegal.com; Mon.-Fri. 10am-7pm, Sun. noon-6pm

Maxfield

Maxfield has everything you might want from a high-end West Hollywood boutique: Chanel couture, vintage designer furniture, and cheeky gifts like a scratch-and-sniff book about marijuana. With its minimalist design and huge modern statues, the outside of Maxfield looks more like a museum than a shop. Inside, you'll find clothing and accessories from both high-fashion designers and locally created street wear. While you're here, check out Maxfield's pop-up shop across the street, which has rotating collections of clothing and accessories, artfully displayed with a thematic focus. Expect to pay top dollar here.

MAP 5: 8825 Melrose Ave., 310/274-8800, www.maxfieldla.com; Mon.-Sat. 11am-7pm, Sun. noon-5pm

Balmain

The Balmain flagship store is everything you might expect from this French clothing designer—tasteful, cutting-edge, and very Parisian. There are lots of gorgeous pieces here for both men and women, mostly tailored clothing with a twist, and a few sparkly party dresses. It's a great place to splurge on a one-of-a-kind item from a brand that has been both classic and trendsetting since 1945. Balmain has boutiques around the world; this is one of only two in the United States.

MAP 5: 8421 Melrose Pl., 323/230-6364, www.balmain.com/en_mo/boutiques/los-angeles; Mon.-Sat. 10am-7pm

MELROSE SHOPPING WALK

Melrose Avenue—the *other* famous shopping street in L.A.—is accessible, diverse, and, luckily for us shopaholics, long. Melrose hosts some of L.A.'s favorite stores, offering everything from hard-to-find sneakers to healing crystals. Ideally, you'll take this route on a Sunday morning, when Melrose Trading Post (a fancy flea market) is up and running at the corner of Melrose and Fairfax.

- **Total Distance:** 1.3 miles

- **Walking Time:** 1-2 hours

1. Start at the east end of Melrose and fuel up with some vegan tacos at **Gracias Madre.**

2. Wander around the **West Hollywood Design District**, speckled with high quality shops and galleries. Get some inspiration for your next home remodel.

3. The highlight of the Design District, the **Pacific Design Center** is an awesome place to visit even if you're not buying an outrageously oversized chair to bring home. Arts meets interior design at the MOCA's satellite exhibition space next door.

4. Keep walking west for a bit, window-shopping and people-watching, before you reach Melrose Place. Here you'll find the hip, popular **Alfred Coffee.** Grab a Stumptown brew to go and take a selfie with its huge "But first, coffee" mural.

5. Also in Melrose Place is the luxe **Balmain,** one of two in the U.S. The beautiful, Parisian pieces are nice to look out even if you can't afford any of them.

6. Go back to Melrose Avenue and cross the street for a fun shopping break at **Duff's Cakemix,** run by the famous *Ace of Cakes* man himself, Duff Goldman. You can bake and decorate your own cupcake masterpieces here. (Or just eat someone else's.)

7. You can't miss the huge, ivy-covered **Fred Segal** store. You also can't leave the iconic California shop without buying some cute clothing, accessories, or home goods.

8. A few blocks east, you'll hit the corner of Melrose and Fairfax, where the **Melrose Trading Post** is held every Sunday 9am-5pm. Angelenos from all over the city head to the parking lot of celeb-attended Fairfax High School to find unique clothing and hand-crafted goods and accessories at reasonable prices.

FURNITURE AND INTERIOR DECOR

West Hollywood Design District

In 1996, the city of West Hollywood smartly designated this little pocket of the city as its "Design District." Spanning Melrose Avenue and Beverly Boulevard between San Vicente Boulevard and Doheny Drive, the Design District is speckled with shops and galleries that pride themselves on high-quality design in both clothing and interior decor. Whether you're in the market for some one-of-a-kind pieces for your home or just enjoy browsing, this is a really nice area to walk around and take in some inspiration.

MAP 5: Melrose Ave. and Beverly Blvd. between San Vicente Blvd. and Doheny Dr., 310/289-2534, http://westhollywooddesigndistrict.com

✪ Pacific Design Center

You can't miss the Pacific Design Center's red, green, and blue exterior: The huge, 1.5 million-square-foot space houses multiple shops and art galleries focused on furniture and interior design. It's a paradise for both the intrepid, deep-pocketed

© AVALON TRAVEL

9. Continue east on Melrose and in a few blocks you'll get to Japanese clothing and accessories store **Joy Rich.** If you're looking for a cool background for your selfie, consider Joyrich's flower-painted exterior.

10. If you're in the mood for a drink, pop into the divey **Snake Pit Alehouse** next door and take a break with a beer (or whiskey) and some jukebox tunes.

11. Once you've refueled, cross the street and find **Anthem,** a big, cool shoe store with fashion-forward footwear for men and women. Check out the creative street art on the sides of the buildings on the north side of Melrose and Sierra Bonita (the same side of the street as Snake Pit).

12. Two blocks down, **House of Intuition** is a one-stop shop for all of your metaphysical shopping needs. Grab some spiritually-minded books, incense, crystals, and jewelry.

13. End your journey at **Wasteland** on Melrose, a haven for gently worn high-end clothing. If you don't have any shopping bags in your hand at this point, now's a good time to stock up.

designer and the artistically curious. The ground floor has Dedon, one of my favorite stores—it's an Australian company that specializes in supercool outdoor furniture, like oversized hanging chairs. While at the Pacific Design Center, you can dine at one of two on-site restaurants operated by famed chef Wolfgang Puck, and also stop by the Museum of Contemporary Art's satellite exhibition space on the Design Center property.

MAP 5: 8687 Melrose Ave., 310/657-0800, www.pacificdesigncenter.com; daily 9am-5pm; free

Kelly Wearstler

Walk through this shop's black marble entryway and grab onto a gemstone-laden door handle to enter a room so understatedly glamorous that you may be tempted to buy a $95 candle. Almost everything in this home decor store is designed by Kelly Wearstler herself, with a few pieces sprinkled in that she picked up on her travels. Some of the vases and jewelry boxes here are truly works of art; it's a special place to pick up a one-of-a-kind piece to take back home. There are very few price tags, so ask store staff for pricing.

MAP 5: 8440 Melrose Ave., 323/895-7880, www.kellywearstler.com; Mon.-Fri. 10am-7pm, Sun. noon-6pm

BOOKS
Book Soup

Book Soup is one of those rare boutique bookstores that has been around for decades. Set right on the Sunset Strip, Book Soup offers thousands of carefully selected titles in dozens of genres including art, film, photography, music, and literary fiction. I particularly appreciate the "Staff Recommended" section, which has a handwritten recommendation card for each title. Book Soup is one of the best places in L.A. to grab a special read for your flight home or buy a few thoughtful presents—complimentary gift-wrapping included.

MAP 5: 8818 Sunset Blvd., 310/659-3110, www.booksoup.com; Mon.-Sat. 9am-10pm, Sun. 9am-7pm

Mystery Pier Books

Wandering into Mystery Pier Books feels like stumbling upon hidden treasure. To get to this small, cottage-like

Book Soup

bookstore, you'll meander down a small alleyway off the Sunset Strip; once you arrive, you'll be surrounded by hundreds of books—all first editions, many of them signed by their authors. This is the place to find rare copies of first-edition books from writers including Shakespeare, Kurt Vonnegut, Bukowski, and many, many more. Take your time to peruse and ask questions—the staff here love to share their vast knowledge of these valuable tomes.

MAP 5: 8826 Sunset Blvd., 310/657-5557, www.mysterypierbooks.com; Mon.-Sat. 11am-7pm, Sun. noon-5pm

Echo Park, Los Feliz, and Silver Lake   Map 6

GIFTS
✪ Los Angeles County Store

If you love Los Angeles, and you want a gift that's unique to our city, come to the L.A. County Store. This millennial version of a country store is filled with locally made L.A.- and California-themed goods. This small shop is in a typical Silver Lake strip mall; inside you can peruse fun knickknacks like children's books about Los Angeles, pillows decorated with hand-sewn maps of Echo Park, and California-shaped cutting boards. Prices are reasonable, especially for this part of town.

MAP 6: 4333 Sunset Blvd., 323/928-2781, https://lacountystore.com; Mon. noon-5pm, Tues.-Fri. noon-7pm, Sat. 11am-7pm, Sun. 11am-5pm

Time Travel Mart

On the hunt for time-traveler sickness pills? Or teeth-darkening strips? You're in luck, because the Time Travel Mart has all that and more. This little shop sells a handful of tongue-in-cheek clothing, goods, posters, and accessories. It's a playful place to stop in and buy a cheeky present for yourself or any loved one with a good sense of humor. And you can feel good about your purchase—all proceeds go to 826LA, a nonprofit that helps kids to develop their creative and expository writing skills.

MAP 6: 1714 Sunset Blvd., 213/413-3388, www.timetravelmart.com; daily noon-6pm

BARBERSHOPS
Franky's

Franky's is a one-stop barbershop that epitomizes rock'n'roll cool. At Franky's, you can get a stylish haircut for a great price, pick up a vintage Guns N' Roses record, and leave with a Smashing Pumpkins tour T-shirt. Franky's friendly and super-casual staff will make you feel welcome while you get your hair washed and cut. Even if you don't need a trim, stop in on your way down Sunset Boulevard just for music and the atmosphere. Walk-ins are welcome.

MAP 6: 3323 Sunset Blvd., 323/668-2088, http://frankysbarberboutique.blogspot.com; Tues.-Fri. 11am-7pm, Sat. 11am-6pm, Sun. 11am-5pm

CLOTHING AND ACCESSORIES
Dean Leather Accessories

While you're exploring the Silver Lake part of Sunset Boulevard, stop into Dean Leather Accessories for very upscale leather goods. As Dean's website says, this is leather with "a vintage feel, yet modern sensibility." Here you'll find a contemporary-looking

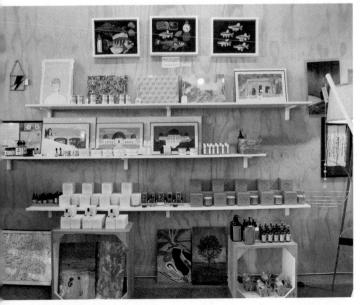

Los Angeles County Store

purple studded purse, made by hand. The watchbands here are particularly beautiful, and there are also classy covers for your phone, tablet, and laptop. There's only one Dean Leather Goods, so anything you buy here will be unique to this shop.

MAP 6: 3918 Sunset Blvd., 323/665-2766, https://dean-accessories.myshopify.com; Mon.-Sat. 11am-7pm, Sun. 11am-6pm

Retrosuperfuture

L.A. sun in your eyes? Wanting to sharpen your look? Come to Retrosuperfuture for sunglasses in trendy, retro, and classic styles. This store sells only sunglasses, and there are lots of beautiful pairs, so if you come wanting to purchase, the hard part will be deciding which pair to buy (many people end up with two). There are a number of high-profile retailers that sell Retrosuperfuture sunglasses, but this is one of only two brick-and-mortar Retrosuperfuture stores (the other is in New York City). Walk in a pedestrian, and leave looking like a celebrity.

MAP 6: 3531 Sunset Blvd., 323/906-9188, http://retrosuperfuture.com; Mon.-Sat. 11am-7pm, Sun. 11am-6pm

Co-Op 28

Co-Op 28 is a boutique gift store that sells vintage, new, and handmade goods, many from local and independent artists. Co-Op 28 takes up the two storefronts, and has an extensive selection of thoughtfully selected jewelry, clothing, furniture, home décor, and more. Head here if you're looking for a crafty gift for yourself or someone special. Staff at Co-Op 28 seem to take pride in their goods, so go ahead and ask about the origins of that vintage-looking guitar. Like many stores in this area, Co-Op 28 may induce a bit of sticker shock, but don't let that stop you from coming in—there are goods at all prices, and a sale rack in the back.

MAP 6: 1728 N. Vermont Ave., 323/669-2828, www.coop28.com; Mon.-Sat. 11am-7pm, Sun. 11am-6pm

Otherwild Goods & Services

Millennials, beware—you'll want everything in this store. But Otherwild Goods & Services is more than a store. It's actually a hybrid retail store and graphic design studio. The store itself offers select wares from local artists, including the very popular "Future is Female" T-shirts and sweatshirts. What's especially cool about Otherwild is that it empowers its customers to make their own goods via workshops that teach crafts like candle dipping, tarot reading, and bracelet making.

MAP 6: 1768 N. Vermont Ave., 323/546-8437, https://otherwild.com; daily 11am-7pm

Otherwild Goods & Services

Sumi's

Sumi's prides itself on offering "artist quality" accessories and gifts. This is where you can find handmade pyrite earrings; a hand-dyed, blue ombre, fair-trade scarf from Ethiopia; or a clementine-colored clutch made in Finland by the store owner's mom. In short, each piece here was chosen with love, and there's a lot to choose from at a range of prices, making Sumi's an excellent stop for the savvy shopper.

MAP 6: 1812 N. Vermont Ave., 323/660-0869, www.sumisanywhere.com; Mon.-Thurs. 10am-8pm, Sat. 10am-9pm, Sun. 11am-6pm

JEWELRY
Artisan L.A. Jewelry

Artisan L.A. is a small shop in the commercial area of Vermont Avenue that offers a beautiful selection of locally made jewelry, as well as custom-made jewelry services. The staff is helpful and approachable, which makes this feel like a true neighborhood gem (pun intended). You may pay more for a piece here than you would at a chain store, but you'll also get a higher standard of quality and service. Julio, the shop owner and jewelry maker, is the heartbeat of this welcoming establishment.

MAP 6: 1856 N. Vermont Ave., 323/644-5699, www.artisanla.com; Tues.-Sat. noon-7pm

FURNITURE AND INTERIOR DECOR
Mohawk General store

If you're in Silver Lake and wanting to shop, check out Mohawk General Store for both men's and women's designer duds. There's a lot of beautiful pieces here, from clothing to shoes to jewelry, swimwear, and intimates. There's also a respectable collection of tasteful home goods, such as brass paperweights and Japanese sake glasses. Mohawk is set up like a studio apartment, which makes it fun to browse for goods that fit all parts of your home. Whether you're looking for a thoughtful gift or something special for yourself, Mohawk will probably have

something you want. You may experience a bit of sticker shock, as Mohawk sits in the midst of many of nouveau-riche hipsters.

MAP 6: 4011 Sunset Blvd., 323/669-1601, www.mohawkgeneralstore.com; Mon.-Sat. 11am-7pm, Sun. 11am-6pm

Bar Keeper

Bar Keeper

Amateur (or seasoned) bartenders, you've found your spot. Bar Keeper is a specialty store that sells new and vintage barware, as well as the liquors to keep your own bar stocked. Right in the heart of Silver Lake, Bar Keeper has all types of bar tools (like muddlers and strainers), tasteful bar glasses in a diversity of shapes, colors, and sizes, and your choice of hundreds of bitters and spirits. Feeling overwhelmed? Bar Keeper's friendly staff will give you some helpful purchasing suggestions.

MAP 6: 3910 Sunset Blvd., 323/669-1675, www.barkeepersilverlake.com; Sun.-Thurs. 11am-6pm, Fri.-Sat. 11am-7pm

BOOKS
Skylight Books

Get lost in the thousands of carefully selected books in this independently owned neighborhood bookstore. Skylight takes up almost a full block right on Vermont Avenue and is packed wall to wall with both best-selling and hard-to-find titles (and there's a live tree growing under the mid-store skylight!). There's a respectable children's book section, fun books about Los Angeles, and some gifts for your smarty-pants friends. Check out Skylight's online event calendar to learn about scheduled book readings, discussions, and signings.

MAP 6: 1818 N. Vermont Ave., 323/660-1175, www.skylightbooks.com; daily 10am-10pm

Stories

A book lover's paradise, Stories has a tome for everyone. Here you'll find a local comic book next to a classic 18th-century novel next to a collection of essays on neo-feminism. This is a really special place for readers and intellectuals, especially if you're looking for new titles to add to your to-read list. It's also a great place to buy a gift—the collection of coffee-table books is especially fun to peruse. There's a cafe in the back, so buy your books, order a latte, and get lost in the pages.

MAP 6: 1716 Sunset Blvd., 213/413-3733, https://storiesla.com; Sun.-Thurs. 8am-11pm, Fri.-Sat. 8am-midnight

KIDS' STUFF
La La Ling

Come to La La Ling for adorable, trendy, hipster-chic children's clothing with fashionably high prices. Searching for a Guns N' Roses, Star Wars, or AC/DC onesie? You've come to the right place. How about a faux-fur-collared leopard-print hoodie for your three-year-old niece? La La Ling has that, too. In addition to clothing, there are cute stuffed animals and also a handful of supplies for parents. La La Ling is a small shop, which makes it an easy and quick stop for some very L.A. kids' gifts.

MAP 6: 1810 N. Vermont Ave., 323/664-4400, www.lalaling.com; Mon.-Sat. 10am-7pm, Sun. 10am-6pm

Downtown   Map 7

MALLS AND MARKETS
Santee Alley

Santee Alley is not for the faint of heart—it's crowded, sometimes hot, and many of the vendors don't speak English. It is, however, for the intrepid shopper. You'll find tons of bargains here on everything from incense to sneakers to suitcases, and you'll have a very real experience of a Mexican street market. Santee Alley is just a few blocks long, but it's packed with shops, stalls, and street vendors, most of whom only take cash (no cards). It's on the outskirts of Downtown, and not a place you want to be after dark.

MAP 7: 210 E. Olympic Blvd., 213/488-1153, www.thesanteealley.com; Mon.-Sat. 9am-6pm, Sun. 9am-5pm

Santee Alley

GIFTS

Q Pop

Both a gallery and unique boutique, Q Pop sells funky items created by Japanese artists and designers. Among its wares are Harajuku fashion from designers in Tokyo and toys from Japanese American sculptors. Q Pop is a place for both trendsetters and kids-at-heart, and it hosts several art shows every year (there's also art for sale). If you're looking for a special gift or something out of the ordinary to take home, swing by Q Pop.

MAP 7: 319 E. 2nd St., Suite 121, 213/687-7767, http://qpopshop.com/main; Wed.-Sat. 2pm-8pm, Sun. 2pm-7pm

2nd Street Cigar Lounge and Gallery

The 2nd Street Cigar Lounge and Gallery is more than just a cigar shop. It's a shop, lounge, and art gallery all rolled into one (cigar, perhaps). The cigars are well-stocked and high quality, and there are big, comfy leather chairs to enjoy them in. Be sure to browse the local art and chat with the friendly staff or patrons.

MAP 7: 124 W 2nd St., 213/452-4416, http://2ndstreetcigars.com; 10:30am-9pm Mon.-Tues., 10:30am-10pm Wed., 10:30am-12am Thurs., 10:30am-2am Fri., 12pm-2am Sat., 12pm-8pm Sun.

CLOTHING AND ACCESSORIES

Raggedy Threads

Raggedy Threads has been one of L.A.'s favorite vintage shops since 2002. Its website says it sells "quality workwear and denim," which is true, but there's a lot more here, too. The clothes are Americana inspired, with lots of overalls, baseball caps, leather boots, and patterned dresses. Raggedy Threads is an especially great place to pick up a one-of-a-kind vintage

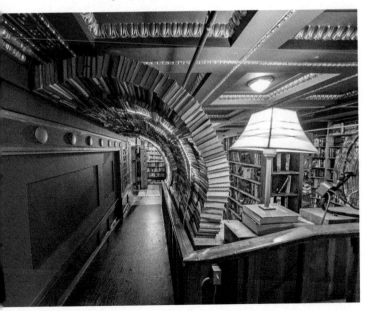

The Last Bookstore

tee, and it's tucked into a cute corner of Little Tokyo's pedestrian mall. Expect to pay L.A. prices for that 1960s satchel.

MAP 7: 330 E. 2nd St., 213/620-1188, www. raggedythreads.com; Mon.-Sat. noon-8pm, Sun. noon-6pm

RIF LA

This is a shop for sneakerheads (i.e., people who collect exclusive sneakers, Nikes in particular). RIF has an "I'm cooler than you" vibe and a lot of its sneakers are super-exclusive, so expect to pay top dollar for that hard-to-find pair of kicks. If you're into sneaker culture, this is a must-stop—it's practically a museum of rare shoes. You might pay more than you'd expect for your pair, but you also might see a music mogul or one of the L.A. Lakers shopping alongside you.

MAP 7: 334 E. 2nd St., 213/617-0252, www. rif.la; Mon. noon-5pm, Tues.-Sat. noon-7pm, Sun. noon-6pm

BOOKS

✪ The Last Bookstore

Make sure you stumble across the Last Bookstore. It has expanded exponentially since it first opened in a small loft in 2005; today, it covers an entire downtown block and houses more than 250,000 titles. In addition to both new and used books, there's other cool stuff for sale, such as vinyl records and graphic novels. The Last Bookstore's labyrinth—featuring a book tunnel and a flying book display—is a great place to take some pics. It may be crowded on weekends and toasty on summer days, but if you love books, it's worth braving the crowd to visit this ironically named shop.

MAP 7: 453 S. Spring St., 213/488-0599, http://lastbookstorela.com, Mon.-Thurs. 10am-10pm, Fri.-Sat. 10am-11pm, Sun. 10am-9pm

Hennesy & Ingals

Hennesy & Ingals

Hennesy & Ingals is a classy, impressive bookstore. Since its first L.A. opening in 1963, Hennesy & Ingals has stayed true to its focus, stocking an in-depth collection of books on art, art history, architecture, photography, interior design, graphic design, and landscaping. This is a good place to find, for example, a book called *Pirates: Culture & Style from the 13th Century to the Present*. This bright new Hennesy & Ingals location was opened in 2016.

MAP 7: 300 S. Santa Fe Ave., 213/437-2130, www.hennesseyingalls.com; daily 10am-8pm

WHERE TO STAY

L.A. hotels have their own personalities, just like everyone else in L.A. The Beverly Hills Hotel, for example, is a pink-and-green bubble of luxury that has been a home-away-from-home for celebrities for decades. Then there's The Standard in Downtown L.A.—with possibly the hippest rooftop pool scene in California. And you can't forget about the beachy bungalows in Santa Monica and Venice.

L.A. has more than its fair share of high-end hotels, but there are also affordable options in all major neighborhoods. In general, hotel rooms cost more the closer you are to the beach, so expect to pay a minimum of $200 per night to stay in Santa Monica or Venice. Room rates will increase as the weather gets warmer.

The good news is that there's no room shortage in Los Angeles—most neighborhoods have a hotel every few blocks and plenty of room for travelers. But don't put off making your reservation, especially if you're coming here during summer months or the winter holidays. Book 90 days in advance if you can to get the best deals and options.

The Beverly Hills Hotel

CHOOSING WHERE TO STAY
Santa Monica
Santa Monica has several grand hotels with ocean view rooms and a sprinkling of budget-conscious inns. Santa Monica is one of the most popular tourist destinations in the city, so rooms fill up quickly here. Try to book your room at least 90 days in advance.

HIGHLIGHTS

✪ **BEST POOL WITH A VIEW:** Mediterranean-inspired **Casa del Mar** has one of L.A.'s only pools with a view of the Pacific as well as a great location near the Santa Monica Pier (page 204).

✪ **BEST BEACH BOUTIQUE: The Rose Hotel** offers minimalist Cali luxury, complete with cruisers for rent, Stumptown coffee, and onsite surf teachers (page 206).

✪ **BEST PLACE TO LIVE LIKE A CELEBRITY:** The private bunga-lows of the **Hotel Bel-Air** are the perfect place to escape like a ce-lebrity—far away from the city bustle but still in close proximity to five-star amenities (page 208).

✪ **BEST OLD HOLLYWOOD GLAMOUR: The Hollywood Roosevelt Hotel** presides like a king over Hollywood Boulevard. Stars like Marilyn Monroe called this hotel home and today's celebs still stay here, too (page 208).

✪ **BEST POOL SCENES:** For a more chic, upscale stay, head to the **Mondrian Los Angeles** in West Hollywood. For hipper, more industrial vibes, it's **The Standard** in Downtown (pages 210 and 212).

✪ **BEST WINE BAR:** In Los Feliz, the trendy **Hotel Covell** is one of L.A.'s hottest boutique hotels. The adjoining Bar Covell has a world-class selection of wine and beer (page 211).

✪ **BEST HIPSTER VIBES:** You'll be greeted by a neon sign, concrete floors, and in-room record players at hipster's paradise **Ace Hotel** (page 212).

✪ **BEST BARGAIN:** The **Freehand Hotel** is a friendly spot with a per-fect location, dorm room options, and lots of friendly travelers (page 213).

PRICE KEY

$	Less than $200 per night
$ $	$200-350 per night
$ $ $	$350-450 per night
$ $ $ $	More than $450 per night

Venice

Venice has done a good job of staying low-key despite its immense popularity among travelers. It's happening here during the day and comparably quite at night. Venice is close to Santa Monica but considerably further from the rest of L.A's more popular neighborhoods.

Beverly Hills

If you're looking for luxury, you really can't go wrong in Beverly Hills. Pretty much every hotel here is posh. If you want to splurge or get a feel for how L.A.'s rich and famous relax, look no further. Depending on where you stay, it might be a hassle to get to more sight-heavy neighborhoods, like nearby Hollywood.

Hollywood

Hollywood is the place to stay if you want to be in the center of it all. It's centrally located between Downtown to the east and Santa Monica to the west, so it's a good home base for exploring the rest of the city. You can choose from a variety of hotels here in multiple price ranges. The downside is that it's harder to find peace and quiet. Book well in advance—everyone else wants to stay here, too.

West Hollywood

If you enjoy a good nighttime scene, consider staying in West Hollywood. There are a handful of unique hotels here, including the iconic Chateau Marmot (a hot celeb scene) and the ivy-covered Petit Ermitage. Feeling particularly adventurous? Book a room on the Sunset Strip and party all night long.

Echo Park, Los Feliz, and Silver Lake

There aren't a lot of lodging options in these residential neighborhoods, but the hip east side isn't a bad option if you're planning on spending a lot of time in Hollywood or Downtown but value peace and quiet or want to feel like a local. It'll be a trek to the beach, though.

Downtown

Staying on a higher floor in a downtown hotel will give you those thrilling cityscape views and put you in walking distance of a plethora of art and cultural gems. You'll also be near several Metro lines and the trains at Union Station.

ALTERNATIVE LODGING OPTIONS

There are plenty of short-term and alternative housing options in Los Angeles. For **short-term rentals** (one week to a couple months), check out Homeaway, VRBO, and AirBnB, all of which offer property rentals directly from the owner. Booking this way is great for cheap, last-minute stays. It's also a great way to experience the city in a uniquely local way; you can book a hip, art-filled loft Downtown or a straight-up mansion in Beverly Hills. Use caution when booking; make sure that anyone you rent from has a good number of positive reviews. Be aware that these options don't always offer the same amenities that hotels do, and privacy can be a factor depending on that rental's specific situation.

If you need to catch an early morning flight, there are plenty of hotel options within two miles of the **Los Angeles International Airport** (LAX), many of which offer shuttle options. The Hyatt Regency Los Angeles Airport is the most luxurious option, and the Best Western Plus Suites Hotel Inglewood is a good budget-friendly choice.

WHERE TO STAY IF...

YOU LOVE THE BEACH...
...stay in **Santa Monica,** where you can ride a bike for miles along the ocean, explore the Santa Monica Pier, and catch some of the prettiest sunsets in the city.

YOU WANT TO GET AWAY FROM IT ALL (AND DON'T MIND PAYING FOR IT)...
...book a state-of-the-art bungalow at **Hotel Bel-Air,** where celebrities go for peace, quiet, and luxurious pampering.

YOU WANT TO PARTY...
...book a hotel on the **Sunset Strip,** where entertainment legends have spent many a long night.

YOU'RE A MOVIE BUFF...
...you gotta stay in **Hollywood** to learn about the history of the U.S. film industry and tour celebrity homes.

YOU'RE INTO THE ARTS...
...book a room **Downtown** to explore huge museums and budding galleries, catch some world-class live theater, enjoy a musical performance at the Walt Disney Concert Hall, or even catch a podcast recording.

YOU'RE LOOKING FOR AN LGBTQ SCENE...
...stay in **West Hollywood,** where gay is the best way!

YOU HAVE A NEW AGE SPIRIT...
...make yourself at home in **Venice,** where being a hippie never goes out of style.

YOU'RE LOOKING FOR A NEW OUTFIT...
...you're in luck. There's fantastic shops scattered across Los Angeles that cater to the needs of a diverse array of shoppers.

Santa Monica   Map 1

Shutters on the Beach $$$$

Shutters on the Beach is a big hotel that brilliantly creates the feeling of a charming seaside cottage. Almost every space is done with blue-and-white themes, and the service is impeccable. Shutters graciously allows the Pacific Ocean to be the true star of the show, but the hotel's welcoming pool deck with ocean views is a close runner-up. Lined with curtained cabanas and cushiony lounge chairs, this is a pool scene that you'll want to luxuriate in for hours—and with full poolside service, you can.

MAP 1: 1 Pico Blvd., 310/458-0030, www.shuttersonthebeach.com

✪ Casa del Mar $$$$

Set in a historic brick-and-sandstone building from the 1920s, Casa Del Mar boasts an expansive, Mediterranean-inspired lobby that is the true heartbeat of the hotel. With grand floor-to-ceiling windows overlooking the Pacific Ocean, two restaurants, a full bar, lots of comfy couches, and live music every night by the fireplace, this is truly a scene. If you can pull yourself away from the lobby, you must check out the heated pool and hot tub, which offer breathtaking day-and-night views of the beach, ocean, and Santa Monica Pier.

Shutters on the Beach

MAP 1: 1910 Ocean Way, 310/581-5533, www.hotelcasadelmar.com

Channel Road Inn $$

Tucked into Santa Monica Canyon, the 10-room Channel Road Inn is a bit removed from the center of town; if you're looking to decompress, come here to sip tea on the patio, read by the fireplace, and get a massage in the garden. When you ring the doorbell to this early-20th-century home, you'll be greeted by a cheery hostess who's wearing an apron because she just got done baking chocolate chip cookies for your room. Channel Road Inn has a daily wine and cheese (and more) happy hour, and also a full home-cooked breakfast every morning.

MAP 1: 219 W Channel Rd., 310/459-1920, www.channelroadinn.com

Sea Shore Motel $

Looking to stay in the heart of Santa Monica without paying Santa Monica prices? Consider the Sea Shore Motel, a sweet pink building that has welcomed travelers from around the world since 1972. The rooms are clean and the service is good in this family-owned motel, but the real draw here is location. Stay at the Sea Shore Motel and walk to all of Santa Monica's major sights, including the Santa Monica Pier, the 3rd Street Promenade, and Santa Monica State Beach.

MAP 1: 637 Main St., 310/392-2787, www. seashoremotel.com

Venice

Map 2

✪ The Rose Hotel $$

Searching for a beachy boutique? Look no further than the Rose Hotel, a two-story hideaway just a block from the beach. This small hotel offers minimalist Cali luxury, with beach cruisers for rent, Stumptown coffee and fresh morning pastries in the lobby, and even a "resident health nut" who will take you surfing. Prices start around $200 for rooms with shared bathrooms, $300 for a simple suite, and $700 for the penthouse. One downside—walls are thin throughout.
MAP 2: 15 Rose Ave., 301/450-3474, www.therosehotelvenice.com

Inn at Venice Beach $$

The Inn at Venice Beach is just a few blocks from the Venice Canals and within walking distance to Abbot Kinney Boulevard. The location is good for travelers who want to be in the heart of Venice but don't want their hotel to feel like a party. Rooms are clean and tasteful, updated to reflect Venice's charmingly ironic vibe. Request a room off the street if you'd prefer not to hear Washington Boulevard traffic.
MAP 2: 327 W. Washington Blvd., 301/821-2557, www.innatvenicebeach.com

Hotel Erwin $$

Location, location, location. Book a room in Hotel Erwin and stay in the middle of it all—steps from Venice Beach, the boardwalk, and the skate park, as well as walking distance from Abbot Kinney Boulevard. If you want to be at the center of the party, this is the place! Don't leave Hotel Erwin without checking out High Rooftop Lounge, located on the hotel's rooftop. Head up at twilight, order a cocktail, and hunker down to watch Mother Nature paint an exquisite sunset over the Pacific.
MAP 2: 1697 Pacific Ave., 301/452-1111, www.hotelirwin.com

Beverly Hills

Map 3

The Beverly Hills Hotel $$$$

Enter The Beverly Hills Hotel by walking through a marble entryway and up a thick red carpet. The hotel lobby is quiet, decorated in hushed pinks and greens. As either a guest or a visitor, you can appreciate the rich history of this first hotel of Beverly Hills, founded in 1912. The pool, for example, was christened in 1955 by starlet swimmer Esther Williams. Dine at the Polo Lounge and you may see a movie star. Reserve a room in either the main

The Beverly Hills Hotel

the Beverly Wilshire

building or the bungalows, which sit on 12 acres of jungle-esque gardens. Even if you're not a celebrity, an afternoon here will make you feel like one. MAP 3: 9641 Sunset Blvd., 310/276-2251, www.dorchestercollection.com/en/los-angeles/the-beverly-hills-hotel

Beverly Wilshire $$$$

What is it about the Beverly Wilshire that feels so darn fancy? Perhaps it's the diamond store sitting conspicuously into the lobby, the multiple Maseratis parked out front, or CUT, the famed steak house by chef Wolfgang Puck. Whatever the cause, the Beverly Wilshire certainly lives up to the "I'm richer than you" reputation it built through the movie *Pretty Woman*, filmed here in 1989. With two fantastic restaurants, a gorgeous pool, an expansive gym, a gleaming spa, and in-house shopping, the Beverly Wilshire is the type of hotel that's hard to leave. But leave you must, because Rodeo Drive's grandest shops are right down the street.

MAP 3: 9500 Wilshire Blvd., 310/275-5200, www.fourseasons.com/beverlywilshire

Sirtaj Hotel $$

Don't tell anyone about Sirtaj, because it's the best-kept secret in Beverly Hills. This modern boutique hotel, just steps from Rodeo Drive, is sleek and colorful, with an Indian-inspired flare. There are 32 rooms that are not huge but definitely large enough to feel comfortable. Its luxury-level rooms have king-size beds and private balconies. If you're looking for a clean, serene hotel with good service and a great location, Sirtaj is your best bet.

MAP 3: 120 S. Reeves Dr., 310/248-2402, www.sirtajhotel.com

Viceroy L'Ermitage Beverly Hills $$$$

L'Ermitage defines understated elegance. It beckons with muted palettes, superb service, and luxurious accommodations right on Wilshire Boulevard, one of the main arteries into the heart of Beverly Hills. While other high-end

Beverly Hills hotels feel a bit stuck in the past, L'Ermitage's vibe is clean and modern. What's special about L'Ermitage is that it gives you privacy while also taking care of your every need. Check out the rooftop pool, which has views of the area's undulating hills.

MAP 3: 9291 Burton Way, 310/278-3344, www.viceroyhotelsandresorts.com/en/beverlyhills

✪ Hotel Bel-Air $$$

The Hotel Bel-Air is a Beverly Hills icon. This is where Marilyn Monroe took some of her most famous pool photos, and where stars of today come for the privacy of state-of-the-art suites snuggled into a tree-lined canyon. Yes, this is a place for celebs, but it's also a place anyone can visit for an upscale lunch at the Wolfgang Puck restaurant, cocktails by the fire at the Bar & Lounge, or a quiet day at the Hotel Bel-Air Spa, known as one of L.A.'s best. My favorite part about the Hotel Bel-Air, besides the suspenseful drive up into Bel-Air to get there, is the graceful swans that glide along the Bel-Air's own personal pond. Nice touch.

MAP 3: 701 Stone Canyon Rd., 310/472-1211, www.dorchestercollection.com/en/los-angeles/hotel-bel-air

Hollywood   Map 4

✪ The Hollywood Roosevelt Hotel $$

Located on the Walk of Fame, The Hollywood Roosevelt Hotel exudes Old Hollywood elegance. In 1929, it hosted the first Academy Awards and has since housed dozens of movie stars, including Marilyn Monroe. Although the Spanish Colonial Revival building feels like a throwback, the pool is quite modern, with a live DJ, cabanas for rent, and a party-like feel on the weekends. The Roosevelt has two swanky bars, three restaurants, and a vintage bowling alley.

MAP 4: 7000 Hollywood Blvd., 323/892-8835, www.thehollywoodroosevelt.com

Banana Bungalow $

For only $33 a night, you can share a comfortable dorm-like room with up to eight other travelers, hang out on a generous outdoor patio, and let loose during nightly planned activities like karaoke, talent shows, and bar crawls. This is a clean space with a secure front door, located right in the heart of Hollywood on Hollywood Boulevard. Private rooms with balconies are available. Freebies include Wi-Fi, breakfast, all-day coffee/tea, and limited parking. There are multiple locations throughout the city.

MAP 4: 5920 Hollywood Blvd., 323/469-2500, www.bananabungalows.com

one of the swanky restaurants in The Hollywood Roosevelt Hotel

Farmer's Daughter Hotel $$

The best thing about Farmer's Daughter might be its location on Fairfax Avenue, across the street from the Grove and the Original Farmers Market. Despite all that, Farmer's Daughter maintains a boutique-y feel. Small touches—bikes to borrow, a lending library, and rubber ducks in the pool—make this place feel special. Because this is such a busy location, you may want to book somewhere else if peace and quiet are your top priorities.

MAP 4: 115 S. Fairfax Ave., 323/937-3930, http://farmersdaughterhotel.com

Mama Shelter $$

Mama Shelter is a cheerful, colorful, on-trend hotel that provides close access to Hollywood hot spots without blowing your budget. Each room is uniquely decorated, and many have great views of the Hollywood Hills. At sunset, bring your camera and head up to Mama Shelter's popular rooftop bar.

MAP 4: 6500 Selma Ave., 323/785-6666, www.mamashelter.com

Magic Castle Hotel $$

Magic Castle is super-popular with travelers looking for clean, unpretentious digs. This is an updated mid-century establishment, with an outdoor pool, free snacks for guests, and excellent service. It's located a block away from TCL Chinese Theatre. As a quirky bonus, it's next door to the Magic Castle, a private club for magicians.

MAP 4: 7025 Franklin Ave., 323/851-0800, http://magiccastlehotel.com

West Hollywood   Map 5

Chateau Marmont $$$$

Tucked into a West Hollywood hillside, the Chateau Marmont is a swanky place to stay in the midst of the Sunset Strip. Its French-styled white building has become somewhat of a neighborhood landmark, and you'll often find paparazzi waiting outside to catch a coveted shot of a budding starlet. The Chateau Marmont was built in 1929 and could perhaps use a few renovations, but what it lacks in updates it makes up for in Old Hollywood charm. The hotel's historic celebrity watering hole, Bar Marmont, is sadly closed indefinitely for renovation.

MAP 5: 8221 Sunset Blvd., 323/656-1010, www.chateaumarmont.com

Sunset Tower Hotel $$$

Come to Sunset Tower to experience Old Hollywood glamour right on the Sunset Strip. Included in the National Register of Historic Places, this art deco-style tower was built in 1929, and during its early years was home to celebrities including John Wayne and Howard Hughes. Today, the Sunset Tower Hotel serves in style, offering luxurious suites, a classy bar, and an irresistible rooftop pool.

MAP 5: 8358 Sunset Blvd., 323/654-7100, www.sunsettowerhotel.com

Best Western Plus Sunset Plaza Hotel $$

Location, location, location. If you're looking to stay on the Sunset Strip and pay less than $300 per night, the Best Western Plus Sunset Plaza is

Chateau Marmont

your place. Its rooms are comfy and clean, the pool is pretty, and staff are super-friendly and helpful. The unpretentious vibe here can be quite refreshing in the midst of the bustling West Hollywood, and the location on Sunset Boulevard puts you within walking distance of all major West Hollywood attractions, and within a few miles of Beverly Hills and Hollywood's Walk of Fame.

MAP 5: 8400 Sunset Blvd., 323/654-0750, www.sunsetplazahotel.com

Petit Ermitage $$$

If you're looking for a classy, California-style hotel with a great West Hollywood location, consider the Petit Ermitage. Its ivy-covered building sits on a relatively quiet residential street that's within walking distance to both the Sunset Strip and the shops and restaurants of Santa Monica Boulevard. Its rooftop—complete with a swanky restaurant and sparkling saltwater pool—is a great place to unwind after a long day of traveling. During summer nights, you can catch a movie there, complete with warm blankets and hot popcorn!

MAP 5: 8822 Cynthia St., 310/854-1114, www.petitermitage.com/home

✪ Mondrian Los Angeles $$

The Mondrian Los Angeles is everything you might want a West Hollywood hotel to be—glamorous and trendy-chic, with sweeping views of the city. If the Sunset Strip is a party, the Mondrian often feels like the center of that party. Perhaps the best thing about the Mondrian is its Skybar lounge, which sits on an expansive wooden pool deck overlooking much of the city. And if you're looking to stay on the Sunset Strip, the location really can't be beat. On weekends, be ready for lots of people coming and going, and frenetic pool parties during the summer.

MAP 5: 8440 Sunset Blvd., 323/650-8999, www.morganshotelgroup.com/mondrian

Elan Hotel $$
Elan is a quiet, clean, and affordable hotel in the heart of West Hollywood. It's not the place for partiers, but it is a place for families, couples, and more introverted travelers. What I like about Elan is that it manages to be upscale yet unpretentious, in a city that has pretension to spare. There's a complimentary wine and cheese happy hour every night and a continental breakfast each morning. Because it's a few blocks from the Beverly Center mall and Melrose Avenue, you'll be within walking distance of some seriously fabulous shopping.

MAP 5: 8435 Beverly Blvd., 323/658-6663, www.elanhotel.com

Echo Park, Los Feliz, and Silver Lake   Map 6

Comfort Inn $
On the border of Silver Lake and Echo Park, this Comfort Inn is not necessarily a hotel you'd write home about, but it's clean and cheap and right on Sunset Boulevard, the main artery connecting Echo Park, Los Feliz, and Silver Lake. This part of Sunset Boulevard has lots of traffic, so it's not quiet, but this friendly two-star hotel puts you within walking distance of great shops and restaurants, and it's just 1.5 miles from Dodger Stadium.

MAP 6: 2717 Sunset Blvd., 213/413-8222, www.comfortinnlosangelesca.com

✪ Hotel Covell $$$
For a while, the Hotel Covell was a well-kept Los Angeles secret; today, it's one of the hottest boutique hotels in town. There are only five rooms here and they're all hyper-designed 300-900-square-foot suites with kitchenettes and hardwood floors. Some are Old West-inspired, while others have a more New York or 1970s Paris feel. Whichever your room, you'll be one of just a few special guests, and Hotel Covell will take care of you. Because these rooms are like small apartments, some guests (particularly those in the film or music industry) choose to stay here long-term. Be sure to check out the adjoining Bar Covell for a world-class selection of wine and beer.

MAP 6: 4626 Hollywood Blvd., 323/660-4300, http://hotelcovell.com/hotel-covell

Downtown Map 7

Omni Los Angeles $$

Omni Los Angeles is a pretty, under-stated, and reliable hotel that's right in the center of everything you'll do in Downtown. Its 17-story tower sits atop Bunker Hill, so you'll have great city views from any room. The Omni is not flashy or trendy; it's quiet, with muted colors and cascading orchids in the lobby. As a guest, you can swim in the heated lap pool year-round, and stay within walking distance to Downtown's best shops, restaurants, and art galleries.

MAP 7: 251 S. Olive St., 213/617-3300, www.omnihotels.com

✪ The Standard $$

In the middle of Downtown L.A. is The Standard, a trendy, modern hotel with a retro-1960s vibe. There are platform beds, roomy tubs, peek-a-boo showers, and a rooftop poolside bar with stunning views of L.A. The Rooftop at the Standard hosts regular parties and is one of the most happening places to be on a Saturday night. There's also a gym, a barbershop, and a restaurant open 24-7.

MAP 7: 550 S. Flower St., 213/892-8080, www.standardhotels.com

✪ Ace Hotel $$

The Ace Hotel is too cool for me…but don't let that stop you from staying at one of L.A.'s hottest hot spots. When

The Standard

you arrive at the front door (with a neon sign that simply says "hotel"), a smiling bellman (with a long ponytail and backwards hat) will guide you inside. Don't be surprised if your room has concrete floors and a state-of-the-art record player. If you're hungry, you don't have to go far: Upstairs, Ace's popular rooftop restaurant, serves good meals all day long (it's also a popular bar after dark).

MAP 7: 929 S. Broadway, 213/623-3233, www.acehotel.com

✪ Freehand Hotel $-$$$

Freehand, both a hotel and a hostel, is the place for travelers looking for something ruggedly luxurious and off the beaten path. You can book anything here from a bed in a shared room to a top-floor suite with city views. Freehand has two great bars—one in the lobby and one on the rooftop deck—and even a tea service to enliven

Freehand Hotel

you after your travels. The atmosphere is communal and convivial; expect to make friends.

MAP 7: 416 W. 8th St., 213/612-0021, https://freehandhotels.com/los-angeles

DAY TRIPS

Los Angeles County is so sprawling and multifaceted that there are even destinations within L.A. County limits that should be treated like day trips—Malibu and Pasadena, for example, are separated enough by distance, traffic, and atmosphere to feel worlds apart.

Malibu

There's something for every traveler in Southern California, so whether you're looking to get to know more of Los Angeles or to get away entirely from the city, you're in luck. Upscale beach bums can lay their towels down in Malibu or Orange County. Culture buffs can spend hours at the Huntington estates in Pasadena. Kids of all ages can have magical adventures at Disneyland or Universal Studios. Couples can get away on a romantic overnight stay on Catalina Island.

PLANNING YOUR TIME

You can easily spend a single day in Malibu, Orange County, or Pasadena. Disneyland or Universal Studios can be done in a day, but expect to be exhausted by the end of it; if you have more time, consider spending a night nearby. It takes the most amount of time and energy to reach Catalina Island (one hour by car, then a 90-minute ferry), so plan on spending at least one night there to fully enjoy it. Except for Orange County and Disneyland, which are about 20 miles from each other, most of these day trips are spread far apart. So, choose one that you're really excited about and add it to your Los Angeles itinerary.

All of these destinations are best accessed by car. If you're driving, plan in advance for traffic. Highways quickly clog during rush hours, so avoid driving 8am-10am and 4pm-7pm on weekdays. Saturdays and Sundays have noticeably less traffic, although the unpredictable traffic jam can always arise—it's a

HIGHLIGHTS

✪ **BEST TRIP BACK IN TIME:** Stroll around the **Getty Villa** and you'll feel like an ancient Roman emperor (page 217).

✪ **BEST SURF CULTURE:** For the quintessential southern California surf experience, head to Malibu's gorgeous **Surfrider Beach** or Orange County's **Huntington Beach** (pages 217 and 234).

✪ **MOST BREATHTAKING GARDENS:** Head to the **Huntington Botanical Gardens** for a tranquil afternoon among roses, succulents, and lush waterfalls—plus two art galleries and a library of rare and collectible books (page 222).

✪ **BEST PLACE TO BE A KID AGAIN:** Put on your Mickey ears at **Disneyland Park,** where magic happens daily (page 224).

✪ **BEST PLACE TO PRACTICE MAGIC:** Explore Hogwarts castle, shop at Hogsmeade, and dine at the Three Broomsticks in **The Wizarding World of Harry Potter** (page 231).

the Chinese Garden at Huntington Botanical Gardens

good idea to give yourself some extra padding on the time no matter where you're going.

Winter months (mostly January and February) tend to be rainy, so plan your beach time accordingly. Also, be aware of Southern California's "June gloom"—June tends to be our most overcast month. If you're looking to get a serious tan, it's better to come in July or August.

Malibu

Since the 1950s, Malibu has played a key role in popularizing American surf culture. In the 1950s and 1960s, Malibu gained a reputation for having some of the best waves in the U.S., and the town's beach culture blossomed rapidly. In 1966, Malibu surfer Miki Dora was featured in the classic American film *Endless Summer,* catapulting Malibu to the forefront of surfer havens. Malibu's popularity as a surf spot only continued to grow throughout the late 20th century. In 2010, Malibu's Surfrider Beach was declared the first-ever World Surfing Reserve.

Malibu is a definitely a surfer's paradise, but there's also plenty for those who prefer to watch from shore. Purposefully less developed than the rest of Los Angeles, Malibu is home to some of Southern California's most beautiful beaches. If you want to spend some real quality beach time, consider

Getty Villa's herb garden

Surfrider Beach

spending the night in one of Malibu's spectacular beachside hotels, which will give you time to taste local sushi, shop for ornate sandals, and ride a barreling wave.

Getting to Malibu will take you 30-90 minutes, depending on traffic.

SIGHTS
✪ GETTY VILLA

The Getty Villa (17985 Pacific Coast Hwy., 310/440-7300, www.getty.edu; 10am-5pm Wed.-Mon.; free admission, advance tickets required, $15 parking) is modeled after an ancient Roman country home and evokes the opulence of its setting in the Pacific Palisades. Make your way through the villa's abundant sculptures and shimmering ancient relics that cover over 7,000 years of history—from the Stone Age to the fall of the Roman empire. The Getty Villa's grand fountain, quiet gardens, and eucalyptus breeze will make you feel like you've just visited the spa.

SPORTS AND ACTIVITIES
BEACHES
✪ Surfrider Beach

Malibu is known as having some of the best surfing waves in Los Angeles, and Surfrider Beach (23050 Pacific Coast Hwy., 424/526-7777, http://beaches.

lacounty.gov) might have the smoothest waves of all. Even if you don't surf these mellow rolls, Surfrider beach is a cozy place to lay your towel, catch some rays, and do some serious pretty people-watching. It's right on Highway 1, so choose another beach if you're looking for a secluded feeling. But if you're looking for a landmark that has been a part of Malibu's surfing scene for decades, head to Surfrider.

Leo Carrillo State Park

Just 28 miles north of Santa Monica on the Pacific Coast Highway, you can explore tide pools and caves at Leo Carrillo State Park (35000 W. Pacific Coast Hwy., 310/457-8143, www.parks.ca.gov, 8am-10pm daily, $12 per vehicle). A point break offshore draws surfers when the right swell hits. Dogs are also allowed on a beach at the northern end of the park.

Zuma Beach

Zuma Beach (30000 Pacific Coast Hwy., 19 miles north of Santa Monica, surf report 310/457-9701, http://beaches.lacounty.gov, sunrise-sunset daily, parking $3-12.50) has a nice big stretch of clean white sand that fills up fast on summer weekends. It's also a popular surf and boogie-boarding break. Grab a spot on the west side of the Pacific Coast Highway (CA-1) for free parking, or pay for one of the more than 2,000 spots in the beach parking lot. Zuma has all the amenities you need for a full day out at the beach, from restrooms and showers to a kid-friendly snack bar and a beachside boardwalk.

Malibu Lagoon State Beach

Malibu Lagoon State Beach (23200 Pacific Coast Hwy., 818/880-0363, www.parks.ca.gov) might be my

El Matador State Beach

favorite beach in Los Angeles. To get to the beach after parking, you'll need to take a little walk around the lagoon to get to the ocean—I think this walk keeps the beach itself from getting too crowded. Waves break far from shore, which provides a calm swimming area for non-surfers. Beautiful birds frequent the marshy lagoon, which is a state-preserved ecosystem. To learn more about the area's history, starting with the Chumash tribe, check out the adjacent **Adamson House and Malibu Lagoon Museum** (310/456-8432, www.adamsonhouse. org; grounds 8am-sunset daily, tours 11am-3pm Thurs.-Sun.; $7 adult, $2 child 6-16).

El Matador State Beach

Bring your camera (or smartphone) to El Matador State Beach (32350 Pacific Coast Hwy., 818/880-0363, www.parks.ca.gov) for some otherworldly sunset shots. The beach is filled with interesting caverns and rock formations that take on a life of their own with each changing tide. Getting to this beach requires a respectable jaunt down an unpaved and sometimes steep trail. So, it's not easy to get to, but if beauty is your top beach priority, El Matador is the place to be.

SURFING

This self-proclaimed "best surf school in the world" is at least one of the best in Malibu. **Aqua Surf School** (2701 Barnard Way, Santa Monica, 310/902-7737, www.aquasurfschool.com; $80-155 pp) offers lessons to people of all ages and has a reputation for being particularly great with kids. Here you can rent a surfboard and wetsuit, and register for either a private or group lesson with one of the school's talented instructors. During your lesson, you'll learn not just about surfing and water safety, but also about local ecology.

HIKING
Santa Monica Mountains

Tuna Canyon (Malibu, http://trails.lacounty.gov) offers a quintessential California hike up rolling hills to wide-angle ocean views. There are some steep inclines in this 1,255-acre park, so it's a good place to get a real workout. To get here, drive up Fernwood Pacific, a winding road, about four miles to arrive at an unmarked trailhead. Once you start hiking, you may come across a stone labyrinth created by some of California's freer sprits. Bring plenty of water on hot days.

Wanting a Zen wilderness experience? Head to **Solstice Canyon** (3455 Solstice Canyon Rd., 805/370-2301, www.nps.gov/samo), a tranquil hiking spot not too far from Highway 1. This generous park offers a handful of hiking trails that take you through charming fields and up the Santa Monica Mountains to find blue ocean views. Wear sunscreen because there aren't too many tall trees.

RESTAURANTS

Moonshadows (20356 Pacific Coast Hwy., 310/456-3010, www.moon-shadowsmalibu.com; 11:30am-10pm Sun.-Thurs., 11:30am-11pm Fri., 11am-11pm Sat.; $15-40) is a Malibu icon. Its floor-to-ceiling windows and wooden patio provide the most beautiful green and blue ocean views, so it's no wonder that celebrities have held meetings here for decades. Take a taste of Malibu's good life—sip on a California chardonnay, chew on freshly grilled octopus, and marvel as the sun sets over the Pacific. You really can't go wrong with an evening at Moonshadows.

Malibu Farm (23000 Pacific Coast Hwy., 310/456-1112, www.malibu-farm.com; 11am-9pm Mon.-Fri., 9am-10pm Sat., 9am-9pm Sun.; $12-24) has not only fresh, farm-to-table (and sea-to-table) meals, but also arguably the best table views in the area. Sitting at the base of the Malibu Pier, Malibu Farm has 360-degree ocean views and breezes to chill even the hottest summer afternoon. The food is organic, delicious, and pricey (as most things are in Malibu). Breakfast and brunch are quite popular, when tables are first-come, first-served. For dinner, make a reservation and be sure to bring an extra layer to stay warm after dusk.

There are a lot of fancy restaurants in Malibu; in my opinion, the decidedly un-fancy Malibu Seafood (25653 Pacific Coast Hwy., 310/456-3430, www.malibuseafood.com; 11am-7:30pm daily; $10-30) rivals the best

of them. This is where to get high-quality, scrumptious seafood without a white tablecloth. This charming shop owned by local fishers serves fried, grilled, and steamed seafood with a side of coleslaw. Malibu Seafood's fish-and-chips have been a local favorite since it opened in 1972.

HOTELS

The Malibu Beach Inn (22878 Pacific Coast Hwy., 800/462-5428, www.malibubeachinn.com) brings understated luxury to your oceanside stay. The hotel itself is among some of Malibu's favorite restaurants and boutiques, just south of the Malibu Pier. Each of the inn's 37 rooms is carefully decorated with blues and green to match the sea. The inn's welcoming staff will help you plan your ideal Malibu excursion.

GETTING THERE AND AROUND

The best way to get to Malibu is by car. There are lots of rental car services around the city and especially by Los Angeles International Airport. Sometimes travelers hire private drivers and/or buses to get to Malibu rather than driving themselves. A 534 Metro bus will take you to Malibu, but it will take hours to get there from most places in the city. Once you get to Malibu, you'll want to have a car because not much is walkable—most shops and beaches are right on Highway 1, which has no sidewalks and is heavily trafficked.

Day Trips

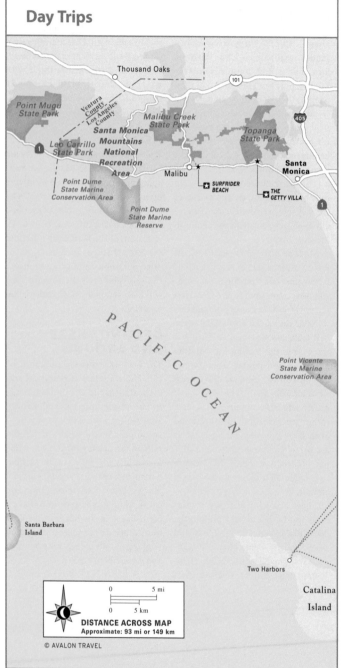

Thousand Oaks

101

405

Point Mugu
State Park

Ventura
County
Los Angeles
County

Malibu Creek
State Park

Topanga
State Park

Leo Carrillo
State Park

Santa Monica
Mountains
National
Recreation
Area

Santa
Monica

Malibu

★ SURFRIDER
BEACH

★ THE
GETTY VILLA

Point Dume
State Marine
Conservation Area

Point Dume
State Marine
Reserve

PACIFIC OCEAN

Point Vicente
State Marine
Conservation Area

Santa Barbara
Island

Two Harbors

Catalina
Island

0   5 mi

0   5 km

DISTANCE ACROSS MAP
Approximate: 93 mi or 149 km

© AVALON TRAVEL

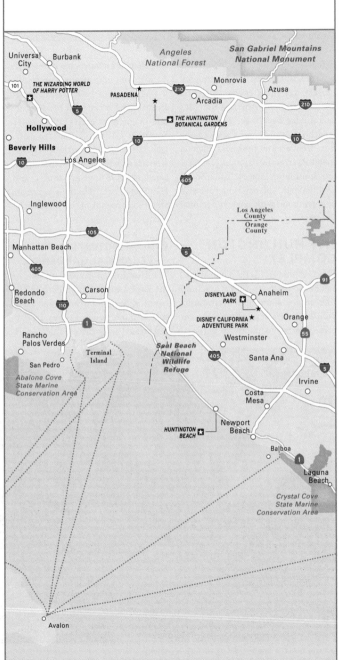

Universal City
Burbank
THE WIZARDING WORLD OF HARRY POTTER
Hollywood
Beverly Hills
Los Angeles
Inglewood
Manhattan Beach
Redondo Beach
Carson
Rancho Palos Verdes
San Pedro
Terminal Island
Abalone Cove State Marine Conservation Area
Avalon

Angeles National Forest
San Gabriel Mountains National Monument
Monrovia
PASADENA
Arcadia
Azusa
THE HUNTINGTON BOTANICAL GARDENS

Los Angeles County
Orange County

Seal Beach National Wildlife Refuge
DISNEYLAND PARK
Anaheim
DISNEY CALIFORNIA ADVENTURE PARK
Orange
Westminster
Santa Ana
Irvine
Costa Mesa
HUNTINGTON BEACH
Newport Beach
Balboa
Laguna Beach
Crystal Cove State Marine Conservation Area

Pasadena

Pasadena offers a quieter and greener taste of L.A. County. The Huntington Library has an extensive collection of European and American art. It's surrounded by 120 acres of specialized botanical gardens showcasing flora from around the world. Plan on spending an entire day or afternoon at the Huntington Library. And if you're a football fan, you can time your visit to correspond with January's annual Rose Bowl.

THE HUNTINGTON COMPLEX

The Huntington (1151 Oxford Rd., San Marino, 626/405-2100, www.huntington.org; 10am-5pm Wed.-Mon.; $13-29), a 207-acre complex, comprises enormous botanical gardens,

art galleries, an independent research library, and educational programs. It was the estate of Henry Edwards Huntington, a railroad and real estate magnate in early-20th-century Southern California, and his wife, Isabella. Your ticket includes admission to the Huntington Botanical Gardens, Huntington Library, and Huntington Art Collections, which are all on the grounds of the Huntington estate.

✪ HUNTINGTON BOTANICAL GARDENS

The Huntington gardens are one of the largest botanical gardens in the country, boasting over 15,000 plant species showcased in 12 separate garden areas. The Japanese Garden—with

the Japanese Garden at Huntington Botanical Gardens

222

its bonsai trees, ambling creek, and humble bridges—is a must-see. Also check out the California desert garden—it has some of the biggest cacti and succulents I've seen. On hot days, bring water and sunscreen, and perhaps wear a brimmed hat. You can bring your own picnic lunch, dine at one of five restaurants, or sip some Earl Grey at the Rose Garden Tea Room (noon-5pm Mon. and Wed.-Fri., 10:30am-5pm Sat.-Sun.; reservations recommended).

HUNTINGTON LIBRARY

Book lovers rejoice! The Huntington Library has some of the largest collections in the world in a few select areas that include English Renaissance 1500-1641, medieval manuscripts, and the American Southwest. What's more, it's a gorgeous, expansive building that has two fascinating permanent exhibitions—one showcasing original manuscripts from authors like Chaucer and Thoreau, the other highlighting great achievements in astronomy, natural history, and medicine. Library visitors can browse the entire collection—register in advance to read books in the special reading rooms.

HUNTINGTON ART COLLECTIONS

The Huntington Art Collections are housed in two separate buildings on the Huntington estate—the Huntington Art Gallery and the Virginia Stelle Scott Galleries of American Art. These galleries are filled with colorful pieces of European and American art from the 15th to the mid-20th century. My favorite permanent collection showcases the furniture, lighting, and stained-glass work of early 19th-century Craftsman-style

masters Charles Sumner Greene and Henry Mather Greene. The Huntington's gift shop sells some home decor items inspired by their exquisite work.

ENTERTAINMENT AND EVENTS
ROSE PARADE AND ROSE BOWL

The Rose Bowl football game has been an annual New Year's Day tradition since 1902. Each January 1, thousands of football fans flock to Rose Bowl Stadium (1001 Rose Bowl Dr., 626/577-3100, www.rosebowlstadium.com) to watch the annual Rose Bowl football playoff game (tickets $200-500). Thousands more line Pasadena streets for the Rose Parade, which honors American military veterans and those serving active duty. This festive parade features dozens of brilliantly designed floats, made almost completely of flowers. The parade and football game always happens on January 1, unless that day is a Sunday, in which case they take place on Monday, January 2.

Rose Parade

FOOD

Pasadena has a handful of great restaurants, and Union (37 E. Union St.,

626/795-5841, http://unionpasadena.com; 5pm-11pm Mon.-Fri., 4pm-11pm Sat., 4pm-10pm Sun.; $30-60) is one of them. Union's minimalist decor allows diners to focus on the fantastic fusion of Northern Italian and Southern Californian cuisines. The menu reflects Union's aesthetic sensibilities—a few starters, some vegetable dishes, several meat entrées, and, of course, the pasta. Don't come to Union without ordering a bowl of pasta—they're all divine.

HOTELS

For the full Huntington experience, stay at The Langham Huntington (1401 S. Oak Knoll Ave., 626/568-3900, www.langhamhotels.com), which is just two miles from the Huntington estate. Amenities include tennis courts, a heated pool, and 23 acres to use at your leisure for strolling, bocce ball, and other lawn games. When you're ready for an afternoon snack, head to the Langham's grand lobby for the traditional afternoon tea service—take your pick of delicate fruit tarts, scones with Devonshire cream, and French macarons.

GETTING THERE AND AROUND

Pasadena is another place you'll want to drive to. The 780 Metro bus and the Gold Line on the Metro rail do go to Pasadena, but once you get to Pasadena you'll really need a car to get around because it's a pretty big area without too much public transportation. Compared with L.A. proper, there's plenty of free parking in Pasadena.

Disneyland Resort

Ah, Disneyland. Southern California wouldn't be as sunny without its "Happiest Place on Earth." The Disneyland Resort is made of up of three main areas: Disneyland Park, the original amusement park that started it all in 1955; Disney California Adventure Park, a California-themed park that opened in 2001 with faster rides meant to appeal to older kids and adults; and Downtown Disney, a shopping and eating district outside the two parks.

If you leave Los Angeles in the early morning and beat rush hour traffic, you can do Disneyland's highlights in a day. Alternatively, if you want the full Disney experience, stay at one of Disney's hotels and explore both parks in full.

TOP EXPERIENCE

✪ DISNEYLAND PARK

Disneyland Park (1313 Disneyland Dr., Anaheim, 714/781-4636, http://disneyland.disney.go.com; 9am-midnight daily; prices vary) attracts a range of visitors. On one end of the spectrum are your die-hard Disney fans—people who get married at Disneyland and purchase some of Disney's most exclusive experiences; on the other end there are visitors who are just want to know what the fuss is all about. No matter where you land on this continuum, a trip to Disney will not disappoint. In one day here, you ride through space, shake hands with Minnie Mouse, and marvel at an incredible, state-of-the-art fireworks display over a castle. Yes, there are long lines and expensive gift stores, but that's part of the package!

ATTRACTIONS

There are eight areas, or "Lands," of Disneyland Park: Main Street, U.S.A.; Tomorrowland; Fantasyland; Mickey's Toontown; Frontierland; Critter Country; New Orleans Square; and Adventureland. In 2019, the park will debut the much-anticipated **Star Wars Land.**

You'll enter onto **Main Street, U.S.A.,** which offers shops, information booths, and other practicalities. Your first stop inside the park should be one of the information kiosks near the front entrance. Here you can get a map, a schedule of the day's events,

and the inside scoop on what's going on in the park during your visit. Don't miss viewing one of the parades down Main Street U.S.A.—it's a super-entertaining, music-filled experience.

Due north of Main Street is Sleeping Beauty's Castle and Fantasyland, with Mickey's Toontown beyond. To the east is Tomorrowland. Adventureland and Frontierland lie to the west of Main Street, with New Orleans Square to the west of Adventureland, and Critter Country in the far western reaches of the park.

Fantasyland rides tend to cater to the younger set. For many Disneyphiles, **"it's a small world"** is the ultimate expression of Uncle Walt's dream, and toddlers adore this ride. Older kids might prefer **Mr. Toad's Wild Ride.** The wacky scenery ranges from a sedate library to the gates of hell. If it's a faster thrill you're seeking, head for the **Matterhorn Bobsleds.**

Cars Land at Disneyland California Adventure Park

You'll board a sled-style coaster car to plunge down a Swiss mountain on a twisted track that takes you past rivers, glaciers, and the Abominable Snowman.

The best thrill ride of the main park and my personal favorite sits inside Tomorrowland. Space Mountain is a fast roller coaster that whizzes through through the galaxy. Get a Fastpass to avoid long lines.

Adventureland sits next to the New Orleans Square area. Indiana Jones Adventure is arguably one of the best rides in all of Disneyland, and the details make it stunning. This one isn't the best for tiny tots, but the big kids love it. Everyone might want a Fastpass for the endlessly popular attraction.

In Frontierland, take a ride on a Wild West train on the Big Thunder Mountain Railroad, an older roller coaster that whisks passengers on a brief but fun thrill ride through a "dangerous, decrepit" mountain's mineshafts.

In New Orleans Square, the favorite ride is the Pirates of the Caribbean. Beginning in the dim swamp, which can be seen from the Blue Bayou Restaurant, the ride's classic scenes inside have been revamped to tie in more closely to the movies. Lines for Pirates can get long, so grab a Fastpass if you don't want to wait. Pirates is suitable for younger children as well as teens and adults.

For a taste of truly classic Disney, line up in the graveyard for a tour of the Haunted Mansion. The sedate motion makes the Haunted Mansion suitable for younger children, but the ghosts and ghoulies that amuse adults can be intense for kids.

DISNEY CALIFORNIA ADVENTURE PARK

Disney California Adventure Park (http://disneyland.disney.go.com; 8am-10pm daily; prices vary) uses unique attractions to bring visitors on a journey through the great state of California. It's right next to Disneyland, and most visitors use a park hopper pass to visit both. While the coaster and Ferris wheel bring thrills, there are also lots of tame rides and upbeat dance shows featuring favorite Disney characters.

Disney California Adventure Park is divided into themed areas. You'll find two information booths just inside the main park entrance, one off to the left as you walk through the turnstile and one at the opening to Sunshine Plaza.

ATTRACTIONS

Adults will enjoy Guardians of the Galaxy Mission: BREAKOUT!, a newer ride with a scream-inducing drop.

Monsters, Inc. Mike & Sully to the Rescue! invites guests into the action of the movie of the same name. You'll help the heroes as they chase the intrepid Boo. This ride jostles you around but is suitable for smaller kids as well as bigger ones.

Get a sample of the world of tiny insects on It's Tough to Be a Bug! This big-group, 3-D, multisensory ride offers fun for little kids and adults alike. You'll fly through the air, scuttle through the grass, and get a good idea of what life is like on six little legs.

For the littlest adventurers, Flik's Fun Fair offers almost half a dozen rides geared toward toddlers and little children. They can ride pint-size hot-air balloons known as Flik's Flyers, climb aboard a bug-themed train, or run around under a gigantic faucet to cool down after hours of hot fun.

Paradise Pier mimics the Santa Monica Pier, with thrill rides and an old-fashioned midway. **California Screamin'** is a high-tech roller coaster designed after the classic wooden coasters of carnivals past. This extra-long ride includes drops, twists, a full loop, and plenty of time and screaming fun. California Screamin' has a four-foot height requirement and is just as popular with nostalgic adults as with kids. **Toy Story Midway Mania!** magnifies the midway mayhem as passengers of all ages take aim at targets in a 4-D ride inspired by Disney-Pixar's *Toy Story.*

Condor Flats, Soarin' Over California is a combination ride and show that puts you and dozens of other guests on the world's biggest "glider" and sets you off over the hills and valleys of California. Get Disney's version of a wilderness experience at Grizzly Peak. Enjoy a white-water raft ride through a landscape inspired by the Sierra Nevada foothills on the **Grizzly River Run.**

Cars Land was inspired by the hit 2006 film *Cars.* Float on larger-than-life tires on the **Luigi's Flying Tires** ride or be serenaded by Mater as you ride in a tractor on **Mater's Junkyard Jamboree.** The **Radiator Springs Racers** finds six-person vehicles passing locations and characters from Cars before culminating in a real-life race with a car of other park visitors.

TICKETS AND PASSES

You can purchase tickets for both Disneyland Park and Disney California Adventure Park online (http://disneyland.disney.go.com) or right at the counter upon arrival.

At Disneyland Park, you'll pay as much as $124 per adult for full-day admission on peak days; on slower days, the price is around $97 per adult. Ticket prices go down the more days you purchase; for example, if you purchase a five-day pass, you'll pay around $64 per day. Disney offers many vacation packages that include hotel accommodations and park tickets. At Disneyland California Adventure Park, ticket prices for single admission vary as well, but tend to hover around $99 per adult.

If you're interested in checking out Disney California Adventure Park as well as Disneyland, your best bet is to buy a **Park Hopper pass** ($172-185 adults, $166-178 children 3-9), which lets you move back and forth between the two parks for a slight discount.

Fastpasses are free with park admission and available near the park's entrances. The newest and most popular rides have Fastpass kiosks right at their entrances. Feed your ticket into one of the machines and it will spit out both your ticket and a Fastpass with your specified time to take the ride. Come back during your window and enter the always-much-shorter Fastpass line, designated by a sign at the entrance. If you're with a crowd, be sure you all get your Fastpasses at the same time, so you all get the same time window to ride. It's possible to claim three Fastpasses at a time. Once you've used up your initial allotment, you can visit a Fastpass kiosk to reload.

FOOD
DISNEYLAND

The best areas of the park to grab a bite are Main Street, New Orleans, and Frontierland, but you can find at least a snack almost anywhere. Make reservations in advance for a table at the **Blue Bayou Restaurant** (New

Orleans Square, 714/781-3463, $55-59). Located in the dimly lit swamp overlooking the Pirates of the Caribbean ride, the Bayou has Cajun-ish cuisine and a reputation for being haunted. The portions are large and the desserts are tasty. Watch your silverware—the "ghosts" in this restaurant like to mess around with diners' tableware.

DISNEY CALIFORNIA ADVENTURE PARK

Most food options are in the Golden State area. For a Mexican feast, try Cocina Cucamonga Mexican Grill ($15). For more traditional American fare, enjoy the food at the Pacific Wharf Cafe ($15) or the Taste Pilots' Grill ($15).

Unlike Disneyland proper, alcoholic beverages are available in Disney California Adventure Park. You can grab a beer at Bayside Brews, or have some Californian wine at the Mendocino Terrace, where you can also learn the basics of wine creation and production. You can have wine and a pseudo-Italian meal at the sit-down Wine Country Trattoria (714/781-3463, $15-36).

DOWNTOWN DISNEY

Downtown Disney is a restaurant, shopping, and entertainment complex outside the amusement parks. There are over 15 restaurants here, most of which are national chains. House of Blues (1530 S. Disneyland Dr., Anaheim, 714/778-2583, www.houseofblues.com, 11am-midnight daily, $15-30) serves typical menu staples like sandwiches, burgers, pasta, and steak and seafood entrées with a Southern spin. A good kid-friendly option, Rainforest Café (1515 S. Disneyland Dr., Anaheim, 714/772-0413, www.rainforestcafe.

com, 8am-11pm Sun.-Thurs., 8am-midnight Fri.-Sat., $11-30) serves the same fare with tropical touches like coconut and mango.

A good non-chain option is Ralph Brennan's Jazz Kitchen (1590 S. Disneyland Dr., Anaheim, 714/776-5200, www.rbjazzkitchen.com, 11am-11pm Mon.-Sat., 10am-3pm and 4pm-11pm Sun., $8-37), serving a Cajun menu with jambalaya, beignets, and various blackened meats and seafood.

If you're looking for some local fare, go for the pastries, sandwiches, and hearty soups at La Brea Bakery (1556 Disneyland Dr., 714/490-0233, www.labreabakery.com; 8am-9pm Sun.-Thurs., 8am-10pm Fri.-Sat., $15-35), an outpost of an L.A. favorite founded by Nancy Silverton. And don't miss Sprinkles (1580 Disneyland Dr., 714/254-0200, www.sprinkles.com; 9am-11pm Sun.-Thurs., 9am-midnight Fri.-Sat., $5-10), which has L.A.'s best cupcakes.

HOTELS
DISNEYLAND

Disney's Grand Californian Hotel & Spa (1600 S. Disneyland Dr., Anaheim, 714/635-2300, http://disneyland.disney.go.com, $417-1,477), located inside Disney California Adventure Park, mimics the famous Ahwahnee Lodge in Yosemite. This massive, Craftsman-style hotel provides guests with West Coast luxury, and is filled with thoughtful touches—like headboards carved from California oak and pool decks decorated with hand-laid stones. For a hotel that's part of a global empire, Disney's Grand Californian provides a distinctly local experience. The hotel is surrounded by gardens and has restaurants, a day spa, and shops attached on the ground floor; it can also get you right out into Downtown Disney and thence to the parks proper. As with all Disney resorts, you can purchase tickets and a meal plan along with your hotel room (in fact, if you book via the website, they'll try to force you to do it that way).

For the most iconic Disney experience, stay at the Disneyland Hotel (1150 Magic Way, Anaheim, 714/778-6600, http://disneyland.disney.go.com, $460-1,016). This nearly 1,000-room high-rise monument to brand-specific family entertainment has everything a vacationing Brady-esque bunch could want: themed swimming pools, themed play areas, and even character-themed rooms that allow the kids to fully immerse themselves in the Mouse experience. Adults and families on a budget can also get rooms with either a king or two queen beds and more traditional motel fabrics and appointments. The monorail stops inside the hotel, offering guests the easiest way into the park proper without having to deal with parking or even walking.

It's easy to find the Paradise Pier Hotel (1717 S. Disneyland Dr., Anaheim, 714/999-0990, http://disneyland.disney.go.com, $344-952); it's that high-rise thing just outside Disney California Adventure Park. This hotel boasts what passes for affordable lodgings within walking distance of the parks. Rooms are cute, colorful, and clean; many have two doubles or queens to accommodate families or couples traveling together on a tighter budget. You'll find a (possibly refreshing) lack of Mickeys in the standard guest accommodations at the Paradise, which has the feel of a beach resort motel. After a day of wandering the park, relax by the rooftop pool.

OUTSIDE THE PARKS

The massive park complex is ringed with motels, both popular chains and more interesting independents. The Anabella (1030 W. Katella Ave., Anaheim, 714/905-1050 or 800/863-4888, www.anabellahotel.com, $332-662) offers a touch of class along with a three-block walk to the parks. The elegant marble-clad lobby seems like it belongs closer to Downtown L.A. than Downtown Disney. A decent restaurant, two pools, a whirlpool tub, and a fitness center are on-site. You can get limited room service at The Anabella, and you can leave your car in the hotel's parking lot to avoid the expense of parking at Disneyland.

If you're looking to stay just outside of Disney's gates, check out the Hotel Indigo Anaheim (435 W. Katella Ave., Anaheim, 714/772-7755, www.ihg.com, $130-180). This affordable modern hotel is a favorite for travelers wanting a clean and friendly place to sleep, without the Disney hoopla. The Hotel Indigo is adjacent to all the Disney attractions—because Disneyland is so big, it will take a 15-minute walk to get you inside the park entrance.

The Hyatt Regency Orange County (11999 Harbor Blvd., Garden Grove, 714/750-1234, http://orangecounty.hyatt.com, $129-289) in Garden Grove is about 1.5 miles (10 minutes' drive on Harbor Blvd.) south of the park. The family-friendly suites have separate bedrooms with bunk beds and fun decor geared toward younger guests. Enjoy a cocktail in the sun-drenched atrium, or grab a chaise lounge by the pool.

GETTING THERE

The nearest airport to Disneyland, serving all of Orange County, is John

Wayne Airport (SNA, 18601 Airport Way, Santa Ana, 949/252-5200, www.ocair.com). LAX is less convenient and a bit farther, but definitely cheaper. Whether you're flying into John Wayne or LAX, you can catch a shuttle straight from the airport to your Disneyland hotel. MouseSavers (www.mousesavers.com) can get you a ride in a van or a bus to your destination at or near Disneyland.

If you're driving from Downtown L.A., Disneyland is about an hour south in Anaheim. It's most accessible from I-5 South where it crosses Ball Road (stay in the left three lanes for parking). The parking lot (1313 S. Disneyland Dr.) costs $20.

Universal City and Burbank

Sitting to the north of Hollywood is the San Fernando Valley, home to the majority of L.A.'s major movie studios. Universal City sits smack above Hollywood, home to Universal Studios Hollywood and NBCUniversal. Studio City lies to the west of Universal City, and to the east is Burbank, with Warner Bros. Studios and Walt Disney Studios. This area is hot, suburban, and sprawling. If you're interested in the film industry, don't miss making a dy trip to tour some of the big studios here. But return to the city center when you're done.

UNIVERSAL STUDIOS HOLLYWOOD

Universal Studios Hollywood (100 Universal City Plaza, Universal City, 800/864-8377, www.universalstudioshollywood.com; hours vary) is the place where movie-lovers go "on the set" of their favorite films and TV shows. The Wizarding World of Harry Potter, one of the park's newest attractions, re-creates Hogwarts castle and Hogsmeade village. Outside of Universal Studios is Citywalk, a touristy area full of chain shops and restaurants. It can be an entertaining place to stroll around before or after your visit to the park. Universal Studios has plenty to see in a day or afternoon—you won't need to spend more than a day here.

TICKETS

Universal offers a handful of ticket packages, depending on whether you want VIP or regular access, etc. Tickets run anywhere from $99 for basic entry to $325 for valet parking, included meals, etc. Purchase tickets online in advance or upon arrival.

entrance to Universal Studios Hollywood

✪ THE WIZARDING WORLD OF HARRY POTTER

If you or your kids love the Harry Potter series, you will fall in love with the Wizarding World of Harry Potter. Universal Studios has essentially recreated the entire Hogwarts village to include many of your favorite moments from this classic book series. The Forbidden Journey is one of the greatest dark rides around—its intricate 3-D design will make you want to brave the line multiple times. Eat lunch at the Three Broomsticks, an ancient-feeling pub, and plan plenty of time for browsing the shops, including Filch's Emporium of Confiscated Goods, Wiseacre's Wizarding Equipment, and Gladrags Wizardwear.

OTHER ATTRACTIONS

Universal's classic ride is the Studio Tour, which takes guests on a ride through the sets of some of Universal's most iconic movies—the ride is 60 minutes long and includes gasp-worthy appearances from King Kong and the shark from *Jaws*. Another ride in which you'll dodge ferocious beasts is Jurassic Park—be ready for its 85-foot plunge finale. The Revenge of the Mummy is another crowd favorite—it has in-your-face fireballs and other special effects.

WARNER BROS. STUDIOS

Warner Bros. Studios (3400 W. Riverside Dr., 818/977-8687, www. wbstudiotour.com; 8am-4:30pm daily, extended summer hours; tours range $55-295) is another one of the major film studios, also active since the Golden Age. The studio has a few different tours to choose from, but the most popular is the "Studio Tour," which lasts three hours and takes you through a real working studio. Each tour includes exclusive access to original props, costumes, picture cars, and sets, like the Central Perk set from *Friends* and some sets from recent blockbuster *La La Land*. There's also a neat DC Universe exhibit, which includes the original Batman Museum (complete with Batmobile). There's certainly a higher chance of seeing celebrities during your tour here than at Universal Studios.

GETTING THERE AND AROUND

Universal Studios Holywood and Warner Bros. Studios are just north of Hollywood. The easiest way to get to them is by car, taking the U.S. 101 north and then Barham Road. It'll take about 15 minutes from Hollywood, depending on traffic. If driving, you'll have to pay $12 to park your car in the official lots at both Universal Studios and Warner Bros. Studios. The two are about 10 minutes away from each other by car. Alternatively, you can take the Red Line of the Metro to the Universal City/Studio City stop, and take a ride-sharing service to Warner Bros. Studios if you want to visit both.

Catalina Island

Catalina is a unique island filled with wild buffalo, golf carts, and beachy charm. Known for its shimmering clear waters filled with bright orange fish, Catalina provides a tranquil respite that's only a boat ride away from the big city. Since it takes about 90 minutes by ferry get to Catalina, I recommended staying the night. It's a small island, so after a day or two you'll be ready to head back to L.A. proper.

SIGHTS

Most Catalina Island visitors are content to walk around, shop, and eat. However, if you're looking to take in the scenery off the main drag, you can spend a few hours at the **Wrigley Memorial & Botanical Garden** (1402 Avalon Cyn Rd., Avalon, 310/510-2897, www.catalinaconservancy.org; 8am-5pm daily; $7 adults, $5 seniors, $3 students with ID and children 5-12). This 37-acre haven includes a pretty memorial to William Wrigley Jr., founder of the famous gum company and lover of Catalina Island. You can walk to the gardens from town center or take a city bus. The **Garden to Sky** hiking trail, which is probably the most popular Catalina Island hike, starts at these gardens—since these are protected lands, you'll need to get a hiking permit at the gardens to do the hike.

In the early 20th century, a buffalo herd was brought to Catalina Island as part of a movie being filmed—and they never left. **Catalina Tours** (205 Crescent Ave., Avalon, 310/510-0211, www.catalinatours.com, 9am-5pm daily) offers touring packages that take you up into the hills in either a Jeep or Hummer for gorgeous ocean views and potential buffalo and bald eagle sightings. A tour is the way to go to see the wilder parts of the island, as most of Catalina is closed to the general public except by permit.

Catalina Island

RESTAURANTS

Descanso Beach Club (1 St. Catherine Way, Avalon, 310/510-7410, www.visitcatalinaisland.com; 11am-4pm daily; $10-16) is the place to eat if you're looking for atmosphere and somewhere not just to dine but to hang out for a few hours. The menu is straightforward American—burgers and the like. People often come in bathing suits, rent cabanas, and lie out in the sun sipping on mojitos for an entire afternoon. The signature drink is called "buffalo milk"—I don't know what buffalos have to do with vodka and Kahlúa, but it sure tastes good.

For a more rustic experience, check out **The Lobster Trap** (128 Catalina Ave., Avalon, 310/510-8585, www.catalinalobstertrap.com; 11am-10pm daily, $10-30). Buoys and fishing nets hang from the ceiling, and you can order a grilled lobster tail with a side of

CATALINA, A TELEGENIC ISLAND

"Twenty-six miles / across the sea / Santa Catalina / is waiting for me." This is the refrain of the popular 1950s tune "Santa Catalina," a love song about Catalina Island. The Four Preps, the quartet who sang this ditty, called Catalina Island the "island of romance." And they were right—Catalina is a romantic place, so close to Los Angeles but feeling like it's in the middle of the ocean.

Because of its romantic nature, Catalina Island has popped up in all sorts of movies and TV shows since the 1920s. As you're strolling the island, you may recall scenes from *Treasure Island* (1934), *Chinatown* (1974), or the soap opera *The Bold and the Beautiful*.

In fact, that's how Catalina Island's famed buffalo population got here—they were brought to the island in 1924 as part of a film and never left. At its peak, this herd counted over 600 buffalo. Just goes to show—you never quite know what you'll find in the entertainment capital of the world.

steamed veggies—no tablecloths necessary. What's nice about the Lobster Trap is that locals come here too; expect a bubbly happy hour, quick service, and good conversation.

SHOPS

Catalina Island has a handful of shopping gems, and **Bay of the Seven Moons** (205 Crescent Ave., 310/510-1450, Avalon, www.catalinachamber.com; hours vary) is one of them. It's a jewelry store/boutique/museum. Most days, you can find the store owner and her dog hanging out, ready to help you find a special accoutrement to take home. There are both locally and globally sourced goods, and likely something for your someone special.

Only on Catalina Island can you find **Afishinados Gallery** (205 Crescent Ave. Ste. 102, Avalon, 888/613-7770, http://shop.afishinados-gallery.com; hours vary), where you can buy their very own fish-themed chairs, paintings, jewelry, and more. As its tagline—"everything fishy, nothing imported"—will tell you, everything here is made on Catalina Island. And don't let its tongue-in-cheek approach fool you—Afishinados has beautiful local artwork that is worth seeing.

SPAS

Island Spa Catalina (163 Crescent Ave., Avalon, 310/510-7300, www.visitcatalinaisland.com; 9am-6pm Sun.-Thurs., 9am-7pm Fri.-Sat.) boasts 15,000 square feet of rejuvenation heaven. With deep tissue massages, oxygen facials, warm sand therapies, and more, Island Spa Catalina is the place in Avalon to reboot and even work out with a group fitness class. If you're a spa lover, don't miss a chance to soak in the outdoor hot tub or bake in the eucalyptus steam room. Afterward, refresh with a colorful smoothie or Mediterranean salad at the spa's **Encanto Café**.

HOTELS

For a tasteful Catalina Island experience, book a night at the **Pavilion Hotel** (513 Crescent Ave., Avalon, 310/510-1788, www.visitcatalinaisland.com), just a few steps from the beach and in the heart of town. Here you can take a dip in a cute pool, snack on wine and cheese at dusk, and lounge on the hotel's deck, gardens, and patio. The Pavilion Hotel does a great job of taking care of your needs, with services like hot breakfast and complimentary luggage pickup from the boat dock.

GETTING THERE AND AROUND

Two main ports have boats leaving regularly for Catalina: Long Beach and Dana Point, both about an hour's drive from Los Angeles. From L.A., you can take the Metro Blue Line to Long Beach. Dana Point is in Orange County—to get there from Los Angeles you can either drive or take Amtrak's Pacific Surfliner train. Once you get to either port, you'll need to buy tickets for the Catalina Express ferry (www.catalinaexpress.com; tickets $60-110 round-trip), which departs every few hours. Once you get to the island, everything is within walking distance—some people rent golf carts or bikes to get around.

Orange County Beaches

Down the coast from Los Angeles, Orange County has charming surf towns, upscale shopping, and seaside seafood dining. The "O.C." (as it's known by locals) is the place to stay if you're looking for a slower pace and some prime beach time. O.C. waters are noticeably warmer than those in Los Angeles proper.

The first beach you'll hit south of L.A. is Huntington, followed by Newport, and then Laguna. These beach towns have distinct vibes and attractions.

GETTING THERE AND AROUND

You can get to Orange County by driving or taking the Amtrak Surfliner train from Union Station. It's nice to have a car to explore these seaside towns, but you can get around fairly easily by bike or car-sharing services. Most attractions are centered around a few miles of each city's beach.

✪ HUNTINGTON BEACH

Huntington Beach, or "Surf City, U.S.A.," as it's known, is *the* place to go in Southern California if you're interested in surfing or surf culture. The crowd skews young and sometimes rowdy, but this is still a very family-friendly beach destination.

SIGHTS AND BEACHES

At the north end is Sunset Beach (between Anderson St. and Warner Ave., 714/834-2400, www.surfcityusa.com; 5am-10pm daily) which is about wide as they come, with a grassy park and pedestrian path extending its 1.5-mile length, just behind a row of beachfront homes. Wild winds minimize good surfing days but provide the perfect fuel for windsurfing and kite surfing, plus fun bodysurfing and stand-up paddleboarding. Find free parking at the lot on Warner Avenue.

Southeast of Sunset Beach, three-mile-long Bolsa Chica State Beach (between Warner Ave. and Seapoint St., 714/846-3460, www.parks.ca.gov; 6am-10pm daily, parking lot closes at 9pm) has smaller waves than beaches to the south, making it a popular spot for beginning surfers. Amenities include fire rings, volleyball courts, restrooms and showers, picnic ramadas (714/377-9422 for reservations), barbecue grills, basketball courts, and

Huntington Beach

a paved bike path. There's also RV camping (800/444-7275, www.reserve-california.com).

Across the Pacific Coast Highway (PCH) from Bolsa Chica State Beach is the **Bolsa Chica Ecological Reserve** (18000 CA-1, 714/846-1114, www.wildlife.ca.gov; sunrise-sunset daily; free), a coastal estuary teeming with more than 200 species of birds as well as hiking trails. It's popular for birders, photographers, and locals on their morning/afternoon walks.

Just before you get to Huntington City Beach, you'll find **Huntington Dog Beach** (between Seapoint Ave. and Goldenwest St., www.dogbeach.org; sunrise-sunset daily, parking lot 5am-10pm), which has been called the O.C.'s "dogfriendliest beach."

Huntington City Beach (103 CA-1 from Beach Blvd. to Seapoint St., 714/536-5281, www.surfcityusa.com; 5am-10pm daily) is 3.5 miles of good surf, volleyball courts, fire rings, and a bike path. A pier in the center of the beach leads into Main Street, where you'll find the **Visitor Information Center and Kiosk**, as well as surf shops and rentals, restaurants, and bars. Huntington Beach is home to the **International Surfing Museum** (411 Olive Ave., 714/300-8836, www.surfingmuseum.org; noon-5pm Sun.-Mon., noon-7pm Tues.-Fri., 11am-7pm Sat.; free), which gives an interesting chronicle of the sport's history.

SPORTS AND ACTIVITIES

Locals can be competitive, so if you're a beginner, consider taking lessons or going out with someone more experienced.

For all your rental needs, head to **Zack's HB** (405 CA-1, 714/536-0215, www.zackshb.com; 8am-6pm Mon.-Fri., 8am-7pm Sat.-Sun.), which offers surfing rentals (surfboards $12/hour and $35/day, wetsuits $5/hour and $15/day), one-hour surfing lessons ($75-100), bike rentals ($10/hour and $30/day), and other general beach rentals.

On Main Street, **Huntington Surf & Sport** (300 CA-1, 714/841-4000,

BEST BEACHES

If there's one thing that comes to mind when visitors think of L.A., it has to be the beaches. Each beach has its own flavor, and the weather is so nice that you can take a beach day almost all year round (except for the few days in winter when it rains).

There's a whole culture around beaches in L.A., and it includes surfers, skateboarders, roller skaters, and pretty people who just like walking around in bathing suits. You can see beach culture in full swing during the summer months in Malibu and Venice especially, where people will be walking around half-dressed with sand covering their legs and feet. My advice is to dive right in (no pun intended)—tousle your hair, don a pair of big sunglasses, and lay your towel out on one of the greatest beaches in America.

- **Best for surfing: Surfrider Beach** (page 217) in Malibu is an iconic, idyllic spot to either jump into the water with a surfboard or sit back in the sand and watch the surfers work their magic (no swimming here, and no public restrooms). This is an unfussy beach that's known for having great wave breaks, and it can get crowded on days with decent waves.

- **Best for families:** On sunny days, **Santa Monica State Beach** (page 161) is filled with kids and families, perhaps because the beach has lots of lifeguard stands. The Annenberg Community Beach House toward the northern end of Santa Monica State Beach has an unrivaled sand-in-your-toes café and a big pool for kiddos to use if they want a break from salt water.

www.hsssurf.com; 8am-9pm Sun.-Thurs., 8am-10pm Fri.-Sat.) offers an extensive menu of surfboards and wetsuits (surfboards $10/hour and $30/day, wetsuits $8/hour and $15/day).

If you're more of a landlubber, bike or skate the 10-mile **Huntington Beach Bike Trail**, which starts at Seapoint Street and goes up the coast to Warner Avenue.

ENTERTAINMENTS AND EVENTS

Every Tuesday night, Main Street is closed to traffic for **Surf City Nights** (Main St., www.surfcitynights.com; 5pm-9pm Tues.), a farmers market and street fair featuring local vendors and artisans, a petting zoo and bounce house for the kids, and live music.

Huntington City Beach hosts late July's **U.S. Open of Pro Surfing** (www.vansusopenofsurfing.com), which draws hundreds of world-class surfers to its multi-day competition.

RESTAURANTS

For a quick bite to eat, stop off at the **Bodhi Tree Vegetarian Cafe** (501 Main St., Ste. E, 714/969-9500, www.bodhitreehb.com; 11am-10pm daily; $6-10) for vegetarian soups, salads, and sandwiches. **Sugar Shack Café** (213 Main St., 714/536-0355, www.hb-sugarshack.com; 6am-2pm Mon.-Fri., 6am-3pm Sat.-Sun.; $7-10) is a great place for breakfast, serving omelets and breakfast burritos.

Located on the pier on Main Street, **Duke's** (317 Pacific Coast Hwy., 714/374-6446, www.dukes-huntington.com; 5pm-8:30pm Mon., 11:30am-2:30pm and 5pm-9pm Tues.-Fri., 11am-3:30pm and 4:30pm-9pm Sat., 10am-2pm and 4:30pm-8:30pm Sun.; $10-20), named after famed Hawaiian surfer Duke Kahanamoku., serves Hawaiian seafood with oceanside views.

- **Best for people-watching: Venice Beach** (page 164) boasts a unique blend of human energy and pure natural beauty. Grab a smoothie and lay your towel out on a sunny summer day—the beach will be packed with people.

- **Best for sunsets: Laguna Beach** (page 239) in Orange County puts on a spectacular sunset show almost nightly; bring your camera, a glass of pinot, and settle in for some of the best views nature has to offer.

- **Best for photos: El Matador State Beach** (page 218) in Malibu is often filled with photo shoots and selfie-taking visitors…because its unique rock-sculptured sands are just that gorgeous. Sunsets here are particularly spectacular. Plan on climbing down a steep path to get to the water, otherwise you can view the beach from the parking lot above.

- **Best for water sports: Newport Beach** (page 237) in Orange Country is a family-friendly town with lots of shops renting various equipment, including jet skis, surf boards, boogie boards, kayaks, and stand up paddle boards. There's also a handful of sportfishing charter companies that will take you out to sea and help you catch a fish for dinner (or just for fun).

- **Best for solitude:** To get to the beach at **Malibu Lagoon State Beach** (page 217), you'll have to walk about a quarter mile around the lagoon itself; this jaunt deters visitors, leaving a beautifully protected beach for your lounging pleasure.

HOTELS

Across the highway from Huntington Beach, you can get ocean-view rooms and standard hotel furnishings at tiny **Sun 'N Sands Motel** (1102 CA-1, 714/536-2543, www.sunnsands.com). Or try the larger and more stylish **Shorebreak Hotel** (500 CA-1, 714/861-4470, www.shorebreakhotel.com), right in front of the pier; it's home to Asian-Mexican fusion restaurant **Pacific Hideaway** (714/965-4448; 7am-11pm Sun.-Thurs., 7am-midnight Fri.-Sat.).

NEWPORT BEACH

Heading south from Huntington Beach along the PCH, you'll hit **Newport Beach,** a small affluent community built around a tiny bay protected by the Balboa Peninsula. This beach town attracts an eclectic mix, from wealthy yachters to families to students from nearby University of California Irvine.

The pier is a super-fun area to spend a family-friendly day in the sun, and Balboa Island is an adorable place to walk around and get ice cream on a hot day. If you love the water, you could spend a few days here—it's a small town, so you won't need anything more than a day or two to see the highlights. Weekends can get crowded, especially during summer, so if you can take your Newport trip during the week you may have more sand to yourself.

SIGHTS

Corona del Mar State Beach (3001 Ocean Blvd., Corona Del Mar, 949/644-3151, www.parks.ca.gov) is one of my favorite beaches in California. The water is an iridescent turquoise, and the cliffs overlooking the beach make me feel like I'm on the coast of France. Parking is close by, and on weekends the beach gets crowded. This is a great beach for kids because the waves are tame. At the right time of day, there are tidepools to explore on the adjacent rocks.

For the quintessential SoCal beach experience, go to Newport Pier (70 Newport Pier, 949/644-3309), a 1,000-foot wooden pier that's the center of much swimming, fishing, and general recreating. Parking is limited on weekends and hot summer days, so come early to get your space and set up a big beach umbrella for a day of bathing, sunning, skating, and biking (rentals available). The Newport Pier area doesn't feel too built up compared with other local beaches, but its boardwalk is lined with some cute shops, restaurants, and multimillion-dollar homes.

Balboa Island (www.balboaisland.com) is one of those adorable places with one main street and everything in walking distance. You can drive across a bridge to get to Balboa or take a quick ferry from the Newport Pier area (I recommend the ferry—it's a fun little trip). Once you're on the island, join the throngs of strolling travelers to find a frozen banana shop, lively pub, or beach-inspired boutique.

RESTAURANTS

Come to Mastro's Ocean Club (8112 East Coast Hwy., 949/376-6990, www.mastrosrestaurants.com; 5pm-10pm Sun.-Thurs., 5pm-11pm Fri.-Sat., $25 and up) for your classic American fine-dining experience. Mastro's is open to the public, but something about it feels quite exclusive. Enjoy dining alfresco under tasteful hanging lights or next to a generous stone fireplace. Many tables have ocean views. The menu is straightforward steak and seafood, all made with care. Make sure to order the warm butter cake for dessert.

Mama D's Italian Kitchen (3012 Newport Blvd., 949/675-6262, www.

Balboa Island

mamadsnewport.com; 4pm-8:30pm Sun.-Thurs., 4pm-9pm Fri., 4pm-9:30pm Sat., $15-25) is *the* place to stuff yourself with delectable pizza and pasta. In fact, the whole place is stuffed—with people, kitschy decor, and some of the best classic Italian food around. Portions are huge, and there's usually a crowd of people waiting for a table in this decidedly unstuffy eatery. If you love creamy dishes, homemade sauces, and traditional thin-crust pizza, it's worth the wait.

Some of SoCal's best Vietnamese food is served right at the counter at the Saigon Beach Restaurant (2233 W. Balboa Blvd. #102, 949/612-8067; 11am-9pm daily; $5-10). If there's such thing as having too much flavor, the food at Saigon Beach might just achieve that feat. Order any kind of *banh mi* (a traditional Vietnamese sandwich) and iced coffee, and you'll be set for the day. The 420 green rice and pretty much all the noodle dishes are also fantastic. Plus, if you eat lunch here you'll have plenty of room in your budget for an upscale dinner.

SHOPS

It's hard to tell what's more beautiful at Amaree's (2241 West Coast Hwy., 949/642-4423, http://amarees.com; 10am-6pm daily)—the marina views or its designer clothing. There's an unmistakable elegance about Amaree's that keeps even the most seasoned shoppers coming back to admire its ever-rotating collection of haute couture garments for men and women. Yes, you will pay top prices for these high-fashion garbs, but Amaree's does a great job of making all customers feel welcome, no matter their budget.

HOTELS

The Newport Beach Hotel (2306 W. Oceanfront, 949/673-7030, www.the-newportbeachhotel.com) is a charming inn in the midst of Newport's beachfront entertainment district. No need for a car here—all your shopping, surfing, and dining needs are within walking distance. The Newport Beach Hotel isn't big and fancy—it's quaint and tasteful, with 15 rooms and five master suites. Amenities include a generous complimentary breakfast

each morning and free use of the hotel's bicycles, boogies boards, and beach toys.

For an authentic Newport Beach experience, stay at Crystal Cove Beach Cottages (35 Crystal Cove, 800/444-7275, http://crystalcove.org). Book your stay well in advance because this preserved early-20th-century colony fills up quickly. There are 14 individual cottages and 10 dorm-style cottages with private rooms. Every cottage is either right on the beach or overlooking the seaside from a bluff, and each has been preserved to maintain its original architectural charm.

LAGUNA BEACH

Want more beach time? Head to Laguna, where every beach (and person) is gorgeous. This upscale beach town is considerably less gritty than the Venice Boardwalk. Since

Laguna Beach

traffic can be thick from Los Angeles to Laguna, I recommended heading down after morning rush hour, spending the afternoon at the beach, having a nice dinner, and then either staying the night or heading back to Los Angeles after the evening rush.

SIGHTS

The Laguna Art Museum (307 Cliff Dr., 949/494-8971, http://lagunaartmuseum.org; 11am-5pm Tues.-Sun.; $7) specializes in art from local and California-based artists. It's not a huge museum but a quaint and friendly place to stop by and see what some Cali-inspired painters, sculptors, and photographers are up to. All of the art is from the 19th thorough 21st centuries. Of course, L.A. proper is really the place to see big and bold art (and lots of it), but if you're looking for a cultural infusion during your Laguna jaunt, the Laguna Art Museum may be just what you want.

For decades, picturesque Heisler Park (375 Cliff Dr., 949/497-0716) has attracted a diverse crowd of visitors looking to stroll its garden-lined trails. Picnickers can dine at the park's picnic tables, and ocean adventurers can explore the tidal pools in the park's marine refuge area. Stretching along the bluffs from Aster Street to Diver's Cove, Heisler Park's oceanside beauty has made it a popular spot for wedding photos and other special events.

RESTAURANTS

From the outside, Nick's Laguna Beach (440 S. Coast Hwy., 949/376-8595, http://nicksrestaurants.com; 11am-10pm Mon.-Wed., 11am-11pm Thurs.-Fri., 7:30am-11:30am Sat.-Sun.; $15-40) might look like your average beach town restaurant with a welcoming patio—what makes Nick's stand

out from the rest is its superior food. There's nothing out of the ordinary on the menu, but somehow Nick's manages to make all of it taste really good. The mac'n'cheese, for example, has just the right balance of cheddar, cream sauce, and truffle oil topped with an herbed crust. The prime rib dip is roasted daily and served with red wine au jus on a brioche bun. Nick's takes limited walk-ins, so make a reservation to avoid a wait.

Las Brisas (361 Cliff Dr., 949/497-5434, www.lasbrisaslagunabeach.com; 8am-11pm daily; $25 and over) is a decent Mexican restaurant serving mostly seafood dishes, but you won't come here for the food—come for a satisfying cocktail and some of Laguna's best ocean views. This is the place where you take a picture of your piña colada with the ocean in the background. Check out the weekday happy hour, which is often accompanied by live music.

SHOPS

Looking for a trinket that can only be found in Laguna? Then check out Gem Mountain Studios (577 S. Coast Hwy., 949/494-0921, www.gmsshop.com; 11am-7pm daily), a charming, blufftop shop overlooking the Pacific. All the pieces—from the shimmering amethyst earrings to an opal sea turtle pendant—are made in-house and capture the spirit of the sea. Prices are reasonable, especially considering the shop's celebrity clientele.

Laguna Beach has more than its fair share of appealing shops—count Kiska Boutique (1330 S. Coast Hwy., 949/290-6620, www.visitlagunabeach.com; 10am-7pm daily) among the best of them. This is the place where Laguna's beach-chic women get their favorite outfits. Kiska's clothing and accessories manage to be trendy, affordable, and high quality—all at the same time. This is a great place to pick up a bohemian-inspired outfit for dinner or add a batik sarong to your beach look.

HOTELS

The **Montage Laguna Beach** (30801 Coast Hwy., 866/271-6953, www.montagehotels.com) provides some of the ritziest luxury in Southern California. With a gorgeous pool and patio, and ocean views at every turn, it's no wonder that this hotel regularly appears on "best" lists not only for California but the entire United States. Start your mornings with a walk on the beach, take an exercise class with an expert trainer, lounge by the mosaic pool, and then finish your day with a romantic dinner and sunset views.

If you're looking for an oceanside hotel without too much hoopla, check out **La Casa del Camino** (1289 S. Coast Hwy., 949/497-6029, www.lacasadelcamino.com). This quirky, Mexican-styled inn has tons of character, great service, and rooftop dining with a view—all just one block from the ocean. Location is really everything—you can go back and forth from your room to the beach all throughout the day. Laguna Beach's main commercial district is about a mile away.

BACKGROUND

The Landscape

Los Angeles City Hall

GEOGRAPHY

The Los Angeles Basin is the meeting point of two tectonic plates, the grinding of which created L.A.'s three main mountain ranges: the San Andres, Santa Monica, and San Gabriel Mountains. L.A.'s 503 square miles make it one of the 10 largest cities in the United States. Los Angeles County, at 4,751 square miles, is even bigger, boasting almost 2,000 square miles of mountains and 75 miles of coastline, which provides beachgoers with heat-palpitating sunsets almost nightly. It's an Instagrammer's dream, and, actually, an oil baron's dream too—that's right, the sands of Los Angeles have a respectable amount of oil, and the county has prolific oil production for its size. There are sporadic oil wells throughout the city (especially nearer to the ocean), and oil rigs dot L.A.'s coastline.

Earthquakes happen intermittently in Los Angeles. They typically measure under 5.0 on the Richter scale, which is the type of earthquake you feel, but doesn't cause structural damage. The last huge L.A. earthquake was the Northridge quake in 1994, which measured 6.7 on the Richter scale. If you do feel the earth start to shake while you're inside, get low to the ground and cover your head and neck; if you're outside, stay away from buildings, trees, and overpasses. But don't worry too much—most of L.A.'s buildings are now earthquake-ready, especially the newer ones.

CLIMATE

There are a lot of wonderful things about Los Angeles, and its weather might just be the most wonderful of all. L.A.'s mild Mediterranean climate means warm, sunny days and cool, dry nights. The average daily high temperature is a reasonable 74°F, and there are about 290 sunny days per year, with very low humidity.

Because the weather is so darn nice, visitors come year-round and there is no real "slow" tourist season. Summer is the high season (especially July and August), when people from around the world lay out blankets and slather on coconut oil on L.A.'s beaches.

L.A.'s annual rainfall is only 15 inches, and Southern California occasionally finds itself in a drought, with directives from the governor for lowering its water usage. When it *does* rain in L.A., the city slows down significantly, I think because most Angelenos don't like driving in the rain. Be prepared for dense traffic and lots of minor traffic accidents on drizzly days.

ENVIRONMENTAL ISSUES

Los Angeles has more than its fair share of environmental challenges. Each summer in L.A. brings at least a few sizeable fires, brought on by hot temps and dry hillsides. The drier the land and hotter the air, the greater potential for a fire. During summer months, visitors should be especially careful when lighting and disposing of cigarettes, especially in areas with brush and trees. There are pretty much no bonfires or campfires allowed in L.A. County, except for in the designated fire pits on Dockweiler Beach.

Fires that clear out large swaths of foliage sometimes make way for mudslides, a natural phenomenon in which the side of a hill or mountain comes crashing down on the land below it, sometimes damaging homes and cars and injuring people. Mudslides usually happen during heavy rains, and there should be warnings from the city government if there is a risk of mudslide on a given day.

To boot, the air quality isn't very good here, and neither is the drinking water. Poor air quality here is caused by the combined forces of car exhaust, the geography of the L.A. Basin, and high summer temperatures. Sometimes you'll see these layers of gray-green air pollution at the pinnacle of a hike or as your airplane lands at LAX. For drinking water, your best bet is to either buy bottled water and carry it with you or buy a water filter in a grocery store and keep it wherever you are staying. Unfiltered L.A. water won't make you sick—it just doesn't taste good.

History

MEXICAN SETTLERS AND 18TH-CENTURY SPANISH MISSIONARIES

In the 1600s and 1700s, the area that we currently know of as Los Angeles was modestly populated with American Indians, Mexican families, and Spanish explorers and missionaries. During this time, most residents lived along the Los Angeles River. There's some debate as to how the city was named, and who named it. We do know that it happened in the 1780s and that L.A.'s given name was either *El Pueblo de la Reyna de los Angeles* (The Town of the Queen of the Angels) or *El Pueblo de Nuestra Señora de los Angeles de Porciuncula* (The Town of Our Lady of the Angels of Porciuncula). Either way, the name was quickly thereafter shortened to *Los Angeles*—the angels.

U.S. STATEHOOD AND THE GOLD RUSH OF THE 1850S

Before California became a state in 1850, it was still very much part of the Wild West. Farmers and gold seekers came here from the eastern United States, and Cali was gaining a sizeable population of *gringos* (white people). This was a time of relative lawlessness. The L.A. area provided much of the agricultural products for prospectors in Northern California.

California was granted U.S. statehood in September 1850, in the midst of the gold rush. At the time, there was heated debate in the United States over whether slavery should be allowed, and California chose to enter

the union as a free, nonslave state. Part of the reason why Los Angeles is so culturally rich today is because so many different types of people came here during this period, seeking both adventure and economic opportunity.

THE RISE OF L.A. AND THE FILM INSTURY

Once Los Angeles became part of the United States, it saw even more population growth, welcoming immigrants from around the world, especially China, Korea, and the Philippines. Each decade leading up to the 20th century brought tens of thousands more residents to L.A., some of whom arrived via new railroads that connected California with the rest of the country.

The 1910s saw the first movies filmed in Hollywood—first silent, black-and-white films, followed in the 1920s by films with sound. By the time the first Academy Awards ceremony was held at The Hollywood Roosevelt Hotel in 1929, most of the world's films were shot in Los Angeles. The 1930s brought even more cinematic excitement with the introduction of Technicolor cinematography, most notably with the films *Gone with the Wind* and *The Wizard of Oz*, both released in 1939. By 1940, L.A. County was booming, with over 1.5 million residents.

THE POSTWAR YEARS

After World War II, Los Angeles experienced dramatic population growth, with the population of L.A. County more than doubling between 1950 and 2000. During these years, Los Angeles became somewhat of a mecca for artists of all kids—writers, filmmakers, photographers, and more. Like San Francisco, Los Angeles became a home for a diversity of people looking to improve their lives and express themselves artistically.

Along with this artistry came a progressive spirit and a commitment to gay rights. In 1979, West Hollywood hosted the world's first gay pride parade; in 1984, it elected the country's first majority-gay city council. Also in 1984, Los Angeles hosted the Summer Olympics, an event that showcased the city to visitors and viewers from around the world. It was a proud moment for L.A. and a smart investment in infrastructure that's still paying off.

CONTEMPORARY TIMES

Today, Los Angeles is one of the world's most popular tourist destinations. Every year, over 45 million people come here for the food, art, beaches, and, yes, movie stars. As evidenced by the constant construction, it's a city that's continually growing and expanding, with no real end in sight. It's a place where trends are born and now, thanks to social media, promulgated faster than ever.

Because most of the world's music and movies are made here, L.A.'s wealthier neighborhoods are filled with celebrities who work in music, movies, sports, and, of course, reality TV (hello, Kardashians!). Whether it's a red-carpet event, a Hollywood scandal, or paparazzi shots of a hunk in Malibu, Los Angeles always seems to be getting attention for something... and that's quite all right for a city full of attention-seekers.

Local Culture

DIVERSITY

In 2016, Los Angeles was home to just over four million residents. L.A. has a depth of cultural wealth brought by citizens from countries around the planet. You'll not only taste this while dining, but hear it in the 185 languages spoken in L.A. households; in fact, most Angelenos speak a language other than English in their homes.

At the edge of the ocean and just hours away from the Mexican border, Los Angeles is a landing spot for new citizens; about 35 percent of people living in this city are foreign-born. As of 2015, California has the largest nonwhite population of any state in America. Here's a rough idea of how L.A.'s population breaks down:

- Hispanic or Latino: 50%
- White: 30%
- Asian: 11%
- Black or African American: 9%

L.A.'s median household income is around $50,000, but this belies huge income disparities between the mega-rich and the thousands of Angelenos making less than minimum wage. L.A. is a place where movie stars step around homeless people to get to the new hot bar on Beverly Boulevard. Touring L.A.'s extravagant streets, you probably wouldn't guess that about one in five citizens here live in poverty.

There are some nonprofits and government agencies across the city that are working to create more equitable living conditions, but the excess and poverty in Los Angeles are not unique to this city—they mirror the enormous income gaps of America itself.

RELIGION

In a city with so much cultural diversity, you can find a place in L.A. to practice just about any religion. According to the Pew Research Center, about 65 percent of Angelenos affiliate with Christian faiths, 9 percent with non-Christian faiths, and 25 percent are unaffiliated.

About a third of the city's residents identify as Catholic, most of them Spanish-speaking. The 3 percent of Angelenos that identify as Jewish have a strong cultural impact on the city, with influential temples, delicious delicatessens, and significant sway in the entertainment industry. And tens of thousands of Angelenos practice other religions including Islam, Buddhism, and Hinduism.

LGBTQ CULTURE

LGBTQ life has become an integral part of L.A. culture. You can, for instance, drive past billboards showing gay couples, sip a latte at a pink-colored LGBTQ-friendly coffee shop, and walk by lots of men holding hands in West Hollywood. Like most of America, L.A. still has a way to go in fully welcoming its transgendered citizens, but it's definitely getting there, with more and more un-gendered bathrooms and the like. In Hollywood, the Los Angeles LGBT Center in Hollywood provides more services for more LGBTQ people than any other organization in the world.

There are gay clubs scattered throughout the city and West Hollywood, with its annual Pride Parade, is the mecca for them all. For a more refined perspective on gay L.A., attend the annual Outfest, which showcases moving films about LGBTQ people and characters. To learn about L.A.'s rich LGBTQ history, take a Lavender Effect or Out-and-About guided tour.

FESTIVALS AND EVENTS

Each weekend here brings multiple food, arts, and music festivals, so your challenge will not be finding things to do, but simply choosing *which* things to do. My favorite resource for weekly events listings is *Time Out Los Angeles* (www.timeout.com/los-angeles). You can also get daily listings from *L.A. Weekly* (www.laweekly.com). Los Angeles hosts multiple big festivals each year, such as the Playboy Jazz Festival and Dia de los Muertos, but there are also lots of smaller events that are equally as entertaining. These include First Fridays, which bring live music and dozens of food trucks to Abbot Kinney Boulevard in Venice.

THE ARTS

You'll see the artistry of L.A.'s denizens in what we wear, you'll hear it in the drums on Hollywood Boulevard, and you'll taste it in fusion foods across the city. There is no shortage of inspiration here; in fact, sometimes the choices for artistic fusion can get overwhelming. Rest assured, talent abounds, so it's hard to make a bad choice when selecting a cultural outing.

THE FILM INDUSTRY

There's a plethora of ways to learn about and experience the film industry while visiting L.A. You can start with studio tours, most of which happen in Hollywood or Studio City (in the San Fernando Valley). Paramount Studios and Warner Brothers Studios are both awesome to see. There are also multiple movie festivals held in L.A. throughout the year, including the AFI Festival and the L.A. Film Festival. Plus, going to the movies in L.A. can be an awesome experience at unique theaters like El Capitan and the ArcLight. Other popular experiences that are tangentially related to the film industry are taking van tours around movie-star neighborhoods (which you can pick up at the Walk of Fame) or visiting Universal Studios, where all rides are movie-themed.

VISUAL ARTS

You could spend weeks in L.A. focusing solely on visual art. The L.A. County Museum of Art (LACMA) is a treasure trove of its own, with over 100,000 pieces from ancient to present times. There are dozens of other impressive visual art museums and also galleries scattered across the city. A good chunk of them—the Broad, the Geffen, the Museum of Contemporary Art (MOCA)—are in Downtown. Speaking of Downtown, the visual arts scene there is bursting at the seams; head to the Arts District for an array of galleries and compelling street art.

COMEDY AND LIVE PERFORMANCE

Los Angeles and New York are our country's joint comedy epicenters. In L.A., you can go to a comedy club seven nights a week and have your stomach hurting from laughter. Because so many world-famous comedians live and work in L.A., you'll often see headliners trying out new material at either The Comedy Store or the Laugh Factory. While the stand-up scene is huge, there are also great improv shows at both the Groundlings Theatre and Upright Citizens Brigade. You're guaranteed a great show at any of the aforementioned spots; if you're feeling adventurous, you can also try a more underground show at venues like the Nerdist Showroom in Hollywood.

MUSIC

In L.A., you can have a huge, grand musical experience (such as seeing Kayne West at the Hollywood Bowl), or an intimate night of jazz at the Dresden in Los Feliz. Citywide, there are live performances from well-known musical artists every night. For punk and rock shows, head to the iconic venues lining the infamous Sunset Strip. Echo Park has great indie clubs, and Hollywood and Downtown have bigger venues like the Palladium and the Walt Disney Concert Hall. And stay on the lookout for the newest and hottest music club—there's always one popping up somewhere.

ESSENTIALS

Getting There

AIR

There are three main airports in Los Angeles: LAX, Hollywood Burbank Airport in the San Fernando Valley, and John Wayne Airport in Orange County.

Los Angeles International Airport (LAX) (1 World Way, Los Angeles, 310/646-5252, www. lawa.org) is by far the biggest and busiest of the three, and usually the cheapest to fly into. Dozens of airlines fly here, and once you land there are lots of choices for ground transportation. LAX is closest airport to the beach towns of Venice, Santa Monica, and Malibu.

Hollywood Burbank Airport (BUR) (2627 N. Hollywood Way, Burbank, 818/840-8840, www. burbankairport.com) has just two terminals, and costs more to fly into than LAX. But the price dif-

Downtown Los Angeles

ference might be worth it if you're looking for a peaceful arrival and convenience. Hollywood Burbank is adjacent to Hollywood and Beverly Hills.

John Wayne Airport (SNA) (18601 Airport Way, Santa Ana, 949/252-5200, www.ocair.com) is a clean, accessible airport that's close to Disneyland, Laguna Beach, and Newport Beach. Like Hollywood Burbank, it will cost you a bit more to fly into than LAX.

CAR

Los Angeles is a notorious for its freeways, which numerous yet congested access points into the city. From the north and south, I-5 provides the most direct

L.A. Freeways

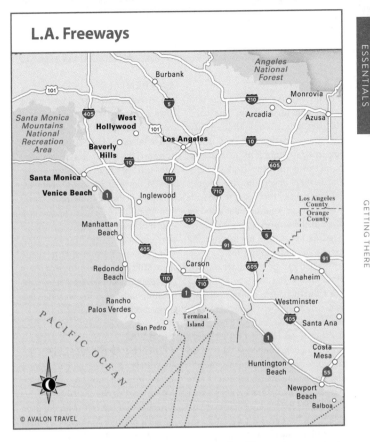

© AVALON TRAVEL

access to downtown. From I-5, US-101 South leads directly into Hollywood; from where Santa Monica Boulevard can take you west to Beverly Hills. Connecting from I-5 to I-210 will take you east to Pasadena. The best way to reach Santa Monica, Venice, and Malibu is via CA-1, also known as the Pacific Coast Highway. I-10 can get you there from the east, but it will be a long, tedious, and trafficked drive.

TRAIN

Amtrak (800/872-7245, www.amtrak.com) has an active rail hub in Los Angeles. Most trains come in to Union Station (800 N. Alameda St.), a 1930s architectural gem. The station bustles during rush hour and takes a breath on weekends. It's on the edge of Downtown, so if you're staying in this part of the city you can take a bus, cab, or ride-share to your hotel.

From Union Station, which also acts as a Metrolink hub, you can take the Metrolink (www.metrolink-trains.com) to or from various spots in Southern California, including Ventura and Oceanside.

Getting Around

CAR

Driving in Los Angeles can be both joyful and tormenting. The painful part is L.A.'s ubiquitous traffic and limited parking; the fun is having access to some of the more scenic, harder-to-reach areas around the city. Unlike other major cities, Los Angeles is just not a city that's easy to navigate without a car. Your best bet is to rent a car at the airport and just plan on needing extra time for driving and extra money for parking fees.

Traffic can be a headache at any time of day, but the worst of it occurs during rush hours—roughly 8am-10am and 4pm-7pm on weekdays. Local drivers are also notorious for their road rage; expect to be cut off and maybe honked at. Most road signs use numbers, but locals, including the radio traffic reporters, use names (e.g., Santa Ana Freeway, Santa Monica Freeway, etc.). There's no visible name-to-number translation on most maps, and names can change depending on which section of freeway you're driving.

Some neighborhoods offer easier parking than others. Santa Monica, for example, has ample public parking at reasonable rates. Downtown, on the other hand, has limited parking and expensive lots, so you may prefer to use a taxi or ride share to take you there, rather than drive yourself. Hollywood, like Santa Monica, has a good amount of public parking, but it comes at a steep price. I like to use ride-shares on Friday and Saturday nights, when parking is particularly challenging because many people are out at the bars and restaurants.

CAR RENTALS

All three airports mentioned above have a shuttle service that will pick you up at the airport terminal and take you to the rental car lot; these shuttles run every 10-15 minutes, so you don't need to book a shuttle in advance. You should, however, book your rental car in advance through the rental company website—it will make the process much smoother and ensure that there is a car waiting for you when you get here. Be prepared to spend up to $100 more on renting a car than you're quoted online; rental companies are notorious for piling on added fees upon checkout.

PUBLIC TRANSPORTATION

Los Angeles is working hard to upgrade its oft-criticized public transportation system. Part of the challenge for this system is that the city is just so darn big—it's not like Manhattan, where there are only a handful of square miles to cover. Nevertheless, L.A. has managed to create a far-reaching bus system that can take you almost anywhere in the city for just a few bucks, if you're willing to put in the time.

The Metro (323/466-3876, www. metro.net, cash fare $1.75, day pass $7, seven-day pass $25) runs both the subway Metro rail system and a network of buses throughout the L.A. metropolitan area. You can pay onboard a bus if you have exact change. Otherwise, purchase a ticket or a day pass from the ticket vending machines present in all Metro rail stations. If you will be riding the Metro often, consider purchasing a TAP refillable

NAVIGATING L.A. TRAFFIC

No great city is free of something terrible; in Los Angeles, our terrible thing has got to be *traffic*.

It's pretty much impossible to visit L.A. without experiencing *some* traffic (if you do it, please let me know how!), but these tips below will at least help you avoid serious traffic jams:

Los Angeles traffic

- **Use apps to find the best routes.** I recommend either the Google Maps app or Waze, both of which show you the fastest (and usually least congested) routes to your destination

- **Avoid the 405 freeway.** This road is notorious for traffic jams, pretty much any time of day or night. Find an alternate route if you can.

- **Don't drive west during the morning commute.** The heaviest traffic in the mornings flows east to west. During this time, roads like Santa Monica, Sunset, and Olympic are jammed bumper-to-bumper on weekdays. So plan your westward drive either before or after the hours of 8am-10am, Monday-Friday.

- **Don't drive east during the evening commute.** Those same workers who travel west to get to work head east between 4pm and 7pm on weekdays. I'm not sure why, but Friday evenings seem particularly congested when driving east. To avoid this mess, plan your eastward drive for the morning or late evening.

If you do end up getting stuck in a major jam, take a deep breath and consider it part of your quintessential L.A. experience—now you *really* know what it's like to be an Angeleno.

card ($1 plus regular fare); you must purchase a TAP card if you want to purchase the unlimited-ride day or seven-day passes.

Some buses run for 24 hours. The Metro rail lines can start running as early as 4:30am and don't stop until as late as 1:30am. See the website for route maps, timetables, and fare details on getting to and from places. The biggest downside is how long it can take; a ride from Hollywood to Santa Monica, for example, takes 45-60 minutes—and that's only halfway across the city.

The rail system is a bit faster, but still time-consuming. There are six different lines—Red, Blue, Orange, Green, Gold, Purple, and Expo—which will take you across the city. The Expo line is the newest; it runs all the way from Downtown to Santa Monica, and is the only line that will take you to the beach. Other notable Metro stops include:

Red Line:
- Hollywood Walk of Fame, at the Hollywood/Highland stop
- Koreatown, at the Vermont/Beverly stop

Yellow Line:
- Union Station
- Little Tokyo
- Arts District

Green Line:
- Los Angeles International Airport

TAXIS AND RIDE-SHARING APPS

Ride-sharing services like Uber and Lyft are among the best ways to get around Los Angeles. Lyft in particular can be surprisingly affordable: Outside of rush hour, a ride from Downtown to Hollywood will cost you about $15-25. Keep in mind that both Lyft and Uber charge based on the amount of time you spend in the driver's car—so if you catch a ride during rush hour and spend 60-plus minutes riding, expect to pay upwards of $50, no matter how far you go.

Taxis are considerably less ubiquitous than ride-shares, unless you're at the airport. If you do want to take a cab, I recommended asking your hotel staff to order/call one.

Travel Tips

ACCESS FOR TRAVELERS WITH DISABILITIES

Los Angeles and Southern California have a good reputation for serving people with disabilities, particularly people who use wheelchairs. Most hotels have rooms for travelers with disabilities, and buses and the rail system are relatively accommodating. Among theme parks, Disneyland is known for its accessibility and Universal Studios is also wheelchair friendly. Museums also do a good job.

The city's sidewalks and streets, however, can be harder to navigate in a wheelchair. Some of which are poorly paved or uneven (mostly in Hollywood, Silver Lake, Echo Park, and Los Feliz). Attractions with broad, well-paved paths include the 3rd Street Promenade in Santa Monica, the Grove and Farmers Market in Hollywood, and the Venice Beach Boardwalk. For more info, check out **A Wheelchair Rider's Guide to the California Coast** (www.wheeling-calscoast.org).

TRAVELING WITH CHILDREN

There is so much to do with kids in Los Angeles. This is, after all, where Disneyland is. Outdoor-loving little ones might like trekking through Griffith Park (which has the L.A. County Zoo and a miniature railroad) or swimming at the Annenberg Community Beach House. Fun museums to explore with kids include the Los Angeles Natural History Museum, the La Brea Tar Pits & Page Museum, the Santa Monica Pier Aquarium, and the California Science Center. And on hot days, don't miss the state-of-the-art playground and splash pad in Santa Monica's Tongva Park.

Be sure to plan on having some entertainment and snacks in the car—you may be spending a lot of time on the road.

WOMEN TRAVELING ALONE

Women traveling alone should be cautious in Los Angeles, as with any other city. Exercise normal precautions: don't walk alone at night, don't get into cars with strangers, and don't get drunk in mixed company.

SENIOR TRAVELERS

Los Angeles is full of activities for seniors. Silver travelers may want to check out **Road Scholar Tours** (www. roadscholar.org), a tour company that specifically caters to seniors. Seniors can also take advantage of discounted Metro transportation and museum admission across the city. Social seniors can spend time with kindred spirits through **Meetup** (www.meetup.com/ topics/seniors), a website which has planned activities for people looking to make the most of their golden years.

INTERNATIONAL TRAVELERS

Travelers from abroad will need different types of visas as determined by U.S. immigration law; the type of visa you'll need will depend on the purpose of your travel (for tourism, business, etc.). While in the United States, your activities will be limited to the reason and purpose stated in your visa, with a few exceptions. America waives visa requirements for visitors from certain countries. For an overview of the types of nonimmigrant visas available under U.S. immigration law, see the nonimmigrant visa classifications on the U.S. Citizenship and Immigration Services website (www.uscis.gov).

Whichever type of visa you have, you need to complete the **customs** and immigrations processes once you arrive in the United States, no matter your final destination. For example, if you're flying to Los Angeles by way of Dallas, you'll complete the customs process in Dallas before boarding your connecting flight to L.A.

Health and Safety

HOSPITALS AND EMERGENCY SERVICES

There are three big medical centers, with 24-hour emergency rooms, in Los Angeles:

- Cedars-Sinai Medical Center, West Hollywood
- Keck Medicine at the University of Southern California, near Downtown
- Ronald Reagan University of California Los Angeles Medical Center, near Beverly Hills

If you're experiencing a medical emergency, you can call **911** to get an ambulance to take you to the nearest hospital (there are others in addition to these three major ones). Once you get to an emergency room, you'll probably sit in a crowded lobby and have a long wait time (usually at least three hours).

Because medical costs can be cripplingly expensive in America, you'll be wise to purchase travel insurance when visiting L.A. from another country.

PHARMACIES

You can find a pharmacy nearby in pretty much every L.A. neighborhood. Major chain pharmacies include CVS, Walgreens, and Rite Aid. They all sell over-the-counter medications and fill out prescription medications.

CRIME

The best way to avoid any kind of theft in L.A. is to never leave any

HOMELESSNESS IN L.A.

Unless you spend 100 percent of your Los Angeles trip in Beverly Hills, you will see a lot of people experiencing homelessness while you're here, especially in Downtown, Hollywood, and Venice. Los Angeles has one of the largest per capita homeless populations in the country. There are a lot of reasons for this. The bottom line is that they're people, too, just like you or me. You will likely be asked for money, and the best thing to do is respond with a courteous yes or no rather than speeding along.

items sitting in your parked car—this will probably keep your car safe while it's parked. Other than that, the basic rules of travel and safety apply: Be cautious on streets after dark, don't walk around after dark alone, and don't take out your phone or other valuables without being aware of your surroundings.

These precautions are especially important in Hollywood and Downtown, which have larger populations of people experiencing homelessness and can get seedy after dark. The Walk of Fame, in particular, will have people looking to take advantage of tourists after dark. That all being said, daylight finds most areas of the city quite safe for exploring.

DRUGS AND ALCOHOL

Partying plays a foundational role in the entertainment industry, and there's no shortage of drugs and alcohol in L.A. nightlife, particularly in Hollywood. You should, of course, enjoy Los Angeles in any way that feels good for you, but be wary of opiates in any form because they can be extremely addictive; also be careful of partiers or dealers looking to take advantage of unknowing travelers (i.e., don't go to a party alone with someone you don't know!).

The most notable development in L.A.'s substance world is California's 2017 legalization of recreational marijuana. This means that anyone can now walk into one of L.A.'s recreational marijuana shops and buy some weed. Because this new allowance went into effect in January 2018, the number of recreational weed shops is still small, but it's steadily growing. Right now, most of these shops are in West Hollywood.

Information and Services

VISITORS CENTERS

There's a handful of visitors centers across the city:

- Hollywood: Discover Los Angeles Visitor & Information Center (Hollywood & Highland, 6801 Hollywood Blvd., www.discoverlosangeles.com/what-to-do/discover-los-angeles-visitor-information-center-hollywood-highland)
- Downtown: Union Station Visitors Center (800 N. Alameda St.)
- Beverly Hills: Beverly Hills Visitor Center (9400 S. Santa Monica Blvd., #102, 310/248-1015, www.lovebeverlyhills.com)
- Santa Monica: Santa Monica Main Visitor Information Center (2427 Main St., 800/544-5319, www.santamonica.com)

POST OFFICES

U.S. post offices are found in all parts of Los Angeles. You can use the post office to buy stamps and mail letters, postcards, packages, and so forth. If you only need to mail a letter or postcard, you can drop those into one of the blue collection bins found on many L.A. street corners. To find a nearby post office, you can use your map app or the post office location finder site, which also shows the location of the blue collection bins.

BANKS AND CURRENCY

Most major banks can be found here, including Bank of America, City National Bank, First Republic Bank, Mercantile National Bank, and Chase Bank. Most banks have ATM locators on their websites, which will be helpful if you need cash. Banks are open at least 9am-5pm on weekdays, with more limited hours on Saturdays and Sundays. All banks are closed on public holidays. Cash advances on your Visa and MasterCard can be obtained from most banks, and credit cards can be used in most of L.A.'s restaurants, shops, hotels, bars, and nightclubs. You can exchange currency and travelers' checks at banks, currency exchange offices, and some hotels.

HISTORY

Davis, Mike. *City of Quartz: Excavating the Future of Los Angeles*. London: Verso, 1990. MacArthur Fellow Mike Davis concentrates on ethnic and class struggles in this sweeping social history of a city that speaks over 100 languages and where beloved Joshua trees are being cut down to make way for desert developments.

Starr, Kevin. *California*. New York: Modern Library, 2005. If you're looking to familiarize yourself with the history of California in one delightful volume, this is it. Renowned historian Kevin Starr takes us from California's first settlement in Santa Cruz Bay in 1535 to the state's current iteration as the fifth-largest economy in the world.

FOOD

Gold, Jonathan. *Counter Intelligence: Where to Eat in the Real Los Angeles*. New York: St. Martin's Press, 2000. Jonathan Gold, food critic for the *Los Angeles Times*, shares 200 of his best restaurant discoveries, including food from 25 countries and the directions for a flawless hot dog. Gold's writing is provocative, colorful, and timeless.

Henderson, Helene, and Martin Lof. *Malibu Farm Cookbook: Recipes from the California Coast*. New York: Crown Publishing, 2014. This delightful compilation of recipes allows you to re-create the sumptuous meals offered at the Malibu Pier's famous seaside restaurant. Lof's photographs are seductive and the book tells a delightful story of how a young woman from Sweden migrated to California and realized her dreams.

ARCHITECTURE AND DESIGN

Banham, Reyner. *Los Angeles, The Architecture of Four Ecologies*. Los Angeles: UCLA Press, 2005. Banham is a professor of the history of architecture who clearly loves Los Angeles. In this tome, he examines the ways its inhabitants relate to the foothills, the beach, the flatlands, and, last but not least, the freeways. Originally written in 1971, it is still current and mesmerizing.

ENTERTAINMENT INDUSTRY

Dunn, John Gregory. *The Studio*. New York: Vintage Books, 1998. In 1968, Richard Zanuck, a vice president at 20th Century Fox, granted Dunn free access to the studio for one year. This humorous and detailed account of that year captures all the showmanship, glamour, and vulgarity of "the business." It reads like a novel and still holds up 50 years later.

Williams, Gregory Paul. *The Story of Hollywood: An Illustrated History.* New York: BL Press, 2011. Williams grew up in Hollywood and started his entertainment industry career as a cinema puppeteer. This book tells the complete story of Hollywood and its glamour, including its decline and urban renewal. The 800-plus vintage photographs enhance Williams's entertaining writing.

FICTION

Chandler, Raymond. *The Big Sleep.* New York: Alfred Knopf, 1939. The setting for this revered noir novel is the sunny streets of downtown Los Angeles. Philip Marlowe is a detective who gets himself mixed up in all manner of murder and mayhem. Chandler's writing is so captivating that most of his novels were eventually made into movies.

Connelly, Michael. *Echo Park.* London: Orion Books, 2006. Connelly is a master of character and pacing. This first-rate legal thriller has all of the multiple plot twists, passion, and corruption you would want out of an L.A.-based page-turner. Connelly is a former police reporter for the L.A. Times who has written 28 novels and won the prestigious Mystery Writers of America Edgar Award.

Ellroy, James. *LA Confidential.* Time Warner Books: New York, 1990. This epic noir crime novel, with its stripped terse style, focuses on three members of the LAPD who get caught up in heroin deals, murder, sex, and corruption. In 1997 it was made into a movie that shot the actress Kim Basinger to A-list fame.

POETRY

Coleman, Wanda. *Bathwater Wine.* Boston: Black Sparrow Press, 1999. Wanda Coleman was born and raised in Watts and is known as the unofficial poet laureate of Los Angeles. She has received fellowships from the Guggenheim Foundation and the National Endowment of the Arts. This collection of angry and extravagant works is at once gutsy, musical, and poignant.

YOUNG ADULT

Block, Francesca. *Love in the Time of Global Warming.* New York: Holt & Company, 2013. Los Angeles is destroyed by flooding in this postapocalyptic teen novel filled with magical realism. Follow Pen, our heroine, in an *Odyssey*-inspired journey in which she searches for her lost family members.

Lacour, Nina. *Everything Leads to You.* New York: Penguin, 2014. In this L.A.-based novel, the protagonist, Emi, dreams of being a set designer. We follow her as she unravels a mystery and falls in love with a new friend. Lacour is the award-winning novelist of the young adult novels *Hold Still* and *Disenchantments.*

Suggested Films

L.A. Story. 1991. Steve Martin and Valerie Tennant star is this romantic comedy/drama about an L.A. weatherman falling in love with an English reporter. Ever the comedian, Martin takes advice from a talking billboard, and his romance is often with Los Angeles itself.

White Men Can't Jump. 1992. Woody Harrelson and Wesley Snipes were nominated for MTV Movie Awards for the best on-screen duo for their magnetic spark in this comedy/drama about basketball hustlers in Venice Beach. Rosie Perez crackles as the oft-ignored girlfriend.

The Big Lebowski. 1998. The Coen brothers wrote and directed this comedy/crime saga starring Jeff Bridges as "the Dude" Lebowski, alongside John Goodman and Steve Buscemi—an epic comic trio. It's everything you ever wanted to know about the culture of bowling (and getting high) in Los Angeles.

Quinceañera. 2006. This heartfelt film zooms in on a 14-year-old Latina woman from East Los Angeles who gets kicked out of her home and taken in by a great-uncle and gay cousin. It deservedly won the Grand Jury Prize and Audience Award at the Sundance Film Festival in 2006.

City of Gold. 2015. The star of this documentary is the Pulitzer Prize-winning food critic and author Jonathan Gold, who takes us on a tour of his beloved restaurants often hidden in strip malls far from the heart of L.A. His passion for the foods of L.A.'s numerous cultures, as well as for the cooks themselves, is palpable.

Internet Resources

NEWS

Los Angeles Times
www.latimes.com

L.A. Weekly
www.laweekly.com

VISITOR INFORMATION

Discover Los Angeles
www.discoverlosangeles.com

Discover Los Angeles County
www.visitcalifornia.com/region/discover-los-angeles-county

FOOD

The Infatuation Los Angeles
www.theinfatuation.com/los-angeles

Los Angeles Magazine
www.lamag.com/digestblog/

Eater Los Angeles
www.la.eater.com

PARKS AND RECREATION

Los Angeles Department of Parks and Recreation
www.laparks.org

Hikespeak
www.hikespeak.com/los-angeles

TRANSPORTATION

L.A. Metro
www.metro.net

L.A. Tourist
www.latourist.com

ENTERTAINMENT

Time Out Los Angeles
www.timeout.com/los-angeles

Thrillist Los Angeles
www.thrillist.com/los-angeles

L.A. Weekly Music
www.laweekly.com/music

Index

Restaurants Index

Nightlife Index

Shops Index

Hotels Index

Photo Credits

Title page photo: © choness/123rf

page 2 (left) © Sean Pavone | Dreamstime.com, (top right) © Erin Bogetti, (bottom) © Gracias Madre; page 4 (top) © Erin Bogetti, (middle) © Daniel Schreurs | Dreamstime.com, (bottom) © Starforeman | Dreamstime.com, (top) © Chon Kit Leong | Dreamstime.com, (bottom) © Erin Bogetti; page 5 © Erin Bogetti; page 6 © Surfr10132 | Dreamstime.com; page 8 (top) © Erin Bogetti, (bottom) © Jared Fairley | Dreamstime.com; page 9 © Tiffanychan | Dreamstime.com; page 10 (top) © Serban Enache | Dreamstime.com, (bottom) © Oskii Monoskii | Dreamstime.com; page 12 (top) © Sara Ashley Locke, (middle) © Guisados, (bottom) © Gert Hochmuth | Dreamstime.com; page 13 (top) © La Luz de Jesus Art Gallery, (bottom) © Disney Enterprises, Inc.; page 14 © Erin Bogetti; page 15 © James Kirkikis | Dreamstime.com; page 16 © Alkan2011 | Dreamstime.com; page 17 © Juan Moyano | Dreamstime.com; page 18 (top) © Erin Bogetti, (bottom) © Gert Hochmuth | Dreamstime.com; page 19 © Disney Enterprises, Inc.; page 20 © Rosana Scapinello | Dreamstime.com; page 21 © Jon Bilous | Dreamstime.com; page 22 © Galinasavina | Dreamstime.com; page 23 © Lunamarina | Dreamstime.com; page 26 © Groovychick69 | Dreamstime.com; page 27 © Sooth Sayre | Dreamstime.com; page 28 © Chon Kit Leong | Dreamstime.com; page 29 © Brphoto | Dreamstime.com; page 30 © Erin Bogetti; page 31 (top) © Erin Bogetti, (second from top) © Erin Bogetti, (second from bottom) © appalachianviews/123RF, (bottom) © Jackbluee | Dreamstime.com; page 32 © Meinzahn | Dreamstime.com; page 33 (top) © Fabio Formaggio | Dreamstime.com, (second from top) © Erin Bogetti, (second from bottom) © Maciej Bledowski | Dreamstime.com, (bottom) © klotz/123RF; page 35 (top) © Jul3s83 | Dreamstime.com, (bottom) © Lograstudio | Dreamstime.com; page 36 © Sarahebelanger3 | Dreamstime.com; page 37 © Erin Bogetti; page 38 © Erin Bogetti; page 39 (top) © Serban Enache | Dreamstime.com, (second from top) © Erik Lattwein | Dreamstime.com, (second from bottom) © Rui G. Santos | Dreamstime.com, (bottom) © Publicimage | Dreamstime.com; page 41 (top) © Kitleong | Dreamstime.com, (bottom) © Kitleong | Dreamstime.com; page 42 © Nito100 | Dreamstime.com; page 43 © Roza | Dreamstime.com; page 44 © Sepavo | Dreamstime.com; page 45 (top) © Sepavo | Dreamstime.com, (second from top) © Erin Bogetti, (second from bottom) © Meunierd | Dreamstime.com, (bottom) © Kristin Teig Photography; page 47 (top) © Scukrov | Dreamstime.com, (bottom) © Meinzahn | Dreamstime.com; page 48 © F11photo | Dreamstime.com; page 49 © Alkan2011 | Dreamstime.com; page 50 © Ryan Forbes Photography, West Hollywood Travel + Tourism Board; page 51 (top) © Gerry Boughan | Dreamstime.com, (second from top) © Jessica Sample, (second from bottom) © Erik Lattwein | Dreamstime.com, (bottom) © The Abbey Food and Bar; page 52 © Divepics | Dreamstime.com; page 53 (top) © trekandshoot | Dreamstime.com, (second from top) © Andreykr | Dreamstime.com, (second from bottom) © Agaliza | Dreamstime.com, (bottom) © Diegograndi | Dreamstime.com; page 55 © trekandshoot | Dreamstime.com; page 56 (top) © Lindsay George, (bottom) © Zverava | Dreamstime.com; page 57 © Celsodiniz | Dreamstime.com; page 58 © Helgidinson | Dreamstime.com; page 59 (top) © Erin Bogetti, (second from top) © Erin Bogetti, (second from bottom) © James Menges | Dreamstime.com, (bottom) © Zepherwind | Dreamstime.com; page 61 (top) © Gerry Boughan | Dreamstime.com, (bottom) © Wolterk | Dreamstime.com; page 62 (top) © Samystclair | Dreamstime.com, (bottom) © Kitleong | Dreamstime.com; page 63 © Rspillman20 | Dreamstime.com; page 64 © Gabe9000c | Dreamstime.com; page 65 © Zepherwind | Dreamstime.com; page 66 © Littleny | Dreamstime.com; page 67 © Supannee Hickman | Dreamstime.com; page 68 © Erin Bogetti; page 69 © Erin Bogetti; page 71 © Erin Bogetti; page 72 © Kitleong | Dreamstime.com; page 73 © Erin Bogetti; page 74 © Danny Raustadt | Dreamstime.com; page 76 © Kendallsev | Dreamstime.com;

Acknowledgements

Thank you, God, for fueling my creative fire.

Thank you, Rachel, for believing in me.

Julia Cameron, thank you for "The Artist's Way" and reminding me why I write.

Mom, thank you for telling me I'm the best at everything I do (even 5th grade synchronized swimming).

Thank you to my family, the soil on which I stand.

Thank you to Rachel Feldman for your grace, kindness, and editorial expertise.

Thank you to Carole Cellucci for showing me new ways to use words.

Thank you to Nikki Ioakimedes for choosing me to create this book.

Thank you to Devin and Jorie for telling me about hidden hipster restaurants.

Thank you to Malena and Vijal for teaching me about steakhouses, cocktail bars, and 5-star hotels.

Justine Jacob, thank you for the years of auspicious edits.

And to L.A.—my muse. Thank you for your effervescent inspiration, golden nights, hummingbird-filled sunrises, and every rolling wave. I love you.

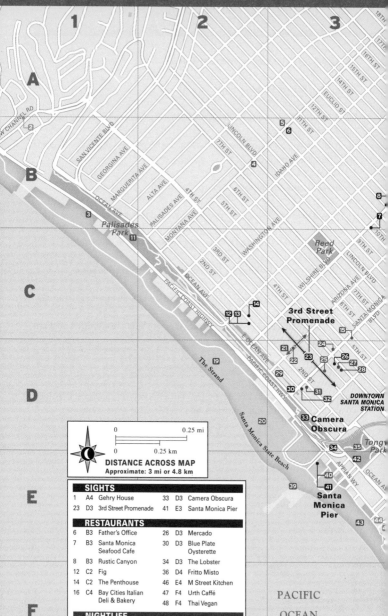

PACIFIC

OCEAN

SIGHTS

1	A4	Gehry House	33	D3	Camera Obscura
23	D3	3rd Street Promenade	41	E3	Santa Monica Pier

RESTAURANTS

6	B3	Father's Office	26	D3	Mercado
7	B3	Santa Monica Seafood Cafe	30	D3	Blue Plate Oysterette
8	B3	Rustic Canyon	34	D3	The Lobster
12	C2	Fig	36	D4	Fritto Misto
14	C2	The Penthouse	46	E4	M Street Kitchen
16	C4	Bay Cities Italian Deli & Bakery	47	F4	Urth Caffé
			48	F4	Thai Vegan

NIGHTLIFE

13	C2	The Bungalow	32	D3	Ye Olde King's Head
28	D3	Harvelle's Blues Club	42	E3	Chez Jay's
29	D3	Onyx Rooftop Bar	55	F5	Library Alehouse

ARTS AND CULTURE

| 10 | B6 | 26th Street Art Center | 51 | F4 | Jadis |
| 40 | E3 | Front Porch Cinema at the Pier | 53 | F4 | Axiom Contemporary |

SPORTS AND ACTIVITIES

3	B1	Annenberg Community Beach House	31	D3	Santa Monica Power Yoga & Meditation
11	C1	Palisades Park	35	D3	Tongva Park
19	D2	The Strand	37	D4	Kundalini by the Sea
20	D2	Santa Monica State Beach	39	E3	Trapeze School of New York
21	D3	Bhakti Yoga Shala	43	E3	Learn to Surf L.A.
27	D3	Santa Monica Beach Bicycle Rentals	54	F4	Beach Yoga

SHOPS

4	B2	Andrew's Cheese Shop	22	D3	Santa Monica Farmers Market
5	B3	Peek Kids	24	D3	Taos Indian Trading Company
9	B4	Co-Opportunity	25	D3	Puzzle Zoo
15	C3	Thunderbolt Spiritual Books	38	D4	Kathmandu Boutique
17	C4	Lunya	49	F4	ZJ Boarding House
18	C6	McCabe's Guitar Shop	52	F4	Mindfulnest

HOTELS

| 2 | B1 | Channel Road Inn | 45 | E3 | Casa del Mar |
| 44 | E3 | Shutters On The Beach | 50 | F4 | Sea Shore Motel |

© AVALON TRAVEL

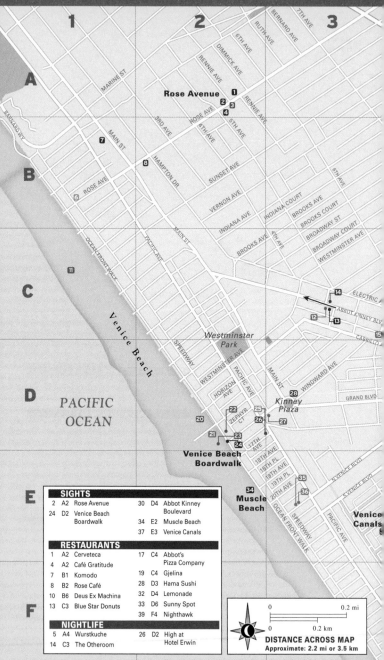

PACIFIC OCEAN

Rose Avenue

Venice Beach

Westminster Park

Kinney Plaza

Venice Beach Boardwalk

Muscle Beach

Venice Canals

SIGHTS

2	A2	Rose Avenue	30	D4	Abbot Kinney Boulevard
24	D2	Venice Beach Boardwalk	34	E2	Muscle Beach
			37	E3	Venice Canals

RESTAURANTS

1	A2	Cerveteca	17	C4	Abbot's Pizza Company
4	A2	Café Gratitude	19	C4	Gjelina
7	B1	Komodo	28	D3	Hama Sushi
8	B2	Rose Café	32	D4	Lemonade
10	B6	Deus Ex Machina	33	D6	Sunny Spot
13	C3	Blue Star Donuts	39	F4	Nighthawk

NIGHTLIFE

| 5 | A4 | Wurstkuche | 26 | D2 | High at Hotel Erwin |
| 14 | C3 | The Otheroom | | | |

0   0.2 mi

0   0.2 km

DISTANCE ACROSS MAP
Approximate: 2.2 mi or 3.5 km

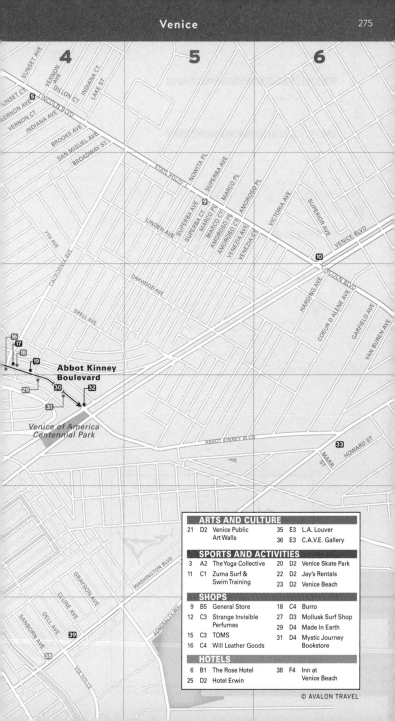

**Abbot Kinney
Boulevard**

*Venice of America
Centennial Park*

ARTS AND CULTURE				
21	D2	Venice Public Art Walls	35 E3	L.A. Louver
			36 E3	C.A.V.E. Gallery

SPORTS AND ACTIVITIES				
3	A2	The Yoga Collective	20 D2	Venice Skate Park
11	C1	Zuma Surf & Swim Training	22 D3	Jay's Rentals
			23 D2	Venice Beach

SHOPS				
9	B5	General Store	18 C4	Burro
12	C3	Strange Invisible Perfumes	27 D3	Mollusk Surf Shop
15	C3	TOMS	29 D4	Made In Earth
16	C4	Will Leather Goods	31 D4	Mystic Journey Bookstore

HOTELS				
6	B1	The Rose Hotel	38 F4	Inn at Venice Beach
25	D2	Hotel Erwin		

© AVALON TRAVEL

SIGHTS

2	Ins	Greystone Mansion & Park
7	A4	Beverly Gardens Park
10	A5	Beverly Hills City Hall
11	A5	Beverly Hills Library
24	C4	Rodeo Drive

RESTAURANTS

14	B4	Nate'n Al Delicatessen
15	B4	Il Pastaio
18	C2	Yazawa
21	C3	Bedford & Burns
25	C4	Nespresso Boutique & Café
29	C5	Mastro's
30	C5	Sweet Beverly
32	C5	Citizen
33	C5	Spago Beverly Hills
36	D4	CUT
38	D5	The Honor Bar
40	E5	Maude
41	E5	Mulberry Street Pizzeria
43	F5	Urth Caffé Beverly Hills

NIGHTLIFE

18	C2	Buena Vista Cigar Club
34	D1	The Club Bar at the Peninsula
35	D1	Vampire Lounge & Tasting Room

0   200 yds
0   200 m

DISTANCE ACROSS MAP
Approximate: 1.1 mi or 1.7 km

Beverly Hills Library

Beverly Gardens Park

Beverly Hills City Hall

Rodeo Drive

BURTON WY

ARTS AND CULTURE

3	Ins	Fredrick Weisman Foundation	13	B4	The Paley Center for Media
8	A4	Wallis Annenberg Center for the Performing Arts	17	B4	Mouche Gallery
			28	C4	Galerie Michael

SPORTS AND ACTIVITIES

1	Ins	Coldwater Canyon Park	31	C5	Spa Montage
9	A5	Beverly Hills Trolley			

SHOPS

5	Ins	The Lady & The Sailor	23	C4	What Goes Around Comes Around
16	B4	Alo Yoga	26	C4	Schutz
20	C3	Kyle | Alene Too	27	C4	Trico Field
21	C3	Leon's of Beverly Hills	42	E5	Beverly Hills Bikini Shop
			44	F5	XIV Karats

HOTELS

4	Ins	The Beverly Hills Hotel	12	A6	Viceroy L'Ermitage Beverly Hills
6	Ins	Hotel Bel-Air and Hotel Bel-Air Spa by La Prairie	37	D4	Beverly Wilshire
			39	D5	Sirtaj Hotel

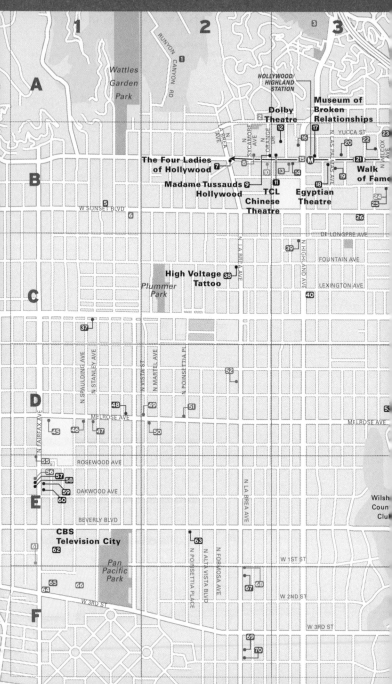

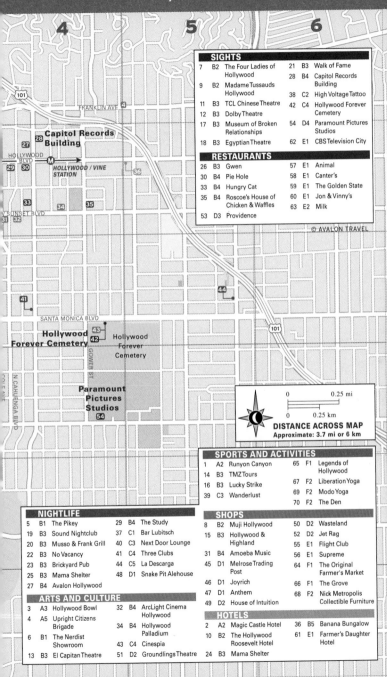

SIGHTS

7	B2	The Four Ladies of Hollywood	21	B3	Walk of Fame
9	B2	Madame Tussauds Hollywood	28	B4	Capitol Records Building
11	B3	TCL Chinese Theatre	38	C2	High Voltage Tattoo
12	B3	Dolby Theatre	42	C4	Hollywood Forever Cemetery
17	B3	Museum of Broken Relationships	54	D4	Paramount Pictures Studios
18	B3	Egyptian Theatre	62	E1	CBS Television City

RESTAURANTS

26	B3	Gwen	57	E1	Animal
30	B4	Pie Hole	58	E1	Canter's
33	B4	Hungry Cat	59	E1	The Golden State
35	B4	Roscoe's House of Chicken & Waffles	60	E1	Jon & Vinny's
53	D3	Providence	63	E2	Milk

© AVALON TRAVEL

Capitol Records Building

28

HOLLYWOOD BLVD

29 30

M HOLLYWOOD / VINE STATION

36

Y'S SUNSET BLVD

31 32 33 34 35

101

FRANKLIN AVE

44

41

SANTA MONICA BLVD

Hollywood Forever Cemetery 43 42 Hollywood Forever Cemetery

N CAHUENGA BLVD

GOWER ST

Paramount Pictures Studios 54

0   0.25 mi

0   0.25 km

DISTANCE ACROSS MAP
Approximate: 3.7 mi or 6 km

SPORTS AND ACTIVITIES

1	A2	Runyon Canyon	65	F1	Legends of Hollywood
14	B3	TMZ Tours	67	F2	Liberation Yoga
16	B3	Lucky Strike	69	F2	Modo Yoga
39	C3	Wanderlust	70	F2	The Den

SHOPS

8	B2	Muji Hollywood	50	D2	Wasteland
15	B3	Hollywood & Highland	52	D2	Jet Rag
31	B4	Amoeba Music	55	E1	Flight Club
45	D1	Melrose Trading Post	56	E1	Supreme
46	D1	Joyrich	64	F1	The Original Farmer's Market
47	D1	Anthem	66	F1	The Grove
49	D2	House of Intuition	68	F2	Nick Metropolis Collectible Furniture

NIGHTLIFE

5	B1	The Pikey	29	B4	The Study
19	B3	Sound Nightclub	37	C1	Bar Lubitsch
20	B3	Musso & Frank Grill	40	C3	Next Door Lounge
22	B3	No Vacancy	41	C4	Three Clubs
23	B3	Brickyard Pub	44	C5	La Descarga
25	B3	Mama Shelter	48	D1	Snake Pit Alehouse
27	B4	Avalon Hollywood			

ARTS AND CULTURE

3	A3	Hollywood Bowl	32	B4	ArcLight Cinema Hollywood
4	A5	Upright Citizens Brigade	34	B4	Hollywood Palladium
6	B1	The Nerdist Showroom	43	C4	Cinespia
13	B3	El Capitan Theatre	51	D2	Groundlings Theatre

HOTELS

2	A2	Magic Castle Hotel	36	B5	Banana Bungalow
10	B2	The Hollywood Roosevelt Hotel	61	E1	Farmer's Daughter Hotel
24	B3	Mama Shelter			

SIGHTS

| 19 | B2 | Sunset Strip |

RESTAURANTS

1	A3	Sushi Park
23	B3	Hamburger Mary's
24	B4	Irv's Burgers
33	C3	Alfred Coffee
35	C3	Lucques
38	C3	Duff's Cakemix
40	D1	Au Fudge
41	D1	Verve Coffee Roasters
43	D1	Gracias Madre
46	D3	Aburiya Raku
50	E3	Joan's on 3rd
51	E4	The Little Door
52	F2	Tagine
53	F3	Matsuhisa

NIGHTLIFE

4	A3	Skybar
7	A3	Saddle Ranch Chop House
8	A4	The Den on Sunset
12	B1	Rainbow Bar & Grill
14	B2	Pearl's Liquor Bar
22	B3	Original Barney's Beanery
26	C2	The Bayou
27	C2	Rage
28	C2	Pump
29	C2	The Abbey

ARTS AND CULTURE

2	A3	The Comedy Store
10	A4	Laugh Factory
13	B1	The Roxy Theatre
15	B2	Whisky a Go Go
16	B2	Viper Room
25	C1	The Troubadour
30	C2	MOCA Pacific Design Center
42	D1	M+B Gallery
48	D4	Taschen
55	F3	Zimmer Children's Museum

SPORTS AND ACTIVITIES

11	B1	Tantris
20	B2	Aura Yoga
54	F3	Hot 8 Yoga

SHOPS

31	C2	Pacific Design Center
17	B2	Mystery Pier Books
18	B2	Book Soup
32	C3	Irene Neuwerth Jewelry
34	C3	Balmain
36	C3	Kelly Wearstler
37	C3	DASH
39	C4	Fred Segal
44	D1	Maxfield
45	D2	West Hollywood Design District
49	E3	The Beverly Center

HOTELS

3	A3	Mondrian Los Angeles
5	A3	Best Western Plus Sunset Plaza Hotel
6	A3	Sunset Tower Hotel
9	A4	Chateau Marmont
21	B2	Petit Ermitage
47	D3	Elan Hotel

0   0.25 mi

0   0.25 km

DISTANCE ACROSS MAP
Approximate: 2.8 mi or 4.6 km

© AVALON TRAVEL

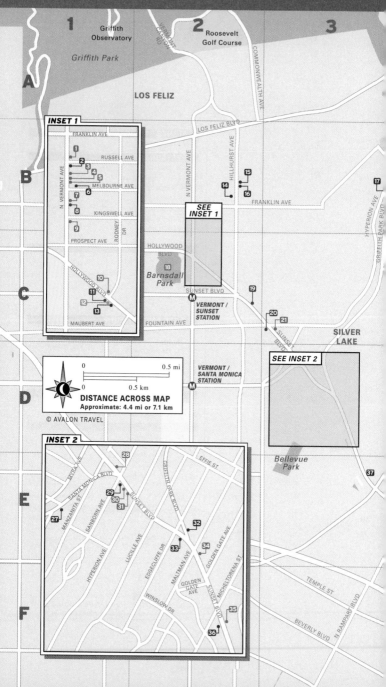

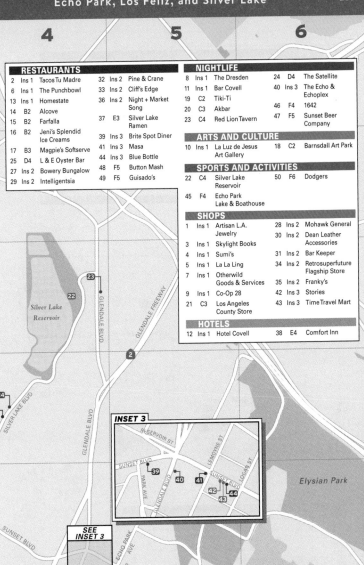

RESTAURANTS

2	Ins 1	Tacos Tu Madre
6	Ins 1	The Punchbowl
13	Ins 1	Homestate
14	B2	Alcove
15	B2	Farfalla
16	B2	Jeni's Splendid Ice Creams
17	B3	Magpie's Softserve
25	D4	L & E Oyster Bar
27	Ins 2	Bowery Bungalow
29	Ins 2	Intelligentsia
32	Ins 2	Pine & Crane
33	Ins 2	Cliff's Edge
36	Ins 2	Night + Market Song
37	E3	Silver Lake Ramen
39	Ins 3	Brite Spot Diner
41	Ins 3	Masa
44	Ins 3	Blue Bottle
48	F5	Button Mash
49	F5	Guisado's

NIGHTLIFE

8	Ins 1	The Dresden
11	Ins 1	Bar Covell
19	C2	Tiki-Ti
20	C3	Akbar
23	C4	Red Lion Tavern
24	D4	The Satellite
40	Ins 3	The Echo & Echoplex
46	F4	1642
47	F5	Sunset Beer Company

ARTS AND CULTURE

10	Ins 1	La Luz de Jesus Art Gallery
18	C2	Barnsdall Art Park

SPORTS AND ACTIVITIES

22	C4	Silver Lake Reservoir
45	F4	Echo Park Lake & Boathouse
50	F6	Dodgers

SHOPS

1	Ins 1	Artisan L.A. Jewelry
3	Ins 1	Skylight Books
4	Ins 1	Sumi's
5	Ins 1	La La Ling
7	Ins 1	Otherwild Goods & Services
9	Ins 1	Co-Op 28
21	C3	Los Angeles County Store
28	Ins 2	Mohawk General
30	Ins 2	Dean Leather Accessories
31	Ins 2	Bar Keeper
34	Ins 2	Retrosuperfuture Flagship Store
35	Ins 2	Franky's
42	Ins 3	Stories
43	Ins 3	Time Travel Mart

HOTELS

12	Ins 1	Hotel Covell
38	E4	Comfort Inn

Silver Lake Reservoir

GLENDALE FREEWAY

GLENDALE BLVD

SILVER LAKE BLVD

INSET 3

RESERVOIR ST

LEMOYNE ST

LOGAN ST

SUNSET BLVD

PARK AVE

GLENDALE BLVD

Elysian Park

SEE INSET 3

SUNSET BLVD

ECHO PARK AVE

ALVARADO ST

SUNSET BLVD

STADIUM WY

Dodger Stadium

Echo Park

Lilac Terrace Park

Echo Lake

ECHO PARK

ARROYO SECO PARKWAY

TEMPLE ST

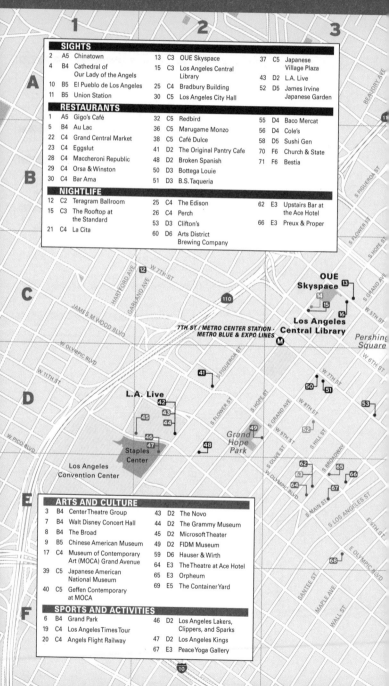

SIGHTS

2	A5	Chinatown	13	C3	OUE Skyspace	37	C5	Japanese Village Plaza
4	B4	Cathedral of Our Lady of the Angels	15	C3	Los Angeles Central Library	43	D2	L.A. Live
10	B5	El Pueblo de Los Angeles	25	C4	Bradbury Building	75	D5	James Irvine Japanese Garden
11	B5	Union Station	30	C5	Los Angeles City Hall			

RESTAURANTS

1	A5	Gigo's Café	32	C5	Redbird	55	D4	Baco Mercat
5	B4	Au Lac	36	C5	Marugame Monzo	56	D4	Cole's
22	C4	Grand Central Market	38	C5	Café Dulce	58	D5	Sushi Gen
23	C4	Eggslut	41	D2	The Original Pantry Cafe	70	F6	Church & State
28	C4	Maccheroni Republic	48	D2	Broken Spanish	71	F6	Bestia
29	C4	Orsa & Winston	50	D3	Bottega Louie			
30	C4	Bar Ama	51	D3	B.S. Taqueria			

NIGHTLIFE

12	C2	Teragram Ballroom	25	C4	The Edison	62	E3	Upstairs Bar at the Ace Hotel
15	C3	The Rooftop at the Standard	26	C4	Perch	66	E3	Preux & Proper
21	C4	La Cita	53	D3	Clifton's			
			60	D6	Arts District Brewing Company			

OUE Skyspace

JAMES M WOOD BLVD

7TH ST / METRO CENTER STATION - METRO BLUE & EXPO LINES

Los Angeles Central Library

Pershing Square

L.A. Live

Grand Hope Park

Staples Center

Los Angeles Convention Center

ARTS AND CULTURE

3	B4	Center Theatre Group	43	D2	The Novo
7	B4	Walt Disney Concert Hall	44	D2	The Grammy Museum
8	B4	The Broad	45	D2	Microsoft Theater
9	B5	Chinese American Museum	49	D2	FIDM Museum
17	C4	Museum of Contemporary Art (MOCA) Grand Avenue	59	D6	Hauser & Wirth
39	C5	Japanese American National Museum	64	E3	The Theatre at Ace Hotel
			65	E3	Orpheum
40	C5	Geffen Contemporary at MOCA	69	E5	The Container Yard

SPORTS AND ACTIVITIES

6	B4	Grand Park	46	D2	Los Angeles Lakers, Clippers, and Sparks
19	C4	Los Angeles Times Tour	47	D2	Los Angeles Kings
20	C4	Angels Flight Railway	67	E3	Peace Yoga Gallery

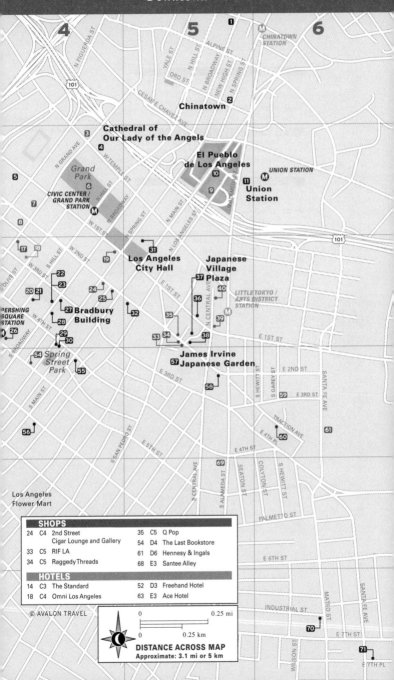

© AVALON TRAVEL

0 — 0.25 mi

0 — 0.25 km

DISTANCE ACROSS MAP
Approximate: 3.1 mi or 5 km

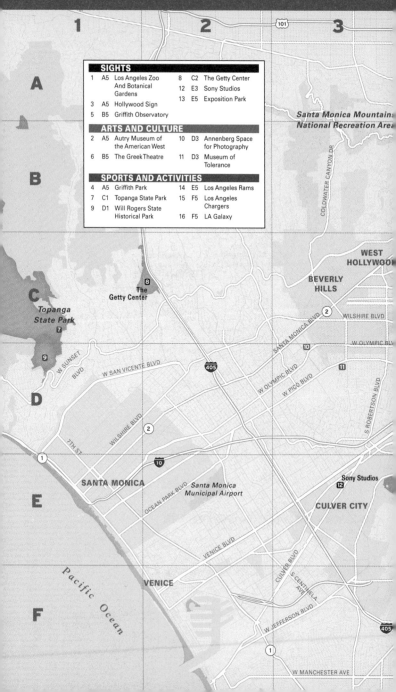

SIGHTS

1	A5	Los Angeles Zoo And Botanical Gardens
3	A5	Hollywood Sign
5	B5	Griffith Observatory
8	C2	The Getty Center
12	E3	Sony Studios
13	E5	Exposition Park

ARTS AND CULTURE

2	A5	Autry Museum of the American West
6	B5	The Greek Theatre
10	D3	Annenberg Space for Photography
11	D3	Museum of Tolerance

SPORTS AND ACTIVITIES

4	A5	Griffith Park
7	C1	Topanga State Park
9	D1	Will Rogers State Historical Park
14	E5	Los Angeles Rams
15	F5	Los Angeles Chargers
16	F5	LA Galaxy

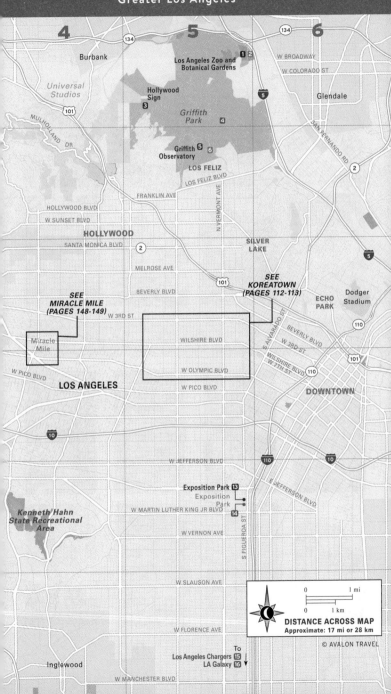

4

5

6

134

Burbank

Los Angeles Zoo and
Botanical Gardens **1** **2**

W BROADWAY

W COLORADO ST

134

5

*Universal
Studios*

MULHOLLAND DR

101

Hollywood
Sign **3**

*Griffith
Park* **4**

Glendale

SAN FERNANDO RD

2

5

Griffith
Observatory **5** **6**

LOS FELIZ

LOS FELIZ BLVD

N VERMONT AVE

FRANKLIN AVE

HOLLYWOOD BLVD

W SUNSET BLVD

HOLLYWOOD

SANTA MONICA BLVD 2

**SILVER
LAKE**

**ECHO
PARK**

Dodger
Stadium

MELROSE AVE

*SEE
KOREATOWN
(PAGES 112-113)*

S ALVARADO ST

BEVERLY BLVD

110

*SEE
MIRACLE MILE
(PAGES 148-149)*

BEVERLY BLVD

101

W 3RD ST

W 3RD ST

Miracle
Mile

WILSHIRE BLVD

WILSHIRE BLVD

W 7TH ST

110

101

W OLYMPIC BLVD

110

W PICO BLVD

LOS ANGELES

W PICO BLVD

DOWNTOWN

10

W JEFFERSON BLVD

110

10

E JEFFERSON BLVD

**Kenneth Hahn
State Recreational
Area**

Exposition Park **13**

Exposition
Park

W MARTIN LUTHER KING JR BLVD **14**

S FIGUEROA ST

W VERNON AVE

W SLAUSON AVE

0   1 mi

0   1 km

DISTANCE ACROSS MAP
Approximate: 17 mi or 28 km

© AVALON TRAVEL

W FLORENCE AVE

Inglewood

To
Los Angeles Chargers **15**
LA Galaxy **16**

W MANCHESTER BLVD

Stunning Sights Around the World

Guides for Urban Adventure

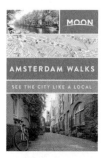
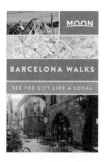
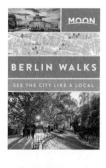

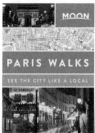

MOON NATIONAL PARKS

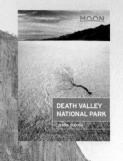

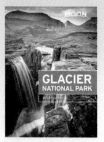

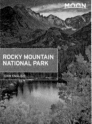

In these books:

- Full coverage of gateway cities and towns
- Itineraries from one day to multiple weeks

- Advice on where to stay (or camp) in and around the parks

Craft a personalized journey through the top
National Parks in the U.S. and Canada with
Moon Travel Guides.

PREPARE FOR ADVENTURE

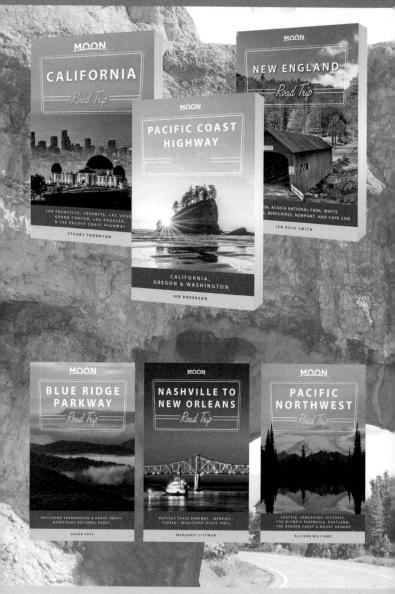

CALIFORNIA *Road Trip*
SAN FRANCISCO, YOSEMITE, LAS VEGAS, GRAND CANYON, LOS ANGELES, & THE PACIFIC COAST HIGHWAY
STUART THORNTON

NEW ENGLAND *Road Trip*
...ON, ACADIA NATIONAL PARK, WHITE ...S, BERKSHIRES, NEWPORT, AND CAPE COD
JEN ROSE SMITH

PACIFIC COAST HIGHWAY
CALIFORNIA, OREGON & WASHINGTON
IAN ANDERSON

BLUE RIDGE PARKWAY *Road Trip*
INCLUDING SHENANDOAH & GREAT SMOKY MOUNTAINS NATIONAL PARKS
JASON FRYE

NASHVILLE TO NEW ORLEANS *Road Trip*
NATCHEZ TRACE PARKWAY · MEMPHIS · TUPELO · MISSISSIPPI BLUES TRAIL
MARGARET LITTMAN

PACIFIC NORTHWEST *Road Trip*
SEATTLE, VANCOUVER, VICTORIA, THE OLYMPIC PENINSULA, PORTLAND, THE OREGON COAST & MOUNT RAINIER
ALLISON WILLIAMS

MOON ROAD TRIP GUIDES

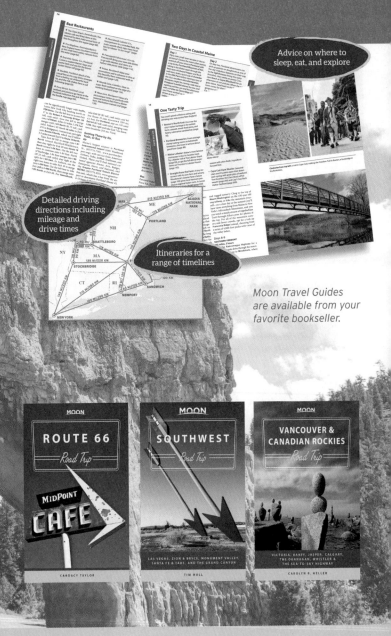

Advice on where to sleep, eat, and explore

Detailed driving directions including mileage and drive times

Itineraries for a range of timelines

Moon Travel Guides are available from your favorite bookseller.

MOON

ROUTE 66
Road Trip

MIDPOINT
CAFE

CANDACY TAYLOR

MOON

SOUTHWEST
Road Trip

LAS VEGAS, ZION & BRYCE, MONUMENT VALLEY,
SANTA FE & TAOS, AND THE GRAND CANYON

TIM HULL

MOON

VANCOUVER &
CANADIAN ROCKIES
Road Trip

VICTORIA, BANFF, JASPER, CALGARY,
THE OKANAGAN, WHISTLER &
THE SEA-TO-SKY HIGHWAY

CAROLYN B. HELLER

Join our travel community!
Share your adventures using **#travelwithmoon**

MOON.COM
@MOONGUIDES

MAP SYMBOLS

Expressway	○ City/Town	✈ Airport	⛳ Golf Course
Primary Road	◉ State Capital	✈ Airfield	🅿 Parking Area
Secondary Road	◉ National Capital	▲ Mountain	⛰ Archaeological Site
Unpaved Road	★ Point of Interest	✛ Unique Natural Feature	⛪ Church
Trail	• Accommodation		⛽ Gas Station
Ferry		⟍ Waterfall	
Railroad	▼ Restaurant/Bar	⬆ Park	❄ Glacier
Pedestrian Walkway	■ Other Location	🎫 Trailhead	Mangrove
Stairs	⛺ Campground	⛷ Skiing Area	Reef
			Swamp

CONVERSION TABLES

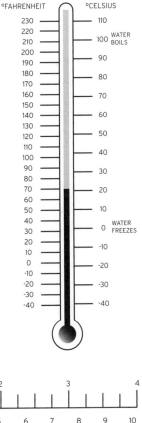

°C = (°F - 32) / 1.8
°F = (°C x 1.8) + 32
1 inch = 2.54 centimeters (cm)
1 foot = 0.304 meters (m)
1 yard = 0.914 meters
1 mile = 1.6093 kilometers (km)
1 km = 0.6214 miles
1 fathom = 1.8288 m
1 chain = 20.1168 m
1 furlong = 201.168 m
1 acre = 0.4047 hectares
1 sq km = 100 hectares
1 sq mile = 2.59 square km
1 ounce = 28.35 grams
1 pound = 0.4536 kilograms
1 short ton = 0.90718 metric ton
1 short ton = 2,000 pounds
1 long ton = 1.016 metric tons
1 long ton = 2,240 pounds
1 metric ton = 1,000 kilograms
1 quart = 0.94635 liters
1 US gallon = 3.7854 liters
1 Imperial gallon = 4.5459 liters
1 nautical mile = 1.852 km

MOON LOS ANGELES
Avalon Travel
Hachette Book Group
1700 Fourth Street
Berkeley, CA 94710, USA
www.moon.com

Editor: Rachel Feldman
Series Manager: Leah Gordon
Copy Editor: Brett Keener
Production and Graphics Coordinator: Krista Anderson
Cover Design: Faceout Studios, Charles Brock
Interior Design: Megan Jones Design
Moon Logo: Tim McGrath
Map Editor: Albert Angulo
Cartographers: Albert Angulo and Brian Shotwell
Proofreaders: Kelly Lydick, Deana Shields
Indexer: Greg Jewett

ISBN-13: 978-1-64049-172-4

Printing History
1st Edition — October 2018
5 4 3 2 1